What's Wrong with Climate Politics and How to Fix It

What's Wrong with Climate Politics and How to Fix It

Paul G. Harris

polity

First published in 2013 by Polity Press

Polity Press
65 Bridge Street
Cambridge CB2 1UR, UK

Polity Press
350 Main Street
Malden, MA 02148, USA

ISBN-13: 978-0-7456-5250-4
ISBN-13: 978-0-7456-5251-1(pb)

A catalogue record for this book is available from the British Library.

Typeset in 10.25 on 13 pt Scala
by Servis Filmsetting Ltd, Stockport, Cheshire

Contents

About the Author

Paul G. Harris is the Chair Professor of Global and Environmental Studies at the Hong Kong Institute of Education. He has written extensively on global environmental politics, policy and ethics, usually with an emphasis on climate change. His work has been published widely in scholarly journals. He is author/editor of many books, including *Climate Change and American Foreign Policy* (St Martin's Press/Macmillan), *International Equity and Global Environmental Politics* (Ashgate), *The Environment, International Relations, and U.S. Foreign Policy* (Georgetown University Press), *International Environmental Cooperation* (University Press of Colorado), *Global Warming and East Asia* (Routledge), *Confronting Environmental Change in East and Southeast Asia* (United Nations University Press/Earthscan), *Europe and Global Climate Change* (Edward Elgar), *Environmental Change and Foreign Policy* (Routledge), *Climate Change and Foreign Policy* (Routledge), *The Politics of Climate Change* (Routledge), *World Ethics and Climate Change* (Edinburgh University Press), *China's Responsibility for Climate Change* (Policy Press), *Ethics and Global Environmental Policy* (Edward Elgar), *Environmental Policy and Sustainable Development in China* (Policy Press), the *Handbook of Global Environmental Politics* (Routledge) and *What's Wrong with Climate Politics and How to Fix It* (Polity).

Preface

Governments and the international community have failed to stem global emissions of carbon dioxide and other greenhouse gases causing climate change. Indeed, climate-changing pollution is increasing globally and it will do so for decades to come without aggressive action by the international community, governments, individuals, and other actors. In this book, I aim to identify the most important reasons for the failure to take such action already, and to suggest some different ways of thinking about the problem and the means by which stronger action can be encouraged. In the process, I will highlight a fundamental driving force of that failure: self-interestedness or, in the literal sense, selfishness. At a very fundamental level, what is wrong with climate politics boils down to selfishness of governments, selfishness of politicians, selfishness of businesses, selfishness of special interests, and, at least among those of us who are affluent, selfishness of individuals. Above all else, what is wrong with climate politics is its inherent tendency to perpetuate and even encourage the selfishness of these actors while too often forgetting the genuine fundamental needs, rights, and obligations of human beings.

Consistent with other books in Polity's *What's Wrong and How to Fix It* series, in this one I use an analogy from medicine – a sick patient requiring treatment to alleviate or cure a serious ailment – to illustrate what is wrong with climate politics and how it might be fixed. As with most complex medical ailments, this one does not have a single cause. It has many causes that have for generations undermined our collective health and that of the whole earth. And much like in the case of difficult illnesses, this one must be given many treatments. But to do that we must first diagnose the most serious ailments and what causes them.

The book comprises two parts. In keeping with the practice of other books in the *What's Wrong* series, Part I diagnoses several things that I believe are *most* wrong with climate politics, namely: (1) the Westphalian international system, which encourages nations to fight for their narrowly perceived interests and makes international cooperation on climate change extraordinarily difficult; (2) the United States and China, which together produce over one-third of global greenhouse gas pollution but which so far have refused to compromise on demands that the other must essentially act first; and (3) the growing pollution that comes from material consumption, energy use, and other aspects of modern lifestyles that are spreading from the developed nations to the developing world as more people join the global middle class.

Part II of the book proposes three of the possible treatments that can be brought to bear to heal the failed politics of climate change, namely: (1) a new kind of climate diplomacy that puts people, including their rights and duties, at the center of climate politics and policy, in the process highlighting the individual human suffering that will come from climate change and the associated duties of affluent and capable individuals everywhere; (2) a formula for a new consensus among developed and developing nations whereby the "common but differentiated responsibilities" of nations (notably the United States and China) to address climate change are matched by the common but differentiated responsibilities of individuals, with the world's affluent classes (including in both the United States and China) taking on greater burdens, thereby potentially breaking the international political deadlock; and

(3) a campaign to help and encourage people to consume more genuine happiness and wellbeing through cultivating full, rewarding lives based on sufficiency and environmental sustainability.

While these treatments are aspirational (again in keeping with other books in the *What's Wrong* series), they are not intended to be utopian. They are potentially workable solutions to what ails the politics of climate change. Having said this, my objective is not to provide a detailed prescription for immediately solving the climate crisis. I doubt a single book could do that. At the same time, I am mindful that we are rapidly running out of time. We need to act boldly very soon. Thus I identify some fundamental problems with climate politics and point to why and how the world might overcome them relatively soon. This will require adjusting the way we think about climate change and how we respond to it. If this book helps to do that, it will have made a small contribution to mitigating the inevitable harms that climate change portends.

Another, more modest, objective of the book is to help readers who might be less familiar with climate politics to get their heads around important issues and events. In that sense, the book has an educational objective. I draw upon the ideas and words of many scholars and experts to illustrate key ideas and forces influencing the world's responses to climate change. However, one objective here is to avoid repeating the theses of other books. One consequence of this may be that some of the themes common to those other books are not as well developed as their advocates might like. As some compensation, notes and references point to where ideas have come from or are elaborated, suggesting paths that readers can follow to pursue them further. All of the ideas we need to address climate change are out there. It is how we put them together, how we prioritize them, and whether we implement them that matter for the future.

This book is about you and me – and other people. It is about our role in climate change. It is a largely human-oriented look at climate politics, identifying solutions to climate change in the behaviors, motivations, needs, and rights of people, even as the ailments that afflict climate politics are often found elsewhere, notably in the flaws of international relations and the rivalries of major nations.

I believe that the treatments recommended here, while certainly not panaceas and far from the only interventions required, would help us to stop the ailments growing worse and potentially could do so in time to avert climate calamity. Perhaps most importantly, we have nothing to lose: the treatments proposed in this book would, if taken seriously and implemented, help to make the world a better place, with a healthier environment and more people who are broadly happier and better off. We would have a world focused on meeting true human needs rather than one that protects special interests and perpetually cultivates short-term desires.

I wish to give my thanks to everyone at Polity who has been involved in bringing this book to readers, especially Louise Knight, who invited me to write it, and David Winters, who kept prodding me to keep my nose to the grindstone. Anonymous reviewers have my appreciation for providing very helpful comments that have improved the final product. As always, I am grateful to K. K. Chan for support at home over more than a dozen years.

Paul G. Harris
Hong Kong

CHAPTER ONE

Introduction

Something is terribly wrong with the politics of climate change. The earth's climate is being altered in profound ways, and there is growing certainty that many communities are facing calamity if we do not change our ways. Yet far too little is being done by the world's governments and other actors to address the causes and consequences of climate change. If the world does not move aggressively to stem emissions of green-house gases, the environment upon which humanity depends for its wellbeing and survival will change in truly profound ways.[1]

The year 2010 puts the failure of climate politics in sharp focus: in that year, global emissions of carbon dioxide (CO_2), the most prevalent greenhouse gas, reached their highest level in human history,[2] and global surface temperatures reached the highest since record-keeping began.[3] Average global temperatures during the decade of 2002–2011 matched that of 2001–2010 (0.46°C above the 1961–1990 average), which was in turn 0.21°C warmer than 1991–2000, which itself was warmer than prior decades, making each succeeding decade warmer than the last, revealing a clear "long-term warming trend."[4] This news comes on the heels of scientists reporting that climate change is not just a problem for the future but one that is affecting humanity and the environment right now.[5] It is much too late to hold back climate change, but the longer we wait to respond to it the more difficult it will be to limit its most adverse impacts, and the more costly it will be to adapt.[6]

Climate change is a *political* problem every bit as much as it is a scientific one, and arguably its technical dimensions are less important than its political ones.[7] Governments and other actors, even while expressing increasing interest and concern about climate change, very rarely act in ways that match the scale of the growing environmental and human tragedy. Indeed, things are only getting worse, despite all efforts to date. There are international treaties and an enormous amount of activity at all levels, but we still do not have definitive political agreements for genuinely mitigating, least of all halting, climate change, and not enough national and local communities, industries, and individuals are willing to do what is necessary to make this happen. Put simply, with too few exceptions, the politics of climate change, despite being increasingly energetic, has failed. In the words of Anthony Giddens, "at present, we have no effective politics of climate change."[8]

What is fundamentally wrong with climate politics? What can be done to fix it? The answers to these questions are nearly as numerous as the experts looking at the problem. Nevertheless, we can identify a few major and chronic "ailments" of climate politics that deserve special attention, and it is to identifying, describing, and treating these ailments that this book is devoted. All of them have a commonality: fundamentally, what ails climate politics is self-interestedness – selfishness of governments, selfishness of politicians, selfishness of businesses, selfishness of other special interests, and ultimately selfishness of individuals. Foremost may be the tendency of the international political and economic systems to perpetuate and even encourage narrowly selfish behavior of nations and other actors, and frequently to forget that human beings are at the root of climate change.[9]

This chapter begins to describe what's wrong with climate politics and starts to propose some treatments that will be examined in detail in later chapters. It briefly describes the "tragedy of the atmospheric commons" and summarizes some of the important steps that are being taken in response to this tragedy. It identifies some of what is "right" about climate politics, albeit with some significant caveats, before describing what is *most* wrong with it and what can be done to treat its most chronic and persistent ailments.

The tragedy of the atmospheric commons

The latest science of climate change paints a bleak picture of the future. In its most recent assessment, the Intergovernmental Panel on Climate Change (IPCC) reported that climate change will result in a range of unwanted impacts, such as more frequent, widespread, and severe droughts and floods; an increasing number of severe weather events; accelerating loss of biodiversity and damage to vulnerable ecosystems; and many adverse impacts on human communities, such as water shortages, the spread of disease-carrying pests, harmful effects on fisheries, and loss of inhabited areas and farmland to the sea – among myriad other unwelcome impacts.[10] While the IPCC predicted that many of these adverse effects would occur much later in the century, recent science tells us that they will occur much sooner – and in many cases may be happening already – and will likely be substantially more severe than the IPCC anticipated.[11] In short, the IPCC science that underlies international negotiations on climate change and most governments' responses to it – despite much criticism that the IPCC has overstated the threat – has been, if anything, far too optimistic. Climate change is a bigger problem than most people realize.

Since the start of the industrial revolution in the late eighteenth century, the atmospheric concentration of CO_2 has increased almost 40 percent, rising from about 280 parts per million (ppm) to more than 390 ppm, with most of that increase occurring since the mid-twentieth century.[12] Predictions point to CO_2 in the atmosphere doubling again by the middle of this century,[13] even as experts tell us that exceeding 350 ppm makes dangerous climate change unavoidable.[14] Indeed, our pollution of the earth's atmosphere has *increased* sharply *since we became aware* of climate change. Incredibly, CO_2 emissions from energy use alone increased 50 percent in only one generation, from about 20 gigatons in 1990 to well over 30 gigatons in 2010, the highest level ever.[15] Despite the global recession, global emissions of CO_2 increased more in 2010 than in any year in history.[16] In 2011, they grew an additional 3.2 percent, reaching their highest level ever – nearly 32 gigatons.[17] Concentrations of greenhouse gases in the atmosphere are now at their highest for the last 650,000 years.[18] Stabilizing carbon emissions at 450 ppm, which some scientists believe is what is needed to limit global warming to 2°C (a dubious benchmark set by governments to avoid the worst effects of climate change), would require cutting global greenhouse gas emissions by 50–85 percent by 2050 (compared to 1990).[19] Yet current trends point to global greenhouse gas emission *increasing* 50 percent by then, to a level approaching 700 ppm CO_2 equivalent.[20] According to the International Energy Agency, there are "few signs that the urgently needed change in direction in global energy trends is underway."[21]

Climate change is not just unfortunate; it is a human-induced tragedy. What makes climate change especially tragic is that nobody intended it to be this way. It is a problem caused by people and industries and nations working hard to advance economically. The problem lies in the convenient but pernicious reality that everyone is free to use the global atmosphere as a dumping ground. In practice, this means that everyone is free to pollute the atmosphere, and we have done so with abandon for hundreds of years. As with most environmental tragedies, all of this is a byproduct of actors behaving quite normally to promote their perceived interests. Neither the corporations that have most callously encouraged our pollution, notably the world's coal and petroleum companies, nor other industries dependent on fossil fuel use, such as the automobile makers, *want* to cause adverse changes to the earth's climate. Climate change is a byproduct of their business practices. People are the main causes of the problem, whether directly through their use of energy or indirectly by their consumption of products and services. Certainly it was (and is) not the intent of individuals, even the wealthiest, to cause climate change. Harm to the atmosphere and all of the communities and people, not to mention ecosystems and other species, that depend on it now and in the future is an incidental consequence of normal human activities intended to promote the interests of those doing the polluting.

Most tragically, those who will be most harmed by climate change – the world's poor people and communities – are least responsible for causing it. Climate change is therefore not only an environmental problem; it is also a great injustice.[22] Nobody wants to do these people harm, but this lack of intent does not mean that this tragedy of the atmospheric commons is not wrong.[23] Surely much of our pollution has been wrong from the time we realized that it was causing climate change.[24] As Stephen Gardiner has described it, climate change is a "perfect moral storm,"[25] with affluent nations and their rich citizens able to shape events at the expense of the world's poor, with current generations able to promote their interests over those of future generations, and with the world lacking a robust theory (or theories) to guide us out of the problem. This storm is building as greenhouse gas emissions continue to increase and the planet continues to warm and undergo other adverse changes from past pollution.

This tragedy of the atmospheric commons has of course

not gone unnoticed. The world has gone to work in trying to address it. It is likely that more scientific resources have been put into studying climate change than any other natural problem. This scientific work has had important results. It has played a key role in efforts by many nations and other actors to begin taking action. Scientists, including those supported by governments and those contributing to the IPCC's work, brought the problem of climate change to the attention of the world and they have been central to helping governments gradually realize its great importance. The inevitable political struggle to decide what is to be done about it – in particular, which nations are most to blame for causing it and therefore are required to take the most action – has resulted in myriad agreements and initiatives among and within nations. However, the politics of climate change have not kept pace with the science. The science – more precisely the changes to the earth's climate and other adverse manifestations of greenhouse gas pollution – is advancing much faster than the politics, with ever more precise and dire predictions of the unfolding tragedy being revealed while domestic and international politics remain unable to respond forthrightly even to the climate science of previous decades.

To put the problem of climate politics in context and to show how much climate diplomacy in particular lags behind climate science, it is worth bearing in mind that the potential problem of human-induced (unnatural) global warming was first theorized in the nineteenth century.[26] By the 1970s, climate change was receiving serious international attention by scientists, and the First World Climate Conference was convened in 1979. The Intergovernmental Panel on Climate Change was created in 1988 and the Second World Climate Conference was held in 1990. International concern was manifested in the 1992 Framework Convention on Climate Change (henceforth the "climate convention"), the 1997

Kyoto Protocol to that convention, and many related agreements that have been reached during the intergovernmental negotiating process ever since. These developments show that the problem is far from new and, more importantly, that scientists and governments have been very actively engaged in it for over three decades.

We can take at least three messages away from this evolution of the climate tragedy and related politics. First, warnings about a warming planet and changing atmosphere, with all the impacts for people and societies that they entail, are by no means new. We have known about the problem for decades, with the dangers to humanity having been widely publicized for more than a quarter-century. Second, the science is telling us that the future will likely be miserable for many ecosystems and for many millions (possibly billions) of people. The more we learn about climate change, the bleaker the future appears to be and the more confident we become of that bleakness. The science will always be uncertain about some things, but the danger is very clear. Third, the international politics, diplomacy, and domestic policies surrounding climate change are grossly inadequate to the task. The science improves by leaps and bounds, the dangers of climate change become more profound each year, but the diplomacy and national responses to climate change plod along at a diplomatic pace, falling further and further behind the aggressive responses that are needed to avert the worst effects. International conferences, even those populated by many of the world's leaders – such as the December 2009 climate conference in Copenhagen, Denmark – have resulted in tepid agreements that do not match the scale of action demanded by the science and which are most often voluntary and therefore unlikely to be fully realized.

Even as the international politics remain weak, failures to implement strong climate legislation within industrialized polluting nations, such as Canada and the United States, reveal problems domestically. With too few exceptions, businesses continue to make things worse, for example by encouraging people to consume things they do not need (even if on rare occasions they are encouraged to consume "green" products), and environmental nongovernmental organizations have not been up to the task of driving and implementing needed changes on the ground.

James Hansen starkly describes the failure of governments to tackle climate change effectively, even those governments that are doing the most.[27] Despite the urgent need to *reduce* greenhouse gas emissions and to phase out fossil fuel use within a few decades, most of these governments say that they can do this through new international agreements akin to the Kyoto Protocol. To this Hansen responds:

> Ladies and gentleman, your governments are lying through their teeth. You may wish to use softer language, but the truth is that they know that their planned approach will not come anywhere near achieving the intended global objectives. Moreover, they are now taking action that, if we do not stop them, will lock in guaranteed failure to achieve the targets that they have nominally accepted.[28]

How can Hansen be so confident in condemning governments? It is because of what they are doing: allowing construction of many additional coal-fired power plants (and permitting environmentally destructive coal mining), developing tar sand deposits, leasing vast new areas for oil and gas exploration, and encouraging hydraulic fracturing for gas, among a range of other actions that will free up enormous amounts of fossil fuels for combustion – just the opposite of what is required.[29] To make matters even worse, governments routinely subsidize these activities, making alternative energies relatively more expensive than they would be otherwise, and of course far more expensive than if the alternatives were subsidized instead.

Thus the tragedy of the atmospheric commons is growing worse, starkly revealing the failures of climate politics.[30] Having said this, it would be unfair to say that absolutely everything is wrong with climate politics. Many developments in recent years offer some reasons for hope, and certainly they can be built upon when aiming to overcome obstacles to cooperation and action to combat climate change. A worry, however, is that some of the ongoing and proposed solutions to climate change may themselves engender additional problems.

What's right with climate politics (with caveats)

Before turning to what most ails climate politics, it is important to recognize positive and fruitful developments, some of which have the potential for substantially mitigating climate change. Without any doubt, there has been tremendous progress in the world's attention to climate change and in efforts to address it. This progress ranges from the scientific to the diplomatic, from international to individual. To begin with, the science of climate change has improved greatly, reaching a very advanced level that provides increasingly detailed guidance to government officials and industry. This is in no small part due to the initiative of governments to invest in studying the causes and consequences of climate change. The number of scientists working on every aspect of the problem has grown over the last quarter-century, and funding for their research has grown significantly, as has the number of outlets for their work, notably expert journals.[31] The result is that knowledge of forces driving climate change and the consequences for ecosystems and societies provides an increasingly clear picture of general changes and, in many instances, quite clear indications of the impacts to come. Consequently, there is now no reasonable doubt that anthropogenic emissions of CO_2 and other greenhouse gases are contributing to unnatural global warming and other manifestations of climate change.

Much of this research has been driven by the international politics of climate change, notably creation of the IPCC, which operates under the auspices of the United Nations (UN) Environment Program and the World Meteorological Organization. The IPCC's periodic assessment reports have in turn been highly influential at all levels of climate politics, although they have also been subject to more than a little controversy. The findings of the IPCC and independent scientists have been translated into interest among leaders, publics, and businesses, and they have to varying degrees driven international responses, especially over the last decade as governments have become more aware of the need for stronger action to limit greenhouse gas emissions. In sum, the science is getting better and it is being taken more seriously.

Having said this, the science of climate change would likely be doing much more good were it not so heavily politicized.[32] Incredibly, millions of people in some countries simply do not believe in climate change or do not believe it is caused by human actions. For some it is considered "natural" or part of God's plan for the earth. "Climate denial" has become one of the myths that underpin conservative political ideologies in some countries, and it has become a mainstay of right-wing political parties in Australia and the United States. Ideology and willful ignorance continue to trump science in these contexts, exacerbating fear in many developed nations, or at least in their legislatures, of the perceived costs of taking concerted action to reverse greenhouse gas emissions. Those same nations are often opposed to major foreign assistance programs that will be needed to help poorer countries adapt to (and eventually help to mitigate) climate change. Special interests have been able to prevent action by making the claim that the economic costs of addressing climate change will far outweigh the benefits. Some of this is caused by ideological blinders, some is outright ignorance – including that which has been actively fostered by special interest groups and the fossil fuel industry[33] – but it is all important for policy responses and individual commitment to take action (see chapter 3).[34]

Despite enormous disagreements over the nature and extent of the problem, and despite profound differences among governments regarding their perceived national interests, diplomats have been able to arrive at a number of climate change agreements, notably the climate convention, the Kyoto Protocol, and subsequent related agreements that now constitute a quite robust international legal infrastructure – the climate change regime – comprising shared principles and norms for nations' cooperation in this issue area (see chapter 2). These international agreements are far too weak, but without them the world might be further behind in tackling climate change. In many cases, the agreements, particularly the Kyoto Protocol, have provided some impetus for nations to begin implementing policies that are already limiting their greenhouse gas pollution, albeit not nearly enough to begin solving the problem. The evidence for this is found most significantly in parts of Northern and Western Europe where some governments have been moving quite aggressively – at least relative to what has been happening historically, if not so much relative to the scale of the problem – to find ways to restrain and even reduce greenhouse gas pollution from within their borders. At the very least, we must give some credit to diplomats and international organizations for working hard in recent decades to create institutions and to start implementing agreements that have the potential to mitigate climate change, at least a bit.[35]

The Kyoto Protocol and other international initiatives have also given impetus, at least in part, to voluntary action around the world, including by regional governments, cities and local communities, civil society organizations, individuals, and more than a few businesses (and entire industries) that are increasingly taking the problem of climate change seriously.[36] Some of these actors are genuine vanguards in leading the fight against climate change.[37] By working together across domestic and international politics, they show that there is significant potential in multilevel governance to address the problem.[38]

Matthew Hoffman has described the plethora of "climate governance experiments" at almost every level.[39] Examples of some of these experiments include: social networking systems for environmental professionals; cooperation among municipalities on climate change mitigation, adaptation, education and the like; voluntary cap-and-trade schemes and carbon markets (where permits to pollute are traded); pledges by colleges and universities to cut greenhouse gas emissions; regional cooperation among nations on technology development and other actions to limit climate change; networks of cities to collaborate and share best practice; shared databases and registries of greenhouse gas emissions; partnerships to use "carbon finance" to enable major urban areas in the developing world to address greenhouse gas pollution; networks of local groups to encourage lowering of "carbon footprints"; government-to-government agreements to develop "carbon capture and storage"; labeling, standard-setting and greenhouse gas registries for use by businesses; partnerships between industries and nongovernmental organizations for greenhouse gas reductions; commitments by cities in Europe to go beyond European Union greenhouse gas cuts; agreements among religious leaders to encourage followers to protect the atmosphere; efforts by institutional investors and insurance corporations to pressure companies to address climate change; cooperative agreements between sub-state regions and foreign governments (for example, between California and the United Kingdom); and associations of business leaders to sharing best practice on climate change and environmental sustainability.[40]

All of these activities notwithstanding, the pace and scale of action on climate change has been far too slow relative to the pace and scale of the problem. Even as greenhouse gas pollution increases, the planet becomes warmer and the adverse effects of climate change manifest themselves, the international community and governments have moved at what might be generously described as a measured pace. International agreements are slow to be reached and they are weak in their requirements for cuts in greenhouse gas pollution, not to mention their inadequate attention to addressing the consequences of inevitable climate change and to helping those who will suffer from it. Most developed nations have taken on commitments under the climate convention, in keeping with their historical greenhouse gas pollution, but for the most part they refuse to take concerted action without commitments from large developing countries, such as China and India, to also take action. Developing nations blame the rich ones and thus refuse to act, with the upshot being that few countries are willing to take robust unilateral action to address the problem.

Even if fully implemented – which is not happening – all international agreements on climate change would not be enough to reverse global warming. This is made worse because the climate regime's regulation of emissions is based on production rather than consumption, providing an incentive to essentially export greenhouse gas pollution from developed to developing nations.[41] Indeed, many of the cuts in greenhouse gas emissions of the affluent nations have been replaced by even more emissions from developing countries, in part because polluting industries from the developed world have moved abroad, with the emissions effectively being reimported via world trade.[42]

Thus, despite the complicated and entrenched climate change regime, and despite the many experiments at all levels by national and local governments, individuals, and business to reduce greenhouse gas pollution and otherwise respond to climate change, the problem grows worse as time passes. International agreements lack teeth and they lack sufficiently wide participation. The political response to climate change has therefore involved baby steps when giant leaps are required.

One potential bright spot is technology. The improved science of climate change, and to some extent the politics, is fostering technological developments that are making stronger action potentially easier and more efficacious. New technologies are making energy use more efficient, for example in more efficient automobiles and factory equipment, and in offering opportunities to avoid pollution through new ways of doing things, for example video-conferencing to replace business travel. Some of the development and deployment of new technology is made possible by government policies, for example when governments encourage installation of windmills and other sources of alternative energy by guaranteeing them tariffs with rates of return sufficient for reasonable profit. Other technologies come from industry research aimed at capitalizing on costly energy supplies, businesses preparing for a future of stricter controls on greenhouse gas pollution, and entrepreneurs who see that there will be fortunes to be made in energy efficiency and other technologies that reduce the world's impact on the atmosphere. Technologies are also being developed, albeit very slowly and controversially, to capture carbon emissions from power plants (so-called carbon capture and storage) and to possibly "geo-engineer" the environment, for example by enhancing carbon uptake by the oceans.[43]

Related to the drivers of new technologies are economic innovations that are being brought to bear against climate change, particularly in schemes for emissions trading in which governments set emissions caps and allocate allowances for pollution from industries, allowing those that fall below their allowances to sell the surplus to others. Sometimes businesses do this internally, and some have pushed for it internationally.[44] The key point is that market incentives are increasingly being created and used to limit and potentially drive down greenhouse gas emissions.

Technological and economic innovations will be a key tool for effectively addressing climate change. However, technology is no panacea and can even pose dangers. "Technophilic optimism," which assumes that technologies will allow economies to simultaneously grow and reduce energy use fast enough to combat climate change effectively, is not supported by historical experience.[45] Paradoxically, even energy efficiency, an important pursuit that needs to be stepped up, has potential drawbacks that will have to be addressed. For example, while more efficient technologies can lead to individuals using less energy in aspects of their daily lives, it can also enable more people to use more energy, leading to an overall increase in pollution. If "low-carbon" cars are developed without limiting the number of them on the roads, a "Jevons paradox" might result: as cars (or other devices) become more energy-efficient, they are likely to be adopted much more widely by consumers and thus more total energy will be consumed than before the new cars were developed.[46] Even industries that become more efficient can become more harmful. For example, the airline industry has substantially improved the efficiency of airliners, but the impact of the entire industry has grown substantially as more people take to the air in more aircraft.

Thus, without careful management of the consequences, energy efficiency can paradoxically result in *more* energy use overall, particularly as the developing world adopts western lifestyles. Development of clean technologies without simultaneously restraining traditional economic growth will not reduce pollution (see chapter 4).[47]

There is even greater potential risk involved in other technological pursuits, notably geo-engineering and carbon capture and storage.[48] Carbon capture from coal-burning facilities requires burning *more* coal (because the extraction of carbon requires additional energy), and the carbon that is stored underground might find its way back into the atmosphere, negating the entire carbon-capture enterprise or possibly making things much worse.[49] Geo-engineering might involve a planetary experiment with unknown consequences for life on earth, and efforts that do not substantially reduce CO_2 emissions doom the oceans, which are already suffering from acidification caused by carbon pollution.[50]

Solving the problem of climate change requires that we use less energy until environmentally benign, nonfossil-fuel-based sources of it become widely available. However, as with some existing technologies, for example nuclear power, the expectation that technologies can solve the problem of climate change and ongoing greenhouse gas emissions in particular diverts our attention away from acting aggressively right now to reduce our impact on the earth's atmosphere. In other words, technology, or the prospect of it, can make governments, industries, and individuals lazy about thinking about behaviors causing climate change and more immediate alternatives to them. People, governments and businesses remain largely in denial, thinking that we can wait a bit longer to tackle this problem.[51] There is a faith that there is still time to find a solution. However, action is needed now – or truly massive effort will be required in the near future – if the world has any hope of avoiding the most dramatic impacts of climate change.

Education has great potential to overcome public apathy and reticence about changing behaviors and accepting (or pushing) government action to limit greenhouse gas emissions.[52] Climate change is not yet fully integrated into curricula at all levels in most countries, even in those where education is of high quality, to say nothing of where basic education is lacking. However, climate-education programs have increased in number, particularly in developed countries, since the 1990s. Likewise, media coverage of climate change issues has generally increased. This coverage waxes and wanes, often increasing just before and during prominent international climate change conferences, and falling thereafter. The steady news generated by climate scientists has inevitably resulted in more coverage in the popular press, on television, and through popular online sources of information.[53]

But not all of this coverage is helpful in informing the public; the press is often most interested in reporting controversies among scientists and their critics. In some nations, particularly the United States, much of the media coverage perpetuates the skepticism of those individuals, industries, and politicians that want to deny the reality of climate change.[54] An example was reaction to the 2009 "Climategate" episode in Britain, occurring not long before the Copenhagen climate conference, in which scientists' email messages were hacked and used by skeptics of climate change to suggest that the science was somehow manipulated to make climate change appear worse than it really is.[55] Alas, if only this were true; instead, scientific findings confirm almost daily that climate change is under way and will have severely adverse consequences for the world. Thus the way that climate change is reported and taught in schools is vitally important because extensive polling research shows that people who understand the basic science of climate change support voluntary and government action to combat it.[56]

Related to both education and media attention given to climate change is another positive development that could feed into more effective climate politics: growing awareness among young people of climate change, and indeed other environmental issues, consistent with some movement toward "post-materialist" values over the last half-century.[57] It is important not to overstate this development; young people of today may grow up to become just as polluting, if not much more so, than their parents. In the poorest communities, this may be inevitable in the short term because more material wealth and energy use is necessary to meet people's basic needs. The extreme danger is that more people around the world are becoming "new consumers" who mimic and multiply atmospheric pollution that has historically been caused by people in the developed world (see chapter 4).[58]

Another thing that is right about climate politics is the recognition (often practiced in the breach, admittedly) that climate change is a matter of justice. Recognition has been particularly clear with respect to international justice. Nations have agreed that there is "common but differentiated responsibility" for climate change, with the developed countries that are historically most responsible for contributing to the problem obligated to take action first and to do much more than those who are less responsible.[59] This is important because it means that the international politics of climate change have recognized the need for and the right to economic development in poor countries. Aggressive efforts to address questions of justice and inequality are central to addressing climate change.[60] A question becomes at what point newly developed countries should take on obligations to reduce emissions alongside the world's developed nations.

These and many other indications of some progress in dealing with climate change (and related caveats) deserve to be recognized. Indeed, there is more progress than noted here, so it is not entirely unreasonable for an optimist to feel some measure of hope for the future. However, each bit of progress tends to present its own set of problems. Generally speaking, the overall problem is that those things that are right with climate politics have one big thing that is wrong with all of them: they are too little, too late. Put another way, what is right with climate politics is currently overwhelmed by, and often undermined by, what is wrong with it.

What's most wrong with climate politics

Despite there being quite a lot that is "right" with climate politics and the world's responses to the problem, things continue to grow worse. Surely the most fundamental failure of climate politics is the fact that global pollution causing climate change continues to *increase at an increasing rate*. Another great failure is that the resources needed to help those most vulnerable to the effects of climate change have been paltry so far, and will surely not meet demand in the foreseeable future (if ever). In a nutshell, what is wrong with climate politics surpasses what is right with it. This poses a big question: What exactly is wrong with climate politics? The answer, or more accurately the answers, to this question would require many books to describe, let alone to analyze fully. Nevertheless, it is possible to distill what is *most* wrong with climate politics. Fixing that would do a great deal to help mitigate both the causes and consequences of climate change. With this in mind, Part I of the book focuses on a few problems that are *fundamental* to the failure of climate politics, notably the self-interestedness of actors, from nations to individuals, and the selfishness that is built into the economic and social structures that influence people's lives. Fundamental to the problem is the all-too-frequent failure to recognize that human beings are at the heart of climate change.

Three diagnoses at international, national, and individual levels are *most* important for understanding the failure of climate politics:

(1) the cancer of Westphalia: the Westphalian international system, which encourages nations to fight for their narrow, short-term perceived interests and makes truly effective international cooperation on climate change extraordinarily difficult;

(2) malignancy of the Great Polluters: the United States and China, which together produce over one-third of global greenhouse gas pollution but which so far have each refused to compromise on the demand that the other commit to doing much more to limit its pollution; and

(3) addictions of modernity: the growing pollution that comes from material consumption, energy use, and other aspects of modern lifestyles that are spreading from the developed nations to the developing world as more people join the global middle class.

These ailments have been collectively chosen as the focus of what is *most* wrong with climate politics because they are fundamental drivers of many of the other problems that are preventing robust action on climate change. Just as physicians must treat the most urgent, systemic ailments of a very sick patient before addressing the less important ones, the diagnosis here is necessarily biased toward a few big problems. The nation-state system preoccupies policymakers, diplomats, experts, and even individuals with top-down, nation-centric solutions and thus distracts us from the roles of other important actors. The United States and China, while not the only national causes of climate change, find themselves at a point in history where they can, by themselves, prevent global solutions to the problem. And the modern (western) lifestyle – entrenched in the United States and most of the developed world, and spreading fast to China and other up-and-coming developing nations – is utterly unsustainable from the perspective of climate change, and indeed from other perspectives, including those of wider environmental health and human wellbeing.

The cancer of Westphalia is extremely pernicious. The selfishness of nations has consistently trumped concerns about the dangers of climate change. International negotiations under the auspices of the United Nations have comprised many international conferences to produce an overarching framework convention followed by more negotiations to reach a protocol. Those negotiations have in turn been followed by yet more negotiations on how to implement the convention and the protocol, and continuing negotiations on what will come next. This process has already lasted a generation, and there is no end in sight. While clearly driving much of the action on climate change, international negotiations as practiced to date are simply not up to the task. The international process is unlikely to end soon – any more than, say, the half-century-long international negotiations on world trade are likely to be abandoned – but the process needs a fundamental rethink and requires a more multifaceted political approach. One of those facets is bringing human beings into the equation much more explicitly. The international negotiations have, in one sense, become a distraction or diversion from local action. They have enabled individuals and communities and entire countries to justify, at least to themselves, that it is rational and acceptable to sit back and wait for global solutions to be agreed by governments before the rest of us take much more concerted action.

With this in mind, chapter 2 describes the nature and impact of the Westphalian system of sovereign nations (so called because it is dated to the Treaty of Westphalia of 1648). Despite increasing action by civil society and various forms of climate-related "governance without government" beyond the nation-state, this system has fundamentally influenced the course of climate politics, both internationally and within nations.[61] The preoccupation with nations and their narrowly perceived national interests is not surprising; this is how most problems crossing borders have been dealt with throughout modern history. Indeed, it has naturally followed that climate change has become the province of the premier collective organization of nations – the United Nations. Chapter 2 describes the UN-brokered climate change agreements and some of the fundamental international principles that underlie international negotiations on climate change. The chapter also explains how the relatively narrow and short-term perceived interests of major nations have prevented the international community from agreeing to the robust policy responses that are required to avert the most serious consequences of climate change. Without a significant shift in emphasis away from the narrow interests of nations toward greater focus on the interests of people (and the environment on which they depend), diplomats will be unable to respond effectively and aggressively to climate change.

Chapter 3 looks at the world's most malignant (in the physiological sense) polluters: the United States and China. The United States was until the mid-2000s the largest national source of greenhouse gas pollution causing climate change, and remains the largest historical polluter. What is more, average per capita emissions in the United States are among the highest in the world (despite having fallen somewhat between 1990 and 2010).[62] China is now the largest national polluter, but its per capita emissions remain much lower than US emissions. Nevertheless, its per capita emissions are above the global average, well above most developing nations, and rising quickly.[63] Because the United States and China together account for more than one-third of global greenhouse gas pollution, it will be impossible to address the problem adequately without their concerted action to stem and ultimately reverse emissions. However, neither of these nations is legally or formally required by international agreements to cut their greenhouse gas pollution. The United States refused to ratify the Kyoto Protocol, and China, as a developing country, is not required by the protocol to undertake greenhouse gas cuts. Instead of collaborating in earnest to mitigate global warming and limit the worst effects of climate change, the United States refuses to take robust action until China agrees to limit and eventually reduce its emissions.[64] China refuses to act until the United States fulfills its historical responsibilities by cutting its emissions and providing major funding to poor countries affected by those emissions. The selfishness of China and the United States, as nations and national communities, has overwhelmed the now-obvious need for subsuming their perceived, short-term national interests to the requirement for bringing the tragedy of the atmospheric commons to an end.

Chapter 4 examines addictions of (and to) modernity that are the driving forces behind greenhouse gas pollution: the world's reliance on fossil fuels and the relationship between that reliance and material consumption. Rather than the numbers of people on the earth being the main cause of climate change, it is how much those people consume beyond their requirements that matters most. A distinction must be made between fulfillment of human needs and environmentally reasonable aspirations which too many people are now lacking, on one hand, and the "affluenza" of material consumption that characterizes the lives of most of the world's affluent people, on the other. One problem with the international political response to climate change is that it diminishes the role of people. As people become affluent, they consume at increasing rates, akin to an addiction that can never be fully satiated. Consumption characterizes modernity, economic systems, and business models. This addiction is not new; what is new is that it is no longer the affliction of the developed nations alone. Today it is also a growing affliction of much of the developing world. As economies of developing nations grow, governments and people there are making the same unsustainable mistakes committed in the developed countries: nurturing a love for modern material goods, private automobiles, air travel, and the consumption of copious amounts of red meat and foods that are high in calories but low in nutrients (western "fast foods").[65] This increasingly speedy spread of material consumption around the world is not only accelerating emissions of greenhouse gases. It is also changing the political calculus for the world's responses to climate change.

A feature of this expanding tragedy is that just when knowledge and awareness of climate change have grown, few people, like few governments, are willing to change their behaviors substantially (if they are already polluting heavily), and the growing number of new consumers in developing nations are (not surprisingly) unwilling to forgo modern lives that engender greenhouse gas pollution just as was done by most people in the developed countries. Nor are many people, notably the affluent who can afford it, normally willing to pay substantially more for energy. People want to enjoy modernity as it is currently conceived, despite the consequences for both environmental and human health. Modern lifestyles, modernity more generally, and related conceptions of how to achieve happiness mirror what nations seek to achieve: more consumption and growth in material output, and the growth of capital to allow even more of this in the future. And even as some countries begin to adopt measures that enable and encourage people to live more sustainably, increasing pollution from growing material consumption and affluence in the developing world overwhelms these efforts. The self-interestedness of people – although not of the world's poor, and not always intentional selfishness – precipitates climate change and stands as a fundamental obstacle to addressing the resulting tragedy.

To be sure, experts will disagree on what is ailing climate politics. But these diagnoses are, at the very least, among the most critical. What can be done to treat them?

How to fix what's most wrong with climate politics

We can point to many treatments for what ails climate politics. It is important to address as many problems with as many solutions as possible. Part II of the book is again biased toward addressing the most urgent ailments with the most essential treatments for escaping the tragedy of the atmospheric commons. As with the diagnoses of the problem, experts will disagree on the best treatments. While the treatments proposed here are not the only important responses to climate change, they are among those that should be administered urgently. Much like an ailment of the human body, treatment can be applied both systemically and locally.

Among the most essential treatments for climate politics are the following, each generally oriented toward a different level of application – international, national, and individual:

(1) people-centered diplomacy: diplomacy and international agreements that put human beings, including the needs of the world's poor and the duties of the world's affluent people, at the heart of responses to climate change;
(2) differentiated responsibility: a formula for international cooperation and domestic policies premised on putting the common but differentiated responsibilities of

individuals alongside the common but differentiated responsibilities of nation-states, thereby diminishing difficult obstacles to action put up by national interests; and

(3) consumption of happiness: a campaign to cultivate human happiness through full and rewarding lives that are premised on sufficiency and environmental sustainability rather than limitless yearning to find satisfaction and pleasure through excessive material consumption.

Chapter 5 begins with the first treatment: people-centered diplomacy. The politics of climate change have focused intently on the role of nations, especially at the international level, as one would expect from traditional international negotiations. This is understandable, but the fundamental drivers of climate pollution are not nations per se. Nation-states as legal entities are ultimately only ideas and institutions. It is *people*, especially the world's affluent people, who unnecessarily drive climate change. In contrast, those who will suffer the most from climate change are not nations or governments per se – the usual recipients of sympathy and of nominal aid related to climate change – but people, especially the world's poor. Their rights to a sustainable and livable environment are being taken away by behaviors of the world's affluent people. An antidote to the cancer of Westphalia involves moving away from the preoccupation with the roles of nations in responses to climate change. At the very least, it requires nations to do more to bring people into calculations of climate politics. Rather than being appendages of climate politics, people – their rights, needs, capabilities, and obligations – ought to be the *primary objects* of international agreements and policies.[66] Put another way, demands for climate justice and fairness among nations ought to be explicitly supplemented with climate justice for and among people.[67] This entails a move away from Westphalian notions toward global (what some might label "cosmopolitan") conceptions of climate politics. Significantly, the remedy is not to abandon the international climate change regime. Instead, the aim is to reorient it more toward people, in the process treating the human causes and consequences of climate change while creating the conditions for more effective cooperation among nations, including the world's greatest polluters – China and the United States.

Chapter 6 examines the distinctions between the common but differentiated responsibilities of nations – an established theme in climate politics – and the common but differentiated responsibilities of individuals. The common but differentiated responsibilities of nations – with the developed ones taking the lead in all actions as the capable developing ones do their best – should be accompanied by common but differentiated responsibilities of individuals: affluent people, regardless of their nationality, should be brought into the global political equation. This better reflects the reality of what causes climate change and it provides a potentially viable way out of the you-go-first syndrome that currently pervades climate diplomacy generally and US–China relations in particular. Under this formula, some (developing) nations would remain legally absolved of responsibility, but their affluent citizens would join affluent people everywhere in taking action. This would bring more of the world's individual polluters into the equation and make agreement among nations politically easier. In short, the world's newly affluent individuals should no longer escape scrutiny. If they were to take action, more political pressure would be felt by affluent people in the developed world, and by their governments, to limit their polluting behaviors.

Focusing on China and the United States, chapter 6 shows how economic development and growth have altered both the practical and moral calculus of climate politics. Not only are these two nations legally exempt from greenhouse gas cuts under existing international agreements, by implication all of their citizens are also exempt. Most will agree that it is not only unsustainable but also absurd that the United States and all Americans continue to enjoy this legal immunity. It might be justifiable for China and especially poorer developing nations to do so because they are far less historically responsible for the problem. However, while per capita emissions of greenhouse gases in most of the developing world remain below those in the developed world, collectively developing countries now produce more than half of all greenhouse gas pollution. As a practical matter, this will have to be addressed in successful climate politics. A solution may be found in focusing on the newly affluent consumers in China, which now number in the hundreds of millions. Global ethics tell us that the pollution of an affluent person in China is just as wrong as pollution of an affluent person in the United States, even while China *as a nation-state* is less obligated (in terms of historical pollution) than is the United States. Thus one treatment for climate politics is to move beyond attempts to persuade China as a nation-state to act alongside the United States, instead working to persuade the Chinese government that affluent people in China (that is, a minority of the population) ought to act alongside affluent Americans (that is, most people in the United States).

Chapter 5 will focus on treatments for what is wrong with climate politics in international negotiations, while chapter 6 will examine treatments for overcoming the political stalemate between the largest national polluters. Those treatments are largely top-down, albeit with people as their objects. In contrast, chapter 7 is concerned with what governments can do and especially with what individuals can do, and why they should, *in their self-interest*, do it. A powerful world economic and social structure, premised on the heavy use of environmental resources, dominates and largely shapes the lives of individuals, corporations, and governments. Capitalism has arguably brought great benefits to humankind, and its spread through globalization has resulted in improvements in human welfare in many developing countries. But one pernicious consequence of the global economy has been environmental destruction and unsustainable levels of pollution that are increasing as developing countries and their people grow and consume more natural resources and more of the material "goods" that characterize modern lifestyles. The economy in which we live simultaneously commodifies the atmospheric commons and encourages dependence upon – nothing short of an addiction to – carbon-based fuels: coal, petroleum, and natural gas. It is extraordinarily difficult to escape from this structure without redefining our goals and our lives.

An alternative to this addiction is a way of life that meets people's material needs, and their personal and societal aspirations, while stopping short of fulfilling their limitless (and unachievable) desires. Everyone needs to be free of poverty; everyone needs and deserves adequate nutrition, shelter, health care, education, and the like. But everyone does not need to consume vastly more than one requires. Indeed, despite common wisdom and messages in advertising and media, affluence much beyond a point of sufficiency does not generally bring happiness and human wellbeing – certainly not enough to justify causing enormous suffering to future generations. This is because affluence is routinely manifested in unnecessary material overconsumption rather than in consumption of experiences that make people truly happy. Indeed, excessive consumption can and does bring unhappiness. In contrast, a life of sufficiency can be both fulfilling to those who have it and environmentally sustainable (even with a larger global population). Climate politics and related government policy would do well to spread this message and to implement programs that make it possible and even easy for people to live more happily *and* more sustainably.

Conclusion

The diagnoses here for what ails climate politics are necessarily partial. They will have to be addressed alongside the many other things that are wrong with the world's responses to climate change. The recommended treatments in this book are also partial and indeed aspirational. But the same could be said about treating urgent health problems faced by individuals who have not responded to traditional treatments, or to more chronic problems, such as weaning individuals and societies off cigarettes. These are ongoing tasks that are well established in many developed societies, thanks to healthcare vanguards who continue to battle their cause. Meanwhile, more and more people are taking up smoking in the developing world, creating an even greater threat to human health. Despite this daunting challenge, most people will agree that the battle against smoking needs to continue, and indeed should be strengthened, to avert a global health crisis. It is also a major ongoing struggle to improve people's health in the West – to get people to "eat their vegetables," exercise, and so forth – even as modern diseases spread rapidly throughout the developing world as people there adopt western diets and lifestyles. Nobody doubts the need to address these health problems, but few would be foolish enough to think that remedying them will be the least bit easy. The cures need to be pursued nevertheless.

The same is true for climate change and associated politics in particular: there is much wrong and there are many potential cures. We need to face up to the disease and get to work on treating its most urgent causes – despite the enormous challenge. The aim of the chapters that follow is to help us focus more on doing just that.

Part I

Diagnoses

CHAPTER TWO

Cancer of Westphalia: Climate Diplomacy and the International System

Among the most troublesome ailments afflicting climate politics is the "cancer of Westphalia." This is an international cancer that influences negotiations and agreements among governments, undermining their willingness and ability to respond to climate change effectively. Fundamental to this ailment is the system of nation-states that encourages governments to view national interests very narrowly and often to see them as inherently opposed to or challenged by other nations' national interests, and which almost always weighs in favor of short-term interests over long-term ones while discounting the importance of environmental stewardship. The practical result has been a very weak climate change regime that is unable to keep up with changes in expert knowledge about the causes and consequences of greenhouse gas pollution and increasingly is unable to respond to climate change that is already under way and clearly visible on the horizon. Like many cancers, this one began early in the life of the international community, grew larger with time and has now metastasized to the point where it permeates nearly every aspect of climate politics, especially at the international level but also in the context of the domestic politics of climate change. Like most cancers, it will be very difficult to rid the system of this one's most pernicious influences. However, despite the lack of time to rid the climate regime of this cancer altogether, it can be treated (as discussed in chapter 5).

This chapter diagnoses the cancer of Westphalia. It

describes the nature of the centuries-old Westphalian system of sovereign nation-states that, despite increasing action by civil society and various types of climate-related "governance without government" (whereby communities and stakeholders organize themselves to take action independently of government regulation or policy), has fundamentally influenced the course of climate politics internationally and within nations. This has happened because the world has responded to climate change the same way that it has responded for centuries to other great problems: through attempts at cooperation among sovereign nations, which since the mid-twentieth century have routinely involved the United Nations and its affiliated organs. The chapter summarizes some of the diplomacy surrounding the United Nations-brokered climate change agreements, describes some of the impacts of those agreements, and touches upon the underlying principles of international justice and common but differentiated responsibilities that have provided a foundation for international cooperation on climate change. This chapter also looks at how the relatively narrow and short-term perceived national interests of nations have made it difficult for the world to achieve the robust policy action that is necessary to avert the egregious consequences of climate change.

The international system

The nature and impact of the Westphalian system of sovereign nations fundamentally influences the course of climate politics at all levels. Nation-states have been the default actors in the world's responses to climate change, and it has been cooperation among nations – or lack of it – that has largely determined what has been done to address the problem, and to what degree. This is a normal response to a global problem requiring collective action because the world remains dominated by sovereign nation-states, particularly in official thinking and discourse. Governments have for centuries responded to collective action problems by trying to cooperate at the international level. Given the international (that is, transboundary) nature of climate change, governments have turned to diplomacy and specifically to the United Nations to find solutions, especially in the form of agreements among nations. This is a logical outgrowth of the Westphalian state system. Indeed, it would have been highly unusual, even radical, if the world had responded to climate change much differently, for example by looking for bottom-up solutions among people and organizations before turning to states for leadership, or by letting people rather than governments decide how to respond. The response to climate change has been consistent with official responses to other problems over the centuries, despite climate change being much less about nation-states than most traditional issues addressed by them (such as border and trade disputes).

The Westphalian international system that dominates world order is not natural. It was crafted by statesmen over centuries and as such is a manmade outgrowth of the historical evolution of relations among groups of people. The Westphalian system may be defined narrowly as the various relationships among the fundamental actors in the system, namely nation-states (such as Britain, China, India, Mexico). Nation-states by definition are political entities, each with a government having sole political authority over a territory and the people living there. A sovereign nation is normally recognized by (most) other nations and nowadays by the United Nations.

While nations had declared their sovereignty at earlier points in history, the modern international system is routinely dated to the Peace of Westphalia of 1648, which ended the Thirty Years War of religion in Europe (1618–1648). The Peace of Westphalia was (and remains) significant because it was premised on those principles that make up the modern global order: parties to the Peace were recognized as being their own masters, rather than being the subjects of foreign religious or imperial powers. Each nation was recognized as being equally legitimate in the eyes of international law, and each agreed to accept, at least in principle, that what happened inside other nations was not their concern. Wars in Europe and elsewhere continued, but diplomacy and international law among mutually recognized nation-states became norms that continue to dominate the world today.

Central to the system of nation-states – the international system – are the principles of sovereignty and noninterference. The government of each nation is recognized as having sovereignty – sole and supreme legal and political authority – in its territory; there is no higher authority than that of the sovereign nation unless a government or governments agree to relinquish sovereignty in specific issue areas, usually by treaty. Fundamental to the system is the principle of noninterference: while nations may take an interest in what happens in other countries (although even doing this can provoke criticism today, especially from China), in principle they have no right to intervene in the internal affairs of another nation without justification. What happens within a particular nation is legally the business of that nation and no other, and each nation has the sole right to conduct its own affairs internally and to conduct its relations with other nations (its foreign affairs).

In reality, of course, these fundamental tenets of the international system are often practiced in the breach; nations are routinely concerned about what happens in other countries and frequently intervene in a variety of ways, ranging from diplomatic protest all the way to military intervention. However, the fundamental principles are self-sustaining simply because nations have a key interest in maintaining them. Very significantly, the Westphalian system creates and reinforces an obsession with the interests of the nation-state above all else.

One cannot understate the power of these principles in the context of climate change. The dominant discourse around the problem, among diplomats, scholars, and even ordinary people, is routinely defined in terms of "state-centric territorialization."[1] Climate change, from this dominant perspective and according to the prevailing discourse, is a problem for nation-states, greenhouse gas emissions are measured in terms of nations, climate negotiations are of course among nations, obligations and interests are of nations, the problem is perceived to create security challenges for nations, the scientists in the IPCC are nominated by governments of nations, and so forth. This "territorial trap" greatly narrows the options for thinking about climate change and finding political and policy solutions to it.[2] For example, the question about how to allocate the distribution of greenhouse limitations has become "unambiguously a statist project, which starts from, and reinforces, the conception that it is states that have both rights and responsibilities in relation to the rest of the world," of course with *diplomats* negotiating responses to climate change while assuming the sovereign equality of nations.[3]

Some nations take the Westphalian principles to extremes. For example, at the 2009 Copenhagen conference of the parties to the climate convention, China refused to accept outside monitoring of even its *voluntary* pledges to improve energy efficiency, justifying this refusal on the grounds of sovereignty and noninterference in its internal affairs. Others were suspicious of China's pledges: could it be trusted to keeps its word if, when giving that word, it simultaneously refused everyone the right to verify it? Whether that lack of trust was justified is not the point. The point is that the norms of the Westphalian system were powerful at the level of diplomatic negotiations and therefore affected their outcome, in this case contributing to a very weak agreement at the conclusion of the Copenhagen conference.

Crucially for our understanding of nations' responses to climate change, in the Westphalian system each nation seeks to promote its "national interests," usually interpreted as the most important objectives of those ruling and living within that political community. Foremost for each nation is its continued existence and the protection of its territorial integrity, without which there would be no sovereign nation-state in the traditional sense. This helps to explain why nations are so protective of controlling their borders: clear territorial boundaries reaffirm the sense of statehood that was codified at Westphalia. Key national interests include economic vitality and all that it entails, including a strong national economy, jobs, financial prosperity, and connections with the world through trade, as well as what we might call the nation's "way of life" – the collection of language, culture, political system, often religion, and other characteristics that define a particular nation and its population's sense of collective identity and purpose. Governments are seen to be legitimate insofar as they are able, at the very least, to defend these vital national interests, and more often than not it is necessary for them to be seen to be doing so by their populations, especially but not exclusively in democratic states in which governments must periodically face the national electorate.

It would be a slight exaggeration to say, especially in this day and age, that national governments and their citizens do not care at all about what happens in other nations. Often they do, as evidenced by, for example, foreign aid regimes, support for international development programs, and the willingness of governments to go to war to aid other countries and even people for humanitarian reasons.[4] But it is also the case that all governments are very heavily inclined to promote the perceived interests of their own nations, whether that is the perceived interests of their citizens in democracies or the interests of the ruling party or elites in authoritarian states. In times of crisis, such as economic recession and when threatened with aggression, the interests of other nations are naturally pushed aside. As some political "realists" might describe it, it is every nation for itself much of the time, and nearly all of the time when the going gets tough.[5] This has real implications for the world's responses to climate change. Climate-related policies have the potential to adversely affect economies and certainly will affect powerful interest groups, leading to political resistance, whereas the effects of climate change will bring great suffering to many nations, harming economic development and human health, and even posing an existential threat to some island countries, of course leading them to push for more urgent action.[6]

Throughout history, communities have sought to protect their survival and promote their other interests through a variety of means. In international relations, a balance of power often arises whereby weaker countries ally together to defend themselves against more powerful potential (and real) adversaries. This is most obvious in wartime – US interventions in Europe during the two world wars of the twentieth century are potent examples – but it also obtains in other issue areas, for example when developing countries teamed up in the 1970s to form the Group of 77 ("G-77") to fight for their economic interests vis-à-vis the western industrial powers. A balance of power of sorts has also been manifested in international negotiations on climate change, with most developing nations allying together to push for action by developed countries, although the traditional "North–South" (rich-nation/poor-nation) dichotomy is breaking down as developing nations divide along lines of responsibility for climate change, capability to respond to it, and vulnerability to its effects.[7]

In addition to balances of power to protect their vital

interests, nations have always sought to address problems requiring collective action through international cooperation, often brokered by the United Nations and its agencies, and through the creation of international regimes, defined by scholars as "principles, norms, rules and decision-making procedures around which actors' expectations converge in a given area of international relations."[8] Perhaps the most visible example of this can be found in the World Trade Organization (and its predecessor, the General Agreement on Tariffs and Trade) and the many norms and rules for trade associated with it. Naturally, governments have responded to climate change in the same manner: by negotiating agreements and developing norms of behavior intended to address climate change in ways that are consistent with the more fundamental underlying Westphalian norms of the international system and the protection of national interests.[9] Alas, the latter norms are often more powerful than the desire to protect the environment.

A key premise of the international system – sovereignty – has always been challenged by war and other forms of intervention, but since about the 1970s it has been put under stress on a continuing and increasing basis by globalization. Globalization, which can be defined in one sense as the erosion of governments' sovereign control over what happens within and across their borders, has engendered the conditions that undermine the ability of nations to shape events, whether individually or even through cooperation. Manifestations of globalization include the increasing integration of national economies through transnational trade, production, and finance, and a speeding up and deepening of connections among economies and people. Globalization is pushed by a western conception of capitalism that unquestionably promotes economic integration of the entire world.[10] It has enabled people to easily and remotely share information and interact almost instantly. It has been accelerated by the microelectronic revolution, manifested in technologies such as desktop and mobile computers, blogs on the World Wide Web, mobile "smart phones," voice-over-internet telephony and the like.[11]

While economic globalization has received most of the world's attention over the last several decades as global trade and finance have accelerated and affected almost every corner of the world, it is the effects of much of that trade – pollution and adverse changes to the global *environment*, including climate change – that are the most profound manifestations of globalization.[12] This is because globalization is as much about the increasingly massive extraction, transport, and consumption of natural resources as it is about mobile phones and the internet. Put another way, *environmental* globalization, particularly climate change, has challenged national sovereignty like almost nothing else. Indeed, for some small-island nations, climate change – and specifically resulting sea-level rise – will likely wipe them off the map one day, making them nations without territories. For them, climate change is the ultimate erosion of sovereignty; it is an existential threat. One argument is that only by cooperating can nations address such a challenge. But with such an enormous collective action problem, it is possible that nations cannot achieve their objectives without expanding the scope of "national" interests to include the natural environment at home and abroad.

Climate change diplomacy

What has the international response to climate change looked like?[13] Governments have come to recognize that there is indeed a tragedy of the atmospheric commons, and they have responded to it as they have responded to so many other widespread challenges affecting more than one country: by trying to work together collectively to formulate and implement solutions. In practice, this has resulted in agreement to study the problem, followed by a framework convention (treaty) that was then refined by protocols and recurring diplomatic conferences and meetings. By some accounts, the model for this response to climate change came from international action to address stratospheric ozone depletion.[14] In that case, diplomats first negotiated the 1985 Vienna Convention for the Protection of the Ozone Layer, a framework agreement that recognized the importance of addressing the problem without assigning any specific requirements for action. Governments subsequently agreed to the 1987 Montreal Protocol on Substances that Deplete the Ozone Layer, which laid out specific cuts in ozone-destroying pollutants, followed over time by more international negotiations leading to a number of amendments to the protocol that were intended to speed up cuts in pollution, add new types of pollutants to those being regulated, agree new means for implementation, and so forth. Collectively, these agreements, and the ozone-protecting norms they helped to solidify among nations, comprise the ozone-protection regime.

Similarly, the climate change regime is made up of a collection of agreements and, importantly, agreed principles and norms that have guided official responses to the problem. Unlike the ozone regime's "progressive development" toward relative success, however, the climate regime is more a case of "arrested development."[15] The ozone regime has resulted in big global cuts in ozone-destroying chemicals, but the climate regime has not resulted in substantial global cuts in greenhouse gas emissions.[16] Indeed, those emissions are on the rise.

Much as was the case with ozone depletion, the international response to climate change was stimulated by the work of scientists who raised the alarm, called for more research,

and provided technical knowledge necessary to inform diplomacy and national action.[17] One of the earliest international
climate-related events was the 1979 First World Climate
Conference, a gathering of scientists interested in climate
change and its relationship with human activities. From that
scientific conference, a program of research was established,
leading to creation of the Intergovernmental Panel on Climate
Change in 1988. The IPCC's first assessment report and the
Second World Climate Conference in 1990 added stimulus
to initial concerns among governments about climate change.
Consequently, in late 1990 the United Nations created the
Intergovernmental Negotiating Committee for a Framework
Convention on Climate Change. Its objective was to negotiate
a treaty that would be the basis for subsequent international
agreements for dealing with the problem. That international
negotiating process resulted in the signing of the climate
convention at the 1992 UN Conference on Environment and
Development (the "Earth Summit") held in Rio de Janeiro.

The primary objective of the climate convention was (and
is) the "stabilization of greenhouse gas concentrations in the
atmosphere at a level that [will] prevent dangerous anthropogenic interference with the climate system. Such a level should
be achieved within a time-frame sufficient to allow ecosystems
to adapt naturally to climate change, to ensure that food production is not threatened and to enable economic development
to proceed in a sustainable manner."[18] The climate convention
came into force in 1994 after ratification by 50 nations. As part
of the convention, developed countries agreed to reduce their
emissions of greenhouse gases to 1990 levels by 2000. This
emissions-reduction pledge was voluntary. Not surprisingly,
therefore, it was not honored by governments, and greenhouse
gas emissions continued to increase for most countries, and,
where they declined, it was for reasons quite unrelated to the
convention, for example due to falls in emissions from within

the former communist nations of Eastern Europe as their economies collapsed during the 1990s.

Importantly, however, the principle that developed nations are foremost responsible for taking action was affirmed by the convention. Particular responsibility was also laid on the developed nations to provide developing countries with "new and additional" resources, specifically financial assistance that would go beyond existing development aid, to help them to limit their own greenhouse gas pollution and to cope with the impacts of climate change. Significantly, despite the potential contradiction with its main aims, the climate convention noted that nations have "the sovereign right to exploit their own resources pursuant to their own environmental and developmental policies," and it reaffirmed "the principle of sovereignty of States in international cooperation to address climate change."[19] By including these caveats, nations indicated formally that fundamental Westphalian norms would come before evolving norms of climate protection.

The climate convention also established a rolling "conference of the parties" to be scheduled periodically by a convention secretariat. This conference of nations has met more or less annually since the mid-1990s, in the process negotiating details of how greenhouse gas emissions limitations should be achieved and deciding how other provisions of the climate convention should be implemented.[20] At the first conference of the parties, held in Berlin in 1995, developed nations acknowledged again that they had a greater share of the responsibility for causing climate change, that they should therefore take the lead in addressing the problem, and that they ought to provide related aid to developing nations. The resulting "Berlin Mandate" affirmed the notion of common but differentiated responsibilities: all nations have a common responsibility to respond to climate change, but the developed countries have "differentiated" (greater) obligation to do so.[21]

At the second conference of the parties, which met in Geneva in 1996, diplomats agreed to start negotiating a legally binding protocol to the climate convention that would include specific targets and timetables for reducing the greenhouse gas emissions of developed nations. The resulting Geneva Declaration served as the basis for negotiating the protocol, which was finalized and signed at the 1997 third conference of the parties held in Kyoto. The Kyoto Protocol required most developed nations to cut their collective greenhouse gas emissions before the end of 2012 by 5.2 percent below 1990 levels, with individual nations (or groups of them) having specific commitments – some cutting more than 5.2 percent, some less – and a few allowed increases.[22] However, not all developed nations agreed to be bound by the protocol. Most prominently and most crucially, the United States, despite its vice president having a direct role in the negotiations at Kyoto, never ratified the treaty due to concerns in Congress about the agreement's potential effects on the US economy (see the next section and chapter 3).

Some of the means by which the Kyoto Protocol's objectives would be achieved were codified at the fourth conference of the parties, which met in Buenos Aires in 1998. These included a number of "market mechanisms," including: emissions trading that would enable parties that exceed their commitments to sell the resulting credits; the Clean Development Mechanism, which allows developed-nation parties to meet their commitments through projects in developing countries; and joint implementation, which allows developed nations to meet their emissions commitments through cuts in other developed nations. At the fifth conference of the parties, held in Bonn in 1999, diplomats agreed to a timetable for negotiating the details for implementing the Kyoto Protocol. This would prove to be difficult. At the sixth conference of the parties in The Hague in 2000, talks broke down in part due to disagreement over the use of carbon sinks (activities that absorb CO_2 from the atmosphere, such as the planting of trees) to meet emissions targets.

In early 2001, the likelihood of the Kyoto Protocol ever being ratified by the United States was put into further doubt with the advent of President George W. Bush. He quickly withdrew all US support for the treaty while also questioning the reality of climate change.

Nevertheless, the sixth conference of the parties resumed in Bonn in July 2001. The resulting Bonn Agreement clarified plans for using "flexible mechanisms," such as emissions trading, carbon sinks, and aid to developing countries, to achieve the protocol's objectives. The seventh conference of the parties, which met in Marrakech in 2001, produced the Marrakech Accords, a complicated mix of proposals for implementing the Kyoto Protocol, largely designed to garner ratifications from enough nations to enable the protocol to enter into force. To satisfy developing nations, diplomats agreed at Marrakech to increase funding for the climate convention's financial mechanism, the Global Environment Facility, and to establish three new funds: the Least Developed Countries Fund, the Special Climate Change Fund, and the Adaptation Fund. However, the implementation measures that were agreed at Marrakech meant that actual cuts in greenhouse gas emissions by developed nations would be far less than the already inadequate 5.2 percent agreed in Kyoto.[23]

Perhaps realizing a certain level of futility about the prospects for major greenhouse gas cuts, at the 2002 eighth conference of the parties in New Delhi the focus of diplomats shifted away from mitigating emissions, and thereby reducing the impacts of climate change, toward *adapting* to climate change, with affluent nations agreeing to help developing countries cope with the impacts.[24] This would allow the developed nations to avoid heavy reductions in their greenhouse

gas emissions – meaning few changes to the way they provide energy to their economies – while making it less likely
that large developing countries would be required to do so
one day. Of course, this meant that the problem would only
grow worse. Also at the New Delhi meeting, as well as at the
ninth conference of the parties held in Milan, Italy, in late
2003, diplomats discussed ways to implement the Marrakech
Accords and to prepare for ratification of the protocol. At the
2004 tenth conference of the parties in Buenos Aires, discussion again focused more on adaptation to climate change
than on efforts to mitigate it through emissions limitations.
Pledges were made by developed-nation diplomats to provide
more assistance to aid poor countries most affected by climate
change, albeit without firm commitments on making access
to those funds easier. Importantly, it was also in 2004 that
Russia ratified the Kyoto Protocol, allowing it to finally enter
into force in February 2005.

Differences between developed and developing nations had
right along been key features of international negotiations on
climate change, with each group of countries expecting more
from the other: the former calling for emissions commitments
from the latter, and the latter calling for serious greenhouse
gas cuts and development assistance from the former. This
was manifested at the climate convention's late-2005 eleventh
conference of the parties – also the first simultaneous "meeting of the parties" to the Kyoto Protocol – held in Montreal,
Canada. Despite attempts by US diplomats to derail the
meeting, it formalized rules for implementing the protocol, streamlined and strengthened the Clean Development
Mechanism, began negotiations for further commitments by
developed nations beyond the Kyoto Protocol's commitment
period (2008–2012), set out guidelines for the Adaptation
Fund, and initiated a process for negotiating long-term action
to combat climate change. Several developing nations, while

still opposed to binding obligations (in keeping with the principle of common but differentiated responsibilities) suggested at this conference that they might be willing to adopt voluntary measures to limit their greenhouse gas emissions.

Despite the high and indeed accelerating level of climate diplomacy, progress in achieving the climate convention's objectives was very limited. Indeed, at the 2006 twelfth conference of the parties in Nairobi, then UN Secretary-General Kofi Annan characterized the climate change negotiations up to that point as displaying a "frightening lack of leadership" from governments.[25] At the thirteenth conference of the parties, held in Bali in 2007, European diplomats pushed for deeper greenhouse gas cuts, the United States opposed them, and developing countries again argued for more financial and technological assistance.[26] In exchange for a streamlining of the Adaptation Fund and sourcing it with a new 2 percent levy on Clean Development Mechanism projects, some developing nations again agreed to consider adopting unspecified future actions to mitigate their greenhouse gas pollution. Developed-nation diplomats accepted new emissions targets and timetables, although, as with the developing countries' pledges, nothing was set in stone.

The Bali conference was noteworthy for diplomats' near-universal and vehement opposition to efforts by US diplomats to put a stop to negotiations on a post-2012 agreement, intended to succeed or extend the Kyoto Protocol, which would obligate developed nations to adopt new limits on their greenhouse gas emissions and to provide more aid to developing nations. Diplomats adopted yet another, supposedly more powerful, plan for more diplomatic efforts – the so-called Bali Roadmap. This roadmap was supposed to guide discussions leading to a new, more comprehensive post-Kyoto agreement in time for the fifteenth conference of the parties to be held in two years' time in Copenhagen.

The discussions at Bali were pushed to a substantial degree by the IPCC's fourth assessment report, which removed any remaining reasonable doubt about the seriousness of climate change. One consequence was a noticeable, almost frenetic, increase in diplomatic activity around climate change, manifested in a large number of international meetings and national discussions to prepare for the Copenhagen conference. One step along the way was the fourteenth conference of the parties, held in late 2008 in Poznan, Poland. The Poznan meeting was noteworthy in one respect: with the global financial crisis hitting economies hard, even European diplomats, who had for a number of years been pushing for more action on climate change, were less supportive of deeper greenhouse gas cuts.

However, the financial crisis did not dampen the enthusiasm that built up among both climate diplomats and environmentalists in the run-up to the 2009 conference of the parties in Copenhagen. Indeed, harkening back to the original signing of the climate convention at the 1992 Earth Summit, the Copenhagen conference included the participation of nearly every nation and more than half of their leaders – 192 countries and 119 heads of state – making it probably the largest gathering of world leaders in modern history.[27] Nevertheless, the result of the conference – the Copenhagen Accord – showed that progress on combating climate change was inversely proportional to the enthusiasm of leaders to attend.

The Copenhagen Accord, which emanated from a process characterized by major differences between and among both developed and developing nations (see the next section), was pulled together in the final hours of the conference by a small group of diplomats and leaders. The agreement did a number of things: it reaffirmed the science of climate change, recognized the need to bring the rise in global greenhouse gas emissions to a halt and to keep the global temperature increase to less than 2° Celsius, and pledged to protect forests as important carbon sinks. Perhaps most significantly, the accord also promised that developed nations were committed to "a goal of mobilizing jointly US$100 billion dollars a year by 2020 to address the needs of developing countries," and it established a Green Climate Fund to administer aid to help those countries adapt to climate change.[28]

Despite these pledges, the Copenhagen Accord lacked ambition in that it was barely more than an incremental move beyond the wording of the climate convention signed at the 1992 Earth Summit. While thousands of nongovernmental representatives and activists outside the conference venue called for action to address climate change aggressively, inside the meeting rooms what mattered was the perceived national interests of a relatively few countries. The accord represented "a lowest common denominator agreement with question-able long-term effectiveness."[29] Even most of the diplomats at the conference characterized the accord as weak and lacking practicality.[30] What is more, the accord was *voluntary*, again harkening back to the voluntary nature of the climate convention itself. Leaders and diplomats at Copenhagen were unable to overcome their short-term national interests.

While there was much diplomatic activity following the Copenhagen meeting, differences remained, with nations unable to agree on robust greenhouse gas commitments, means for ensuring that they are implemented, long-term financing of the Green Climate Fund, or even agreement on what level of global warming all these efforts should aim to prevent – with some small-island nations arguing that the nominal goal of limiting warming to 2° Celsius (already a nigh-impossible target to achieve)[31] would mean certain catastrophe for their communities.[32] These differences were reflected in the December 2010 sixteenth conference of the parties in Cancun, Mexico, which recognized that much more needed to be done to combat climate change, proposed action to protect forests in developing nations when doing so, and continued negotiations on how to implement the Green Climate Fund while failing to decide on whether or how to replace the Kyoto Protocol with a stronger agreement.

The seventeenth conference of the parties, which met in Durban, South Africa, in late 2011, produced the "Durban Platform for Enhanced Action." This platform was essentially more of the same: pledges to continue negotiations on implementing previous agreements and treaties for achieving the objectives of the two-decade-old climate convention. The most significant outcomes of the conference were agreements to move toward implementing the Green Climate Fund and to continue steps toward financing it, albeit without saying where the money would come from; to keep the Kyoto Protocol commitments alive for several more years, probably to 2017 but possibly to 2020; and to begin negotiations by 2015 on a successor treaty, which is supposed to include some kind of legal commitments on greenhouse gas emissions limitations by *all* nations, for ratification by 2020.[33]

During the conference, the European Union was willing to accept a new commitment period under the Kyoto Protocol in exchange for an agreement that would include legally binding emissions commitments from large developing countries. The Europeans were pitted against China and India, which expressed dismay at the continued unwillingness of developed nations to implement past agreements, arguing that a new treaty would be premature without more action from the historical polluters. China's chief negotiator implied that his country might be willing to accept legally binding commitments "after 2020" if a number of preconditions were met – essentially requiring developed countries to meet all of their past commitments and obligations even as China's emissions continue to grow.[34] The United States eventually joined the consensus, many of its delegates no doubt hoping that their own country would take more action in the not-too-distant future.

As with so many other climate conferences, these pledges to reach and implement new agreements over the coming decade were not legally binding; they were promises to be kept by future governments. The Durban action plan reaffirmed the need to restrict global warming to no more than 2° Celsius above normal, but diplomats simultaneously recognized that warming of at least double that was on the cards under existing national commitments, even as scientific reports released around the time of the conference – showing large increases in global carbon emissions and the virtual inevitability of much greater global warming[35] – suggested that the skepticism of developing-nation diplomats and environmental groups that greeted the close of the conference was justified.[36]

What the Durban conference made clear beyond any doubt was that no new greenhouse gas commitments, least of all the types of robust cuts in emissions needed to avert dangerous climate change, would be agreed before 2015, and that those new commitments, whatever they might be, would not be implemented before 2020. The conference was another "significant step forward" (to quote Britain's chief delegate), but it was once again much too little much too late.[37]

The outcome at Durban revealed the fundamental problem with climate change conferences: diplomats routinely put their own nations' short-term interests, or at least the interests of those with power in their home countries, well ahead of the long-term interest that the world has in averting catastrophic climate change. Indeed, within hours of returning from the Durban conference, Canada's environment minister announced that his country would become the first to withdraw from the Kyoto Protocol, renouncing legally binding commitments that Canada had accepted years before.[38] He justified this action on the grounds of cost and the lack of participation in the protocol by the world's largest polluters. No doubt he was also hoping to protect growing exports of petroleum from the Alberta's tar sands, despite their considerable adverse impact on the global environment.[39]

Climate change vs. national interests

Recent conferences of the parties, notably the sixteenth at Cancun in 2010 and the seventeenth in Durban in 2011, and the preparatory meetings in between, sought to revive international negotiations and to recover from the failure at Copenhagen. But the general trend of climate diplomacy prevails: national interests trump climate-related ones. It seems that the world remains quite far from the turning point toward, let alone being willing to move swiftly down, a path of concerted action by enough nations. Generally speaking, throughout the climate change negotiations, beginning in the late 1980s when the climate convention was being devised, the relatively narrow and short-term perceived interests of major nations have prevented the international community from agreeing to the robust policy responses that are required to avert the most serious consequences of climate change, least of all implementing such policies. There have been a number of recurring themes in this respect, including rivalries among groups of nations.

The traditional and most obvious rivalry has been between developed and developing countries over questions of poverty, economic development, and international justice. Repeating themes of the New International Economic Order from the 1970s, when developing nations called for a restructuring of the international economic system so that it might exploit them less and instead bring them more benefit, the climate change negotiations have been a battleground for promoting the relative national interests of developed and developing countries. However, unlike in the case of the failed New International

Economic Order, developing nations have been successful in getting many of their concerns incorporated into the climate agreements, most obviously in the principle of common but differentiated responsibilities but also in the formal recognition of their demands to be free of mandatory greenhouse gas cuts and to receive "new and additional" funding to help them prepare for and cope with the effects of climate change.[40]

These developments may be welcome recognition by developed nations of some of the legitimate interests of developing countries and their populations. Nevertheless, despite fostering support for the climate change regime among many developing-country governments, this recognition has not achieved the aims of the climate convention. By promoting nominal justice among nations, *environmental* justice – starting with putting an end to the harm being done to the earth's atmosphere – has mostly been given lip service and effectively ignored. Developed nations have been predictably slow in acting on the principle of common but differentiated responsibilities – their collective greenhouse gas emissions have not fallen – and the developing countries have not been given anywhere near enough help to cope with climate change, least of all being given the incentives and resources needed for them to make major shifts toward sustainable development that would keep their own greenhouse gas emissions down.

The diplomatic struggle between developed and developing nations has been exacerbated by rivalries within each of these groupings. These rivalries reveal the extent to which national interests – and specifically quite narrow, short-term, and ecologically distant conceptions of them – have shaped and continue to shape the course of international and domestic climate politics and associated policies. In the early days of the climate negotiations, developed countries were in general agreement that it was necessary to do something about climate change. But none of them wanted to do very much individually, and certainly not anything that might conceivably undermine their individual economies. They put national economic competitiveness before global environmental health.

In recent years, this more or less similar diplomatic position among developed nations has changed. For example, the positions of Western Europe and North America have grown farther apart in many respects. European Union members have increasingly viewed responding to climate change, by becoming less dependent on fossil fuels and by trying to avert a catastrophic increase in global temperatures, as part and parcel of their national interests, and they have increasingly taken more seriously their obligations to those nations least responsible for climate change and most affected by it.[41] In contrast, North American nations (Canada and the United States, among some other affluent countries) have shown much less interest in pushing for larger cuts in their greenhouse gas emissions – despite the attempts of the United Nations and even the Pentagon to argue that climate change poses very serious threats to the national security of most countries, including developed ones.[42] (Due to the focus in climate politics on national interests, taking this national security-oriented approach is arguably a partial antidote, if only it could catch on.[43] Insofar as this argument is true, it is another testament to the importance of the nation-state in shaping responses to climate change.)

Thus the Europeans' inclination to do more – to live up to their obligations to get their greenhouse gas pollution down, most importantly – is juxtaposed with the United States doing almost nothing, putting European nations in an economic position that many entrenched business interests there argue is a highly compromised one.[44] From this perspective, if European countries implement changes while the United States does not, they become less economically competitive. This is just one common perception, notably among energy-hungry industries. Alternatively, by becoming highly energy efficient and less dependent on fossil fuels, Europe might create new economic opportunities and make itself resilient for future petroleum price shocks or shortages. The latter argument is significant in Europe but not all powerful. Typically, then, while climate change almost certainly poses an enormous long-term threat to most nations, whether developed or developing, short-term perceived national interests, often revolving around existing economic configurations and actors, continue to trump or at least greatly undermine moves toward robust international action on climate change.

This placement of individual national interests before the common interest in combating climate change is just as visible, and perhaps even more so, in growing differences within the developing world. As Timmons Roberts argues, whereas in earlier stages of the climate diplomacy, such as during negotiation of the Kyoto Protocol, when there was substantial solidarity among developing countries on key issues, the Copenhagen negotiations showed that "negotiating blocs have fractured along lines of *responsibility* for climate change, *capability* to address it, and national *vulnerability* to climate risks."[45] These differences are epitomized in the great disparity in the positions of members of the Organization of Petroleum Exporting Countries, whose economies are utterly reliant on the world economy's addiction to oil, on one hand, and many members of the Alliance of Small Island States, some of which face the most severe effects of climate change, ranging from storm surges and total inundation of water supplies to forced mass migrations (to who-knows-where) and territorial obliteration by sea-level rises on the other hand. This was exemplified at the Copenhagen conference when some of the latter countries were flabbergasted by opposition from some of the former nations to calls for more forceful cuts in global greenhouse gas pollution.

The crack in developing country solidarity was further revealed at Copenhagen when China proved to be the biggest obstacle to agreement on more aggressive global emissions cuts. As the largest national source of greenhouse gas emissions, whether China gets its pollution under control is crucial to the world's climate future, and thus to the future of those countries and people most vulnerable to climate change. China has traditionally joined with the G-77 countries in climate negotiations – and nominally still does in a diplomatic grouping referred to as "G-77 plus China" – and it was once in apparent solidarity with their plight. This changed quite markedly in recent years as China (along with Brazil and India) increasingly put its own economic interests before the existential interests of some of its G-77 brethren.[46] Again, narrow national interests trump common (environmental) ones.

Despite all of these problems, from a diplomatic perspective one might want to argue that the glass is half full – that there is indeed diplomatic progress of all sorts, with many agreements to go with it, and that there are frequent promising signs of action by the world's governments – until one realizes that global warming is accelerating, that its causes are not diminishing but instead increasing markedly, and that climate change will get far worse before it gets better. Greenhouse gas emissions from most developed countries continue to rise, albeit only slightly overall, when they need to drop precipitously. Some European countries have reduced their emissions a bit – Germany, for example, deserves credit for its efforts – but these reductions look impressive only if one overlooks the total greenhouse gas pollution coming from consumption within their economies (that is, if one ignores their total carbon footprint, including emissions from imported products).[47]

Furthermore, most large developing nations have increasing greenhouse gas emissions, which is to be expected as their economies grow. But the profound problem is that they have collectively overtaken the developed nations to produce the majority of global greenhouse gas pollution.[48] Amazingly, China's annual *increase* in emissions alone exceeds the *total* annual emissions from some large European countries.[49] On top of historical emissions from the world's developed nations, this newer pollution from large developing nations is environmentally catastrophic, with tragic consequences for millions of people (and their nations) in the future, most profoundly those in the developing world itself.

One thing that is striking about climate diplomacy is how much effort has gone into it. The resulting treaties and other agreements are almost certainly the most complex, extensive, and detailed series of international negotiations ever. The commitment to climate diplomacy is a reflection of how serious the world takes the problem. But it also shows the limits of diplomacy when national interests perceived to be vital are at stake: if great effort over a generation cannot bring about even a modest reduction in global greenhouse gas emissions when major cuts are needed, it seems that no amount of diplomacy, short of a change in the priorities of diplomats, can result in agreements that will tackle climate change in a truly effective way. To quote Matthew Hoffman, despite

> all the efforts of negotiators and urgency surrounding this issue, multilateral treaty-making has consistently failed to produce treaties and agreements that effectively address climate change. It may be time to concede that there is a mismatch between this type of treaty-making and the problem of climate change; that global treaty-making, as attempted in the last two decades, cannot catalyze the societal and economic transformation necessary to avoid the potentially catastrophic consequences of climate change.[50]

As noted in the previous chapter, Hoffman has pointed to a proliferation of alternative responses at all levels, from regional international programs to actions by local communities, businesses, and civil society groups. These are significant, but even if put together they are grossly inadequate, given the scale of action that is required. A different approach would be to reform the international response so that it abets and bolsters these alternative responses, specifically by taking the interests of human beings more seriously (see chapter 5).

It would be an exaggeration to say that countries and their governments care *only* about national interests. There is evidence that the desire to behave ethically and to promote the common good have motivated nations, especially in recent generations, as evidenced by international aid programs and instances of humanitarian intervention, and even more so that ethical concerns have restrained the behavior of nations at times, for example with respect to noncombatant immunity during wartime.[51] The same is almost certainly true of climate change. For example, some European nations and the European Union have at times taken a lead in pushing for more action on climate change because that has been perceived as the right thing to do.[52] Several nations are indeed restraining their greenhouse gas pollution, usually at significant cost. However, far more often nations' foreign (and domestic) policies on climate change have been motivated by their own short- and medium-term interests as perceived by national leaders, political processes, or powerful economic interest groups and industries.

William Marsden describes the climate change negotiations this way: "Sent forth by their nations are armies of diplomats who are themselves hardwired in the narrow diplomatic traditions of defending their country's self-interest."[53] The point is that national interests, traditionally conceived and usually oriented toward economic growth, almost always win out over the interests of the natural environment, the interests of other nations, the interests of people living in those other countries, and especially the interests of vulnerable people of the future. While there are multiple reasons for the focus on national interests, the underlying cause of this phenomenon is the long metastasizing cancer of Westphalia. The world is divided into sovereign nation-states that by definition exist to promote their own individual interests.

This leads to the conclusion that the world's "society of states," which often tempers selfish behavior and encourages international cooperation, has not been enough to overcome the threats to national interests that are assumed to come from responding to climate change in the minds of most of the world's diplomats and leaders.[54] That is because international society is firstly about nation-states and not about the world's vulnerable environment and people. More generally, many pressing environmental problems, including climate change, "are global in nature and are therefore the antithesis of the nation-state just as much as the nation-state is the antithesis of the emerging global environmental agenda."[55] Thus a more fruitful way around the problem of climate change – a way to treat the cancer in the brief period that remains to possibly avert the worst effects of the problem – would be to reconceive national interests, and specifically to bring people more directly into the picture.[56] As a means of doing this, an important remedy for what is wrong with climate politics is to be found in the continuing historical evolution of *international* society toward a more *global* one that places other major interests – interests in a stable atmosphere and the protection of those who will suffer from climate change – alongside, if not before, the traditional interests of individual nations (see Part II).

Conclusion

Sovereignty and the protection of the exclusive interests of people within national borders worked to address many transborder problems in the past, and often they still do, explaining why Westphalian norms took hold and persist. But in the modern world, plagued as it is by worsening climate change, "the national interest" can no longer be separated from "the interests of all nations" and those who live in them. By definition, global environmental problems, chief among them climate change, do not respect borders. It is impossible for any one nation, or even a small group of them, even the most powerful ones, to stop climate change. Greenhouse gas emissions that permeate the earth's atmosphere mean that pollution from within any given nation's territory affects other nations. If those nations most affected are unable to adapt, the consequences can be quite severe, even profound. The interests of people within borders mean that a responsible nation-state must consider ways to address greenhouse gas pollution originating in other nations. Practical sovereignty, at least in this context, is a thing of the past.

Nevertheless, for the most part the fundamental pattern of international climate politics has changed very little since it began in the 1980s, despite being fleshed out with increasingly detailed and wide-ranging agreements. The world's response to climate change, while hardly an exclusive undertaking of diplomats and national governments, has largely been a function of them. Some subnational and nongovernmental responses have been motivated by international moves toward action, but just as often they are likely to be motivated by recognition that those moves are inadequate.[57] The climate change regime has reached a stage of what Oran Young calls "arrested development."[58]

A number of factors have contributed to the world's inability to address climate change effectively, not least the complexity of the problem, climate skepticism and denial cultivated by special interest groups and industries, and the world's addiction to fossil fuels. But a fundamental cause lies in Westphalian state-centric norms that underpin climate diplomacy and related policy responses. These norms exacerbate the other problems. For example, one might argue persuasively that what is most wrong with climate politics is the success of those groups sowing doubt about climate change. They have poisoned the policy process, especially in the United States, making American officials incapable of acting to defend genuine long-term national (and human) interests. Thus the story of climate diplomacy is symptomatic of the cancer of Westphalia. A fundamental ailment is that the interests of the environment, and specifically the earth's climate, not to mention those people who are vulnerable to an unhealthy environment and most susceptible to the effects of climate change, are routinely subjugated to the perceived interests of nation-states, or more precisely the interests of those actors within them that have the most power, whether these be old-fashioned monarchs (as in some petroleum-exporting nations), oligarchs and corrupt officials (as in Russia, China, and many other developing countries), industry and its lobbyists (as in Japan and many European countries), or selfish interest groups and sycophantic politicians (as in the United States).[59]

The underlying state-centric norms of climate politics mean that solutions are officially conceived in terms of nations. But nations routinely behave selfishly when their perceived interests are at stake, and especially when their short-term vital interests are threatened. They routinely do things that they (or more specifically their officials) believe will promote their national interests. They only rarely act to promote wider common interests when doing so might conceivably incur significant costs to themselves, especially in the short term, which is what acting on climate change might do. Even when nations agree on common concerns for justice, for example in their agreement to the principle of common but differentiated responsibilities to act on climate change, the question is usually about how to promote justice among nations rather than among people or between people and the environment.

Put succinctly, the diplomatic response to climate change has revealed a fundamental clash between the global interest of addressing climate change, largely by averting its worst effects through a massive cutback in global greenhouse gas emissions, and the selfish interests of nations that prefer business as usual. One of its key features has been to largely ignore the rights and obligations of human beings – an incredible shortfall considering that protecting human rights and ensuring the common good (at least within borders) is supposedly the *raison d'être* of any state.[60]

The failure of international negotiations to achieve agreements that will do more to avert catastrophic climate change – their stated objective from the outset – can be largely attributed to the cancer of Westphalia. The norms that serve as the basis of international relations have proved to be more powerful than the nascent and evolving norm of environmental stewardship. This cancer affects the entire body of the climate change regime. The cancer has not prevented international cooperation. Indeed, it largely explains why the response to climate change is so much about nations and their interests. But the cancer has made that response feeble relative to the seriousness of the problem.

The most significant example of how the cancer of Westphalia can metastasize to produce this effect can be found in the diplomacy, policies, and behavior of the United States and China. While these two nations are very important by themselves, their refusal to act robustly to combat climate change affects almost every other nation. The cancer spreads, debilitating the whole international community. The next chapter examines the roots of this American and Chinese malignancy.

CHAPTER THREE

Malignancy of the Great Polluters: The United States and China

This chapter looks at how the United States and China have contributed to the climate change problem, summarizes their related policies and diplomacy, and provides some explanations for their behavior.[1] In doing this, the chapter shows how the cancer of Westphalia has become worryingly malignant in the two nations where its effects can do the most harm and prevent wider global action on climate change. If it were possible to identify one actor that has done the most to arrest the development of the climate regime, it would have to be the United States. Its dithering on the issue has resulted in other nations, even those few that are willing to take substantially more action, restraining themselves. Despite the United States being the world's greatest historical polluter of the earth's atmosphere, its national policies to address climate change are pitiful relative to the scale of the problem. Its greenhouse gas emissions are far above what they were in 1990 – the level to which the US government promised to bring them when it signed the climate convention in 1992 – and it has done little, whether through its actions at home or its diplomacy abroad, to encourage other countries to reduce their own contributions to climate change. The failure of the United States to act has been compounded by the economic rise of China and its pathological obsession with the fundamental interstate norms of sovereignty and nonintervention. Indeed, while the United States is a perfect example of national interests – in truth meaning special interests within a particular nation –

winning out over global environmental interests shared by all, China is perhaps the best example of how the cancer of Westphalia has infected every sinew of the state, even to the point where Westphalian norms have come to trump clear Chinese interests in a better global environmental future.

Together the United States and China produce about 40 percent of global greenhouse gas emissions.[2] Consequently, it will not be possible to address climate change effectively if they fail to stem climate pollution coming from the behaviors of their citizens and businesses. Likely the single most effective way of tackling climate change in the near term would be for these two countries to work closely together toward that end. There is some nominal cooperation between them, but generally speaking the opposite is the case.[3] The United States uses China's failure to limit its greenhouse gas pollution as an excuse for failing to do so itself. China uses the US's failure to act on its historical responsibility to cut its greenhouse gas emissions, arising from two centuries of pollution by Americans, and its refusal to provide major financial assistance to developing countries that would help them to cope with climate change as excuses for not taking more action. In short, rather than taking strong action at home and working together abroad to limit climate change, the shared policy of the United States and China is to say to one another, self-righteously and in all earnestness, "you go first." This is a recipe for deadlock and goes a long way toward defining what most ails the politics of climate change.

The United States and climate change

The policies and actions of the United States on climate change have not changed significantly since the issue came onto the international agenda in the 1980s, despite the efforts of officials, activists, and diplomats through four presidents' administrations. The US government's rhetoric has varied in significant ways, but the declared concern about climate change from some presidents and officials has routinely exceeded actual policy responses and behavior. As a consequence, in spite of a slowing economy, US greenhouse gas emissions increased 11 percent between 1990 and 2010, even as per capita emissions fell from 19.7 to 16.7 tons during the same period and overall emissions of CO_2 dropped due to a shift away from coal toward natural gas, lower energy use in transport, and milder winters.[4] Improved automobile efficiency, air quality regulations that have restricted the use of coal, and other policies encouraged by the federal government have helped to limit US emissions; things could be worse. But the reductions that have resulted from such policies are at least an order of magnitude too little. There is very little by way of a national policy to begin the major shift toward large reductions in the country's greenhouse gas emissions that is necessary to comport with objectives of the climate convention and with the dire predictions of climate scientists.

When the climate convention was signed at the 1992 Rio Earth Summit, the US government made a voluntary pledge to reduce American emissions. At the same time, however, US officials told summit participants that "the American way of life is not negotiable."[5] This fundamental contradiction – gradual acknowledgement of the practical need for US action without actually doing much, particularly at the national level – has largely characterized the US response to climate change. The George H. W. Bush administration, skeptical of the whole idea of climate change, was opposed to any kind of *binding* greenhouse gas emissions requirements for the United States. It was feared that they would make the United States less competitive internationally.[6] This has been a recurring theme in US climate policy, particularly among members of the US Congress, with responding to climate change being viewed more as an economic issue than an environmental one.[7] Indeed, President Bush refused to attend the Earth Summit until binding emissions limitations were removed from the text of the climate convention. Ultimately, much like the Reagan administration before it, the George H. W. Bush administration's response to global warming was to call for more scientific research, which some interpreted as simply a recipe for pushing any requirement for US action well into the future.

The administration of President Bill Clinton took climate change much more seriously. In an effort to demonstrate US initiative, Vice President Al Gore participated in the Kyoto negotiations in 1997. However, Clinton and Gore had their hands tied by domestic opposition to action that would restrain US greenhouse gas emissions.[8] In the lead-up to the Kyoto conference, the US Senate, which is required under the US constitution to ratify international treaties signed by the United States before they can become US law, passed the Byrd–Hagel Resolution. The resolution opposed any international agreement requiring the United States and other developed countries to limit or reduce their greenhouse gas emissions without also imposing commitments on developing countries, as well as any agreement that would adversely affect the American economy.[9] Consequently, the United States could not formally join the Kyoto Protocol. Congress was influenced by financially and politically powerful interest groups, especially the American oil, coal, and automobile industries, which were opposed to any US action on climate change and questioned the validity of climate science.[10] In spite of serious efforts by the Clinton administration to act on US global commitments to take climate change more seriously, to accept binding commitments to reduce US greenhouse gas emissions, and to reflect these commitments in policy and diplomacy, members of Congress were able to prevent much real action by the United States during Clinton's eight years in office.[11]

In contrast to Clinton's presidency, the George W. Bush administration, including the president himself, was vociferously opposed to any US action on climate change. Within two months of taking office, Bush withdrew the US signature from the Kyoto Protocol and dismissed the science of climate change as being inconclusive. All of this was part of the administration's wider opposition to environmental regulation and to restraints on energy use in particular, positions championed by Bush's vice president, Dick Cheney, and possibly reflecting that both men had close ties to the petroleum industry.[12] As a means of raising doubt about the validity and accuracy of climate science, the administration "mastered the political manipulation of science" by advocating what it called "sound science," thereby implying that the work of climate scientists was unsound, and it even went so far as to actively suppress climate scientists.[13] It would take some years before President Bush succumbed to basic facts and came around to the view that global warming was a reality, but the damage was done. To this day, most Republican lawmakers, and indeed most Republican voters, remain highly skeptical of mainstream climate science and the IPCC in particular.[14]

In short, the George W. Bush administration did all that it could to protect the fossil fuel industry from having to change its ways, and US emissions continued to increase. Internationally, in keeping with the administration's very strong opposition to international regulation, it used its influence in the United Nations and in the climate change negotiations to oppose action whenever it could, to the point where the US delegate was uniformly booed by fellow diplomats at the 2007 conference of the parties in Bali. Put simply, the eight years under George W. Bush were wasted, with no progress at the national level.

Significant action by the US on climate change seemed possible with the advent of Barack Obama in 2009.[15] However, as with the Clinton administration, the Obama administration faced opposition from powerful interest groups seeking to maintain the status quo.[16] Despite much-improved knowledge of climate change, widespread support for action among scientists, significant public support for doing more, and calls for action from defense experts to address the threats to US interests posed by climate change and to reduce the country's reliance on petroleum (much of it imported from volatile regions of the world), the Obama administration found it nigh impossible to act concertedly to address the problem. In 2010, Congress abandoned attempts to pass the Waxman–Markey American Clean Energy and Security Act. The most significant action by the administration was the creation of stricter standards for automobile fuel efficiency, potentially putting the US on a course to reduce its gargantuan consumption of gasoline.

The administration sought to have a larger impact in international negotiations, and President Obama himself attended and actively participated in negotiations at the 2009 conference of the parties in Copenhagen. However, while he was instrumental in negotiating the Copenhagen Accord, he disappointed environmentalists by being unwilling to put US weight behind strong new initiatives to strengthen the climate change regime and, in particular, to require developed countries to reduce their greenhouse gas emissions substantially. The accord pledged to provide additional financial assistance to developing countries to help them cope with the inevitable impacts of climate change, but it was unclear where that money would come from in the US government's shrinking budget, or whether Congress would approve climate-related spending during difficult economic times.

It seems that Obama's heart was in the right place. For example, in addition to pushing for higher automobile fuel-economy standards, he tried to do an end run around Congress by having the Environmental Protection Agency regulate carbon dioxide as a pollutant under existing laws. However, Congress and industry sought to block implementation of these regulations.[17] Overall, despite great hopes that the United States under Obama might take a lead in tackling climate change, or at the very least make strides in moving beyond his predecessor's climate skepticism, there was a high degree of continuity between Obama's and his predecessors' climate-related policies.[18]

This is not to say that nothing has happened in the United States. Certainly, agencies of the federal government, such as the Environmental Protection Agency and the Department of Defense, have shown that they understand the dangers of climate change. Some actions by these agencies, federal support for scientific research and occasional efforts by US diplomats (during Democratic administrations) in support of stronger international agreements have had some effects. But where action is really starting to happen – often in response to the failure of the US central government to do much – is at the local, state (that is, US states, such as California and Massachusetts), and regional (for example, the US Northeast) levels.[19] A number of US states have enacted greenhouse gas emissions targets, including for automobiles and power plants, and at least half of the states have strengthened renewable-energy standards that require electric utilities to generate a portion of their power from renewable sources. Several US states have joined regional cap-and-trade programs with Canadian and Mexican provinces. It seems that leaders and legislators in some US states view climate change as a bigger threat than do many national policymakers, and many state officials, along with local communities and industries, see economic opportunity in moving toward renewable energy. Having said this, these subnational endeavors will not take the United States very far toward the level of cuts in greenhouse gas emissions that are necessary from the whole country.

A number of factors explain why the United States has been either a laggard or a spoiler on climate politics globally.[20] The US policymaking process requires major consensus or a large majority in favor of action in Congress to pass legislation, but this is impossible due to the increasingly partisan politics between those who want the United States to address climate change (many Democratic lawmakers, excepting those from coal-mining and automobile-manufacturing states) and those who view action on climate change as a threat to economic growth or do not believe in the problem at all (most Republicans, particularly those on the radical right).[21] Pressure to implement strong regulations that would bring US greenhouse gas emissions down is not high in Washington, due to concern among policymakers and lawmakers about US international competitiveness, Americans' addiction to cars and inexpensive gasoline, and limited concern about climate change in the United States compared to many other nations. The situation is made much more difficult by extremely powerful interest groups, including lobbyists for the petroleum, coal, and automobile industries, which have fought to maintain the benefits of business as usual, including enormous government subsidies that reduce the cost of fossil fuels and thereby feed the US dependency on them for most of its energy.

Lobbying against national action on climate change has been coupled with a pernicious and effective industry-funded campaign to foster climate skepticism and denial, leading to confusion among both the public and many policymakers.[22] The skeptics are supported by right-wing media outlets, and they are able to take advantage of "balanced" media coverage from reputable news outlets that until recently gave equal weight to both the consensus among the world's scientists and the tiny minority of fringe groups and doubters who question the reality of global warming.[23] Many of the climate skeptics and deniers in the United States see action on climate change as a route to undermining personal and economic freedoms; their efforts to sow doubt are not always about climate science per se but instead about promoting and protecting an extreme free-market ideology that brooks no restraint by government.[24] This cultivated American doubt about climate change, and indeed active denial of it as a real problem, helps to maintain business as usual, specifically continuing dependence on fossil fuel energy, as the default national interest in the minds of many US politicians. This is critically important because voters have a role in US policy choices. If they are skeptical about climate change, their representatives in government have little incentive to implement policies to combat it.

The very hot summer of 2012 in the United States, and a devastating hurricane on its East Coast that autumn, raised concern about climate change among Americans, with more of them believing that it is a serious threat to the country. However, although only a string of hot summers and more frequent severe storms seem likely to persuade their representatives in Congress to think likewise.[25]

China and climate change

In 2006, China overtook the United States to become the largest national source of CO_2 emissions, and it now accounts for a quarter of the global total.[26] By 2010, China's greenhouse emissions were 20 percent above those of the United States, and predictions put them at about 50 percent above the United States in 2050.[27] China's CO_2 emissions from fossil fuel use increased by nearly 80 percent in the first decade of the century, and two-thirds of the total global increase in emissions in 2008 originated in China alone.[28] The majority of this pollution comes from the burning of coal, which is by far the country's largest source of energy.[29] China's coal-fired power sector is the world's single-largest unnatural source of CO_2 emissions.[30] As a consequence, even though China's cumulative historical carbon emissions are only one-fourth those of the United States, its per capita emissions are well above those of most developing nations and now exceed the world average.[31] Indeed, the country's per capita CO_2 emissions increased from 2.2 tons in 1990 to 6.8 tons in 2010, reaching a level approaching per capita emissions of many developed nations, equal to those of Italy and exceeding those of France.[32] They will be double those of the European Union by about 2020, and by the early 2020s China's total historical emissions will match its share of the world's population, with its aggregate historical contribution to climate change surpassing that of the United States by mid-century.[33]

A large source of growth in China's emissions is the production of exports, but a majority of products are consumed domestically and well over half of the growth in the country's CO_2 emissions come from domestic sources, notably carbon-intensive construction and other capital investment for household and government consumption (with less than a third related to exports).[34] Consumption is almost certain to increase enormously in coming years as millions of Chinese join the global middle class.[35] This trend is starkly revealed by the growth in car ownership in China. The number of passenger cars doubled every 30 months during the 1990s, and by one estimate the number of automobiles in China expands by 20,000 each day.[36]

In the run-up to the 2009 Copenhagen conference of the parties, China agreed to voluntarily implement a 40–45 percent reduction in its carbon intensity (CO_2 emissions per unit of output) by 2020 compared to its 2005 emissions. However, this pledge amounted to little more than continuing business as usual. For example, from 1991 to 2006, the country's total CO_2 emissions doubled, even as carbon intensity dropped by 44 percent.[37] Its CO_2 emissions doubled again between 2006 and 2010, growing by 10 percent in 2010 alone.[38] In just the four years up to 2006, demand for energy in China grew more than it had in the preceding 25 years put together.[39] Consequently, even if the government's Copenhagen pledge is fully implemented, China's total emissions will increase, possibly sharply, unless trends in economic growth and energy use in recent years change dramatically.[40] Even if growth in China's economy were to slow down significantly – to 5 percent, half the rate in recent years – and emissions intensity were to continue improving as pledged by the government, the country's emissions would not peak before 2030, let alone fall.[41]

China first became involved internationally in addressing climate change during the 1980s when it collaborated with the United States to study the impacts of CO_2 emissions, thus beginning a process of growing Chinese involvement and interest in climate-related issues.[42] Scientific questions predominated during the 1980s, but in the 1990s climate change become a politicized developmental issue for China.[43] Its climate change diplomacy became more active when it joined with other developing countries to influence negotiations for the climate convention and the Kyoto Protocol. As a developing country, China is not legally required to limit its greenhouse gas emissions under these agreements. It defends this position and, as demonstrated at the Copenhagen conference, it has shown few signs of allowing this approach to change substantially in successor agreements. Chinese officials were strident at Copenhagen in opposing new binding

limits of any kind for developing countries. They were ada-
mant that China's pledge to improve its own energy efficiency
was a *voluntary* one, and they made it very clear that they
would strongly oppose international monitoring of this pledge
– leading to suspicion about how serious the government
was in implementing the promised improvements. (This was
not an unwarranted suspicion, Chinese officials' righteous
indignation notwithstanding, given the failure of Beijing to
implement many of its own domestic environmental policies
and regulations.)[44] For the Chinese, verification of its pledges
or commitments by outsiders would be tantamount to a
sacrifice of its sovereignty.[45]

Not only has China opposed binding international greenhouse gas limitations for developing countries, it has opposed
binding *global* cuts in climate-changing pollution. At the
Copenhagen conference, Chinese officials blocked a proposed
binding agreement to reduce global emissions of greenhouse
gases by 50 percent by mid-century.[46] China's opposition to
these global cuts was likely a function of its relatively new role
as one of the largest national sources of greenhouse gas pollution: to achieve global cuts of 50 percent (which would be
far less than what scientists say is needed to avert dangerous
climate change), China would have to reduce its own emissions quite dramatically, at significant long-term economic
cost relative to the cost of doing nothing.[47]

In part due to this opposition to a global greenhouse gas-
reduction target, some observers and participants in the
Copenhagen conference openly blamed China for the failure
of the gathering to result in a stronger international treaty.[48]
Whether China deserved such blame may be subject to debate,
and of course the Chinese strongly denied such a proposi-
tion.[49] What was beyond question, however, was that China's
new role as the largest national source of pollutants causing
global warming made its policies and actions central to efforts

by governments, industry, and individuals to address climate change more effectively. Like the United States, China is in a position to make or break the climate change regime: to "make" it by taking on a leadership role in finding a path to real global greenhouse gas cuts, or to "break" it by refusing to act on the practical connection between its own burgeoning pollution and future climate change.

Given this reality, it is not surprising that developed nations have pushed China to be more aggressive in limiting its greenhouse gas emissions and to submit to external auditing of the implementation of those limits that it does agree to, ideally to be followed by measurable reductions. This is a practical necessity. However, the Chinese do not interpret this as being fair. From their perspective, such demands contradict the argument that it is the developed nations that are to blame for climate change. They believe that before China can fairly be expected to do more, developed countries should first take robust action to limit their own greenhouse gas emissions and compensate developing countries for the suffering that will accrue from historical atmospheric pollution. In this context especially, China still considers itself to be part of the developing world. Despite its newfound wealth, China's international position on climate change remains that of a developing nation focusing intently on domestic economic growth while pointing the finger at the developed world, particularly the West, as responsible for addressing climate change. Consequently, China's diplomatic position does not reflect its new status as the world's largest polluter, nor does it account for the hundreds of millions of newly affluent consumers in China who are consuming and polluting at near-western levels, and in many cases far beyond that (see chapter 6).

Despite its strong opposition to being *required* to limit its pollution, the Chinese government has promulgated policies domestically that move the nation more or less in the direction of greenhouse gas limitations, consistent with broader national developmental goals.[50] Indeed, China has arguably done more than almost any other country to rein in energy use and to limit reliance on fossil fuels. Beijing has mandated improved energy efficiency in factories and automobiles, fostered the adoption of hydro, wind, and solar energy on a large scale, and shut down many factories and power plants burning coal. It has been heavily involved in the Kyoto Protocol's Clean Development Mechanism, receiving over half of the world's investment in the mechanism's projects.[51] However, the expansion of highways and car ownership far outstrips new efficiencies in automobiles, for each coal-fired plant that is shut down several others (albeit more efficient ones) are built, alternative energies are facing difficult hurdles (such as wind farms without adequate connections to electricity grids), and it seems that many of the country's projects under the Clean Development Mechanism may be scams to garner money from western countries rather than actually to cut greenhouse gas emissions.[52] As Bo Miao and Graeme Lang describe the situation, despite the Chinese government's efforts to promote less polluting sources of energy, for the time being it would not be plausible to realistically expect China to reduce its consumption of coal and other fossil fuels substantially, meaning that the country's greenhouse gas emissions will "continue to soar."[53]

Nevertheless, there is ample evidence that the Chinese government takes the issue of climate change seriously, as reflected, for example, in the creation of the National Coordination Committee on Climate Change in 2003; release in 2007 of a national climate change program and formation of a Leading Committee on Climate Change, headed by the prime minister (the first time the head of government took the lead in addressing an environmental problem); and publication in 2008 of a blueprint for policies and actions to address climate change by the powerful National Development and Reform Commission, among other things.[54]

The government's climate change policy process is typically centralized and complicated, involving a dozen agencies and ministries concerned with everything from national development and environmental protection to finance and foreign affairs. Despite the focus on climate change domestically, Miao and Lang point out that the government does not have an "orchestrated national policy incorporating effective regulatory instruments" for addressing the country's greenhouse gas emissions.[55] As in most nations, while the issue of climate change has moved up the policy agenda, it never seems to become a top priority, routinely losing out to economic growth and development.

In a nutshell, China's policies on managing climate change are officially guided by six principles: (1) addressing climate change within the broader framework of the country's "national sustainable development strategy"; (2) adhering to the principle of common but differentiated responsibilities; (3) addressing both climate change mitigation and adaptation; (4) integrating climate change-related policies with programs for "national and social economic development"; (5) relying on technological advancement for effectively mitigating and adapting to climate change; and (6) "actively and extensively" participating in international cooperation on climate change.[56] Generally speaking, what comes from these principles is indication that climate change is taken seriously by the government but also that the issue does not take priority over other national objectives. If climate change mitigation and adaptation can be made consistent with those objectives, China will take action. If advantages for economic growth and other objectives can be wrung from the climate change issue, China will exploit them (for example, by extracting funding and technology from the West for both economic development and greenhouse gas mitigation). In short, China's alternative energy policies and other climate-related actions are not motivated by climate change per se.[57] As Colin Hunt notes, "limiting energy use and phasing out old power plants has not been motivated by China's climate change objectives but rather by concerns over energy security, energy costs and environmental factors such as air pollution."[58]

China's greenhouse gas emissions will not be as high as they might be without conscious efforts by the government to encourage more environmentally sustainable development domestically. Whether this will be enough to actually bring the increase in China's emissions to a halt any time soon, and then to start reducing them, may be an open question for optimists. Unfortunately, policies in China aimed at controlling energy use and expanding the use of renewable energies, while impressive compared to many other countries, the United States included, have been far too little compared to the scale of global greenhouse gas cuts that will be needed to avert catastrophic climate change. Worryingly, in 2010, China's top official on climate change matters, Su Wei, declared that the country's emissions would have to increase, adding that the government would continue to be guided by the principle of common but differentiated responsibilities and that "China 'could not and should not' set an upper limit on greenhouse gas emissions."[59]

Consequently, agreement from China to take on new binding obligations to cap or limit – least of all reduce – its greenhouse gas emissions, or to submit to independent verification of those emissions, seems quite unlikely.[60] Bold moves by the United States and other developed countries toward reducing their greenhouse gas emissions remain prerequisites for a major change in Chinese policy – barring a shift in how the problem of climate change is perceived by governments (see chapter 6).

"You go first" and climate deadlock

A grand bargain between the United States and China will likely be needed, and soon, if the ailments of climate politics are to go into remission. But instead of such a bargain, China and the United States continue to use one another as reasons for doing far too little. Their mantra is, in so many words, "you go first." Instead of working together seriously to reduce greenhouse gas emissions and thereby mitigate the worst effects of climate change, the United States refuses to take robust action until China agrees to limit and eventually reduce its greenhouse gas emissions. Likewise, China refuses to act until the United States, in accordance with its historical responsibility, cuts its emissions and provides major funding to poor countries affected by past atmospheric pollution. Cooperative activities between the two nations, such as joint research projects and participation in the Asia–Pacific Partnership on Clean Development and Climate, are little more than distractions from the level of action and cooperation that is required.[61]

The US position is based on legitimate if disingenuous practicality: China's emissions must be brought under control to address the problem adequately. China has refused – legitimately so, from a Westphalian state-focused perspective – to do more because it is relatively poor and responsibility lies with the developed nations, the United States especially. With respect to the principle of common but differentiated responsibilities, China focuses on the differentiated (greater) responsibilities of the United States and other developed nations, whereas the United States tends to focus on common responsibilities of all capable nations to act, often directing its attention toward China. This "ping-pong game between the U.S. and China" (to quote a European delegate at the Durban conference of the parties in December 2011) is an "enduring feature" of all climate change negotiations.[62] These two nations' positions add up to a recipe for climate deadlock.

This deadlock is largely a consequence of the US and Chinese obsession (shared by other nations, of course) with Westphalian norms, leading them to focus on their individual perceived *national* interests (or, more precisely, to interests of some parts of their societies) above the interests of people everywhere, and to fixate on their own legal *sovereignty* to the exclusion of the welfare of the natural environment. It is not surprising, in principle, that these nations would seek to promote their own interests as traditionally perceived and interpreted. Communities have always sought to do so. What is so unhealthy is the degree to which they ignore the interests of others (including those of the future) affected by global environmental changes, promote the interests of well-connected actors over the general welfare, and generally exclude the global environment from prudential calculations. While harmful, this sort of behavior is not abnormal; it largely explains the tragedy of the atmospheric commons. What is abnormal and relatively recent in the broad sweep of history is a preoccupation with legal sovereignty that is out of sync with the environmental challenges that nations and their citizens face in the twenty-first century, and which cannot be fully understood or addressed by sole reference to narrow national interests. The obsession with national sovereignty demonstrates the power of a socially constructed idea over rationality in world politics.[63]

The perceived national interests of the United States and China have routinely revolved around economic growth and related issues, such as protection of jobs, keeping costs for citizens low, and promoting international economic competitiveness. Typically, the national interests of the United States in the context of climate change (and indeed other contexts) have been largely interpreted as ensuring US economic growth and the nation's dependence on relatively inexpensive fossil fuels (relative to, say, Western Europe). The American focus on the economy was manifested in the 1997 Byrd–Hagel Resolution and, a decade later, in attempts to pass the Waxman–Markey Act.

The Byrd–Hagel Resolution, while not directed at China alone, specifically listed China and four other developing nations as among those that had been exempted by the climate regime from emissions limitations. The resolution's most important provision was opposition to mandatory greenhouse gas emissions limitations that would put the US at a competitive disadvantage relative to other nations, the large developing ones in particular. The Senate had two major concerns about developing nations.[64] First, there was a strong worry that those countries would have an unfair economic advantage because they would not be facing the same restrictions on economic output as the United States. There was also concern that US manufacturing industries, and the jobs that go with them, would move abroad to take advantage of lower environmental regulations in developing nations. Second, senators believed (or said as much) that an effective climate treaty would require greenhouse gas emissions limitations by developing nations. During floor debate on the resolution, many senators specifically pointed to future emissions from China as justification for their position. They pointed out that China would surpass the United States by 2015 to become the world's largest national producer of greenhouse gas emissions (which happened even sooner than they anticipated).

The sentiment of the Byrd–Hagel Resolution remained potent. It was manifested strongly during the George W. Bush administration when the president, reflecting the view of many other US politicians (especially Republicans), proclaimed that the Kyoto Protocol was unfair and irresponsible because it did not require China and other large developing

countries to reduce their greenhouse gas pollution.[65] Worries
about the Chinese were clear. According to Anthony Giddens,
the administration was "inclined toward climate change
skepticism anyway, and influenced strongly by industrial lobbies," and was concerned that China might gain a competitive
advantage that could threaten US interests.[66] The same worries were expressed during debate over the Waxman–Markey
Act, which failed to pass due to growing Congressional opposition to its key feature, a domestic emissions cap-and-trade
scheme. Debate among senators revealed a preoccupation
with economic interests vis-à-vis China in particular. For
example, Senator James Inhofe (Republican) said that the act
would be "economically ruinous for the United States. . . .
Because the stronger it is, the more manufacturing jobs
will leave the United States to go to China. . . . China wants
the United States to accept draconian emission reduction
targets that will continue to cripple the U.S. economy."[67]
Representative Ginny Brown-Waite (Republican) put it more
succinctly, declaring that the Waxman–Markey Act "should
really be called the Let's Send More Jobs to China Act."[68]

These sentiments reveal that Congress often views
American climate relations with China through the lens of
threats to American industries and more generally in terms
of US competitiveness relative to China.[69] Consequently, a
key aim of the Waxman–Markey Act was protecting "energy-
intensive, trade exposed" industries in the US and effectively
to impose tariffs on nations exporting to the United States if
their products were to compete with similar goods produced
in the US at higher costs due to future climate-related regulations.[70] Despite the failure of the act to pass, it showed the
direction that many members of Congress and some powerful US industries hope to move in the future should domestic
greenhouse gas regulations come into force. Not surprisingly,
China has been vocal in opposing this sort of legislation.

Domestic political considerations are the primary drivers of the US's climate change policies. As suggested by the Byrd–Hagel and Waxman–Markey legislation, the "national" interests of the United States are routinely equated with powerful political and economic interests. This is especially important because, unlike in many other countries, and certainly unlike in China, Congress must support US involvement in international agreements. In particular, the Senate must give its "advice and consent" before the United States can join international treaties.[71]

Senators (and members of the House of Representatives) tend to vote to promote the interests of their home states and constituents. This is highly germane, given the reliance of many US states on fossil fuels. More than half of US senators come from states whose economies significantly rely on coal production and even more of them come from states that rely on cheap US coal for electricity generation, with this "natural resource dependence" thus profoundly influencing their stands on climate policy.[72] Senators from states that are dependent on the oil or coal industries consistently vote against legislation that would mandate greenhouse gas cuts at the national level.[73]

Furthermore, interest groups put pressure on senators via campaign contributions (especially in the case of business interests) and vote drives (in the case of political groups). This gives access to all manner of special interests, but petroleum companies and those that rely on fossil fuels, such as the automobile industry, have been especially effective in capturing votes in both the Senate and the House of Representatives, doing just enough to prevent serious and widespread action. In short, US national interests related to climate change are modified and arguably undermined by Congressional politics. While these pressures do not always prevent laws and regulations that help to limit US greenhouse gas pollution, they do show that the US national interest related to climate change is actually a function of complicated domestic politics.[74]

Economics and trade are not the only things that motivate US climate change policy and underlying perceptions of the nation's interests. Another factor fits neatly into the "realist" conception of international politics: the relationship between China and the US on climate change occurs in the context of their broader relationship. They see each other as competitors internationally, both economically and politically. While this competition is tempered by their bilateral trade, their many common interests, and particularly their mutual economic interdependence, neither wants the other to establish an advantage from international climate politics that could leave it relatively weaker in the long term. This helps explain why so much of the attention in the United States is focused on China: not only is China the largest national source of greenhouse gas emissions, it is also a major economic competitor globally and its economic rise is being matched by rapid growth in its military capabilities, which can challenge US interests in East Asia and beyond. This clearly worries many US officials and legislators, heightening their opposition to the Kyoto Protocol and other climate change agreements that, while not directly strengthening China, incur financial costs for the United States and not for China, leading to China's relative gain.[75]

While US administrations (notably under the Bushes) and many members of Congress have consistently opposed binding US greenhouse gas emissions limitations out of fear that implementing them might harm the economy, Daniel Bodansky argues that US opposition to such commitments is in part a reflection of "deeper opposition to international con- straints on US sovereignty," thereby making it unlikely that the United States will accept treaties "even when they other- wise enjoy very widespread support."[76] This points to a deeper US "interest" that emanates from Westphalian sovereignty norms: a long-standing and enduring suspicion about, and opposition to, international treaties that might constrain the United States itself. This is partly historical, derived from the early decades of the US republic and admonitions of the nation's first presidents to avoid "entangling alliances."[77]

Nowadays, this historical attempt to limit interactions with the outside world that might undermine US security or freedom of action is manifested in opposition among the political right to anything coming from the United Nations. For many Republicans, the UN-brokered climate change agreements and the Intergovernmental Panel on Climate Change are seen as plots or conspiracies.[78] This opposition to international regulation is partly selfish and partly a manifestation of the US political system. Treaties ratified by the Senate must be implemented by the US government, which can be sued by environmental groups if it fails to do so, unlike in many other countries, notably China, where it is more a matter of trust that international environmental agreements will be adhered to. As Bodansky describes it, US opposition to binding climate change treaties "is a structural problem which is unlikely to change anytime soon."[79]

Perceptions of national interest and concerns about national sovereignty are very similar in China – a focus on economic growth and opposition to interference in the nation's internal affairs – but arguably the perceptions and sentiments are even more intense, given China's history of poverty, hardship, and occupation by foreign powers. China is very much focused on the principle of common but differentiated responsibilities, and its interpretation of the concept largely determines how far it is willing to go in accepting limitations to its greenhouse gas emissions. The Chinese government interprets the principle very strictly as requiring, according to the National Development and Reform Commission, that developed countries take the lead in reducing greenhouse gas emissions as well as providing financial and technical support to developing countries. The first and overriding priorities of developing countries are sustainable development and poverty eradication. The extent to which developing countries will effectively implement their commitments under the [climate convention] will depend on the effective implementation by developed countries of their basic commitments.[80]

China very much puts itself in the developing country category in this respect.

There are a number of other fundamental concerns underlying China's positions, notably sovereignty and non-interference in its internal affairs, social stability, support for the ruling party and the government, demonstrating leadership among developing countries, challenging the international authority of the United States, environmentally sustainable development as a medium- and long-term objective, and obtaining aid and technology from developed nations.[81] After ensuring Chinese sovereignty, the government's overriding short- and medium-term priority in the context of climate change (and in most other policy contexts) is economic growth. Although China's leaders are concerned about climate change, the issue "has not surpassed economic development as a policy priority."[82] Development is in turn tied to the ruling party's policy objectives, such as lifting more Chinese people out of poverty, using the nation's growing economy to increase military capabilities to ensure territorial integrity and, very fundamentally, the party's assumption that economic growth is essential to political stability and to its survival.[83]

China's attachment to sovereignty norms, including in the context of climate change, cannot be overstated. Much of its foreign policy related to climate change is driven by the Chinese obsession with sovereignty and the government's total opposition to "intervention" of any kind, however slight.[84] The government is preoccupied with preventing real *and* perceived interference in its domestic affairs or anything that could conceivably (in the Chinese mind) be construed as undermining national integrity.

China's historical relationship with the outside world plays a big part in setting the tone for all of its responses to climate change, both diplomatic and domestic.[85] Demands by the United States and other developed nations for China to take on binding greenhouse gas limitations are resisted by the country's profound sense of historical grievance toward the outside world for past interventions in its internal affairs. China's "century of national humiliation" featured the Opium Wars of the nineteenth century and invasions during the first half of the twentieth century, and it extends to perceptions by Chinese that the outside world sought to hold back the country's development in the second half of the twentieth century and continues to do so today (notwithstanding the West's deep economic engagement with the country in recent decades).[86] Consequently, the Chinese government is opposed to outside monitoring of its greenhouse gas emissions, as world leaders learned at the Copenhagen conference in 2009. The head of the Chinese delegation at the Copenhagen conference, Xie Zhenhua, summarized the results of the meeting this way: "For the Chinese this was our sovereignty and our national interest."[87] In short, the Chinese government will oppose international policies that could in any way be interpreted as intervention or as undermining China's sovereignty.[88]

China's reticence about allowing outside monitoring of its emissions is also a function of the central government's weak capacity in this respect, exacerbated by the long-standing problem of a lack of transparency related to statistics of almost any kind. The Chinese government simply cannot guarantee that its pledges will be fully implemented. Thus the seemingly reasonable demand from some western nations at the Copenhagen conference (and since) for China to agree to monitoring of its greenhouse gas targets is, from the Chinese perspective, partly unreasonable and partly unworkable.

China's domestic policies related to climate change are driven by objectives other than fighting climate change, such as energy security, technology innovation to enhance economic competitiveness, and profiting from the Clean Development Mechanism. In other words, China's climate change policies are only incidentally or indirectly related to climate change per se. This may change as the impacts of climate change experienced in China manifest themselves and the co-benefits of taking strong action, such as reducing local air pollution from coal-fired power plants, become more evident.[89] However, the official calculus is likely to remain for quite some time that mitigation of greenhouse gas pollution is more costly for the economy and especially for the regime than is adaptation to the effects of climate change. This would help to explain China's focus on adaptation over mitigation in international climate negotiations.

What is more, China is no longer a champion of the developing world in the context of climate change. This was reflected quite dramatically at the 2009 Copenhagen conference of the parties, where China opposed international actions dear to the many poor countries, especially the small-island states, which demanded that China and some other large developing countries adopt emissions cuts. But it seems that it was even worse than that. In addition to opposing a global emissions-cut target (no doubt fearing China would one day have to join in meeting it), the Chinese delegate in top-level negotiations at Copenhagen reportedly tried to block inclusion of the small-island and low-lying nations' target of limiting global warming to 1.5° Celsius, possibly dooming some of them to physical extinction.[90] As an advisor to the Maldives' government put it, "the truth is that the small island states and most vulnerable countries want China and its allies to cut their emissions because without these cuts they will not survive. Bluntly put, China is the world's No1 [number one] emitter, and if China does not reduce its emissions by at least half by mid-century, then countries like the Maldives will go under."[91] Despite continued rhetoric about developing country solidarity, China is now unquestionably a champion of its own interests – determined largely by domestic economic and political calculations – regardless of the costs for those nations and people that are most vulnerable to climate change.[92]

Conclusion

At least in the context of climate change, Westphalian norms have become malignant. They permeate thinking of national governments around the world. This is especially true of the United States and China, which are blinded by conceptions of "national interests" and sovereignty to the exclusion of wider interests of humanity and the environment, and indeed arguably to the exclusion of their own long-term interests threatened by climate change. As Cass Sunstein sees things, "circumstances for an international agreement are distinctly unpromising if the leading emitters [China and the United States] do not perceive themselves as likely to gain a great deal from emissions reductions."[93] Each of these countries focuses on the common (greater) responsibility of the other and the differentiated (lesser) responsibility of itself. The US withdrawal from the Kyoto Protocol under George W. Bush is a case in point: doing so relieved pressure on China to do anything, and China's resulting inaction has fed into US concerns about economic competitiveness.[94] That is, the concept of common but differentiated responsibilities, so central to international agreements on climate change, is interpreted by these two countries in a way that gives each, at least from its own perspective, an excuse for inaction, thereby excluding an enormous portion of global emissions from regulation and sending the wrong signal to nations more willing to act. The policy process in both countries reinforces the notion that action on greenhouse gas pollution is against their national interests until the other side does something, thus bolstering each nation's distaste for international regulation.

The you-go-first relationship between the United States and China has become a structural impediment to either of them going as far as necessary to limit and ultimately cut their greenhouse gas pollution quite drastically. This keeps well over a third of global greenhouse gas emissions beyond control. China and the United States are "locked into a 'game of chicken,'" with neither of them willing to concede first.[95] For other nations this situation creates "a profound political conundrum: unable to change the US or Chinese positions, the push for a global deal is likely to fall at the first hurdle."[96] China and the United States' myopic focus on their own perceived national interests and their mutual obsessions with maintaining total sovereignty, in keeping with traditional Westphalian norms, means that other nations that *are* willing to take more action – many European countries and the European Union, most notably – are unable to do so without taking the apparent risks that might arise from going first to the substantial degree that is required. They lack any assurance that the United States and China will follow, as they must if others' actions are to reverse climate change.

Thus the cancer described in the previous chapter metastasizes to most of the world's major polluting nations, preventing them from taking robust action and effectively putting the vast majority of the world's greenhouse gas pollution beyond adequate control. Climate politics are held hostage to

American and Chinese officials' perceptions of what is best for their own nations.

One way to treat this malignancy is to find ways for the Americans and the Chinese to break free from "the state" as traditionally conceived and to focus more on *people* as the drivers of climate change and as those who will suffer the most from it. Chapters 5 and 6 suggest that this should involve diluting "national" interests with the interests, rights, and obligations of human beings. But first the next chapter looks more deeply at the role that people play in all of this.

CHAPTER FOUR

Addictions of Modernity: Affluence and Consumption

The fundamental driving force behind climate change is the material consumption of people. While the *number* of people on the earth is vitally important to understanding what causes climate change and how best to address it effectively, what matters more is *how much* (and what) people consume – specifically how much they consume beyond their needs – and the fact that material consumption is increasing much faster than population is growing. During the twentieth century, the world's population increased by six times, from one to six billion people, but consumption of fossil fuels increased by 16 times.[1] Individuals deserve to meet their basic needs; this is a fundamental right.[2] However, we should distinguish the provision of basic needs – enough healthy food, clean water, adequate shelter, education, and health care (which for more than 1 billion people remain unmet) – and other reasonable and justifiable aspirations (such as leisure time, entertainment, and advanced education) from the "affluenza" – the influenza of affluence – that has infected most of the world's developed societies and is now spreading very rapidly to the developing world. As people become affluent, they consume things at a faster pace, always wanting more, akin to any other addiction that can never be fully satisfied. This addiction is nurtured by industry through clever marketing strategies and by governments through fossil fuel subsidies and policies that encourage growth in material consumption.

The world's spreading addiction to consumption, especially

material consumption that unsustainably extracts resources from the natural environment and leads to greenhouse gas emissions and other types of pollution, is not a new phenomenon. What is new, however, is the spread of this affliction via the vectors of economic and technological globalization from its original centers of activity in the developed world, especially western nations, into and across the developing world, most profoundly into China and other large, rapidly industrializing nations. Growing material consumption characterizes modernity, national and international economic systems, and business models. It involves the stoking of desires for material goods and luxuries, extracting environmental resources, manufacturing products and thereby satisfying demands of "modern" lifestyles. The resulting pollution goes into environmental commons, including the atmosphere, at little or no direct economic cost to consumers or manufacturers but with serious adverse consequences for poor communities and future generations.

Members of the world's growing middle class are developing a love for material luxuries, private automobiles, novel gadgets and appliances, air travel and excessive consumption of meat and processed foods derived from imported commodities. The accelerating spread of affluent consumption around the world is rapidly increasing global emissions of greenhouse gases, vastly outpacing any planned cuts by developed-world governments. This globalization of material consumption is now the most powerful driver of greenhouse gas pollution. It is changing the political calculus of how the world responds to climate change.

Population and consumption

At the root of climate change is pollution from and caused by individuals. Short of major changes in the way people live, and assuming a world of continuing traditional economic growth, more people mean more greenhouse gas pollution. Paradoxically, global population is an issue that has received relatively little attention from scholars studying the human dimensions of climate change.[3] What is more, people seem to be an afterthought in many international environmental agreements, and questions of population growth and its relationship to material consumption are often downplayed because such questions are controversial and get to the heart of how people live (including sex, lifestyle, and consumer choice), which governments often believe should not be subject to diplomatic scrutiny, let alone international regulation.[4] Despite this resistance to discussing population explicitly, it cannot be ignored.

The world's population doubled in the 150-year period from the start of the Industrial Revolution to the turn of the twentieth century, toward the end of which it doubled much more quickly – in less than four decades.[5] Just 50 years ago, the world's population was a relatively small 3 billion; now it stands at 7 billion.[6] Population continues to increase by about 75–80 million people each year, with most predictions putting it at roughly 9 billion by mid-century, when it may peak.[7] However, according to recent United Nations estimates, it could exceed 10 billion by century's end.[8] Almost all of the increase in world population during the first half of this century – about 3 billion people – will occur in developing countries.[9] This means that the world will include more of the people who are most vulnerable to the impacts of climate change. In contrast, in the developed world, where the ability to cope with climate change is greatest, most nations' populations will decrease unless those societies choose to allow more immigration from the developing world. Eventually, almost certainly during this century, world population is likely to stop increasing, and it will start to decrease if downward trends in human fertility spread across the developing world. However, even if this happens, due to increasing material consumption, the human impact on the planet will continue to increase enormously – short of very substantial changes to past trends.

Thomas Malthus famously predicted at the turn of the nineteenth century that growth in the human population would exceed the ability of nature to provide for human needs, resulting in famine and other ills: "The power of population is indefinitely greater than the power in the earth to produce subsistence for man."[10] Malthus overstated the influence of population in terms of numbers, but, "despite being killed off many times" his warning "continues to resonate."[11] In the late 1960s, Paul Erlich warned of a "population bomb."[12] Like Malthus, he was concerned about the ability of the earth to feed everyone. Malthus and Erlich were wrong in important ways; population has not grown as fast as expected, and global food production has more than kept pace with actual increases in human numbers. However, recurring famines in some of the world's poorest places are reminders that, in many localities, humanity has exceeded the ability of the environment to sustain it. The earth can probably provide enough food for the predicted population in 2050, but the question is whether it can sustain humanity at the levels of prosperity and consumption currently enjoyed in the developed nations and in affluent pockets of the developing world.[13]

Malthus's and Erlich's warnings highlight the ecological consequences of population growth, reminding us that the overall impact of humanity will likely outpace the carrying capacity of the earth if population and the inevitable consumption of food and other resources grow unchecked.[14] It may have taken longer than Malthus and Erlich anticipated, but their predictions have come true in an important sense: the world is running up against the ability of the earth to provide key resources and natural services. This is not so much a direct function of population, as Malthus expected, but a result of growing affluence in a global capitalist economy, along with the associated appetite for material resources and the pollution that results.

There is ample evidence that humanity is living beyond the ability of the earth to sustain it in perpetuity. Fifty years ago, the world's population of 3 billion was using half the resources that could be sustainably provided by the earth's ecosystems, but, by the time population reached 5 billion in the mid-1980s, humanity was using "all of the Earth's sustainable production."[15] At *current* levels of consumption and pollution, the world's population is running an ecological *deficit*, having reached the earth's carrying capacity in 1986.[16] In other words, people are consuming the planet faster than it can "reproduce" itself. The statistics are worrying. Since the mid-1960s, the total ecological (or environmental) footprint of humanity has doubled, and it is now using up the environment (natural resources and pollution sinks) 50 percent faster than the earth can sustain.[17] At current rates of resource consumption and pollution, humanity is using the equivalent of 1.5 Earths, with this level likely to equal two Earths within two decades.[18] The impact of carbon emissions – calculated in terms of the land and sea that would be required to sequester (or absorb) them – accounts for over half of the world's ecological footprint, and it is the fastest-growing part of it, increasing eleven times in the last half-century.[19]

Research on the relationship between population and climate change is complex, but, generally speaking, slowing the growth of the world's population would likely reduce greenhouse gas emissions compared to what they would be with faster growth.[20] One must say "likely" because this assumes that behaviors leading to greenhouse gas emissions do not increase to the point where they cancel out the effects of slower growth in population. Because the effects of population

changes take considerable time to have an impact, the beneficial effects for climate change of declining birth rates will be
most felt in the second half of the century.[21] Very significantly,
half the world's current population is under the age of 25, and
they "will, quite literally, shape the future."[22] While the elderly
will henceforth outnumber the young, it is the latter that
will determine the size of the world's population later in the
century, and it is their behaviors that will largely determine
whether greenhouse gas pollution rises or falls.[23]

It is debatable whether the earth can sustain its current
population in perpetuity, let alone the 9 billion or more people
who will likely be alive in 50 years, without dramatic changes
in lifestyles. After all, humanity is *already* living well beyond
the carrying capacity of the earth. However, if individuals and
societies choose to live more simply and sustainably, it is possible that the planet can indeed sustain everyone.

There is undoubtedly a finite ecological limit to human
population, but the greatest concern should be how much
and what humans consume, and consequently how much
they harm the environment and specifically how much they
cause and contribute to greenhouse gas pollution. More specifically, the chief concern in coming decades is how much
people consume beyond their needs. On top of population
growth in general are the growing ecological and specifically
carbon footprints of the world's affluent people, now exceeding 1 billion individuals. If we compare rich and poor nations
– bearing in mind that the same applies to rich and poor individuals – the disparities in material consumption are huge:
90 percent of personal consumption worldwide occurs in the
developed nations where only about 20 percent of the global
population resides.[24] People in the developed nations on average use 32 times as many resources and produce that much
more waste than do people in developing countries.[25] Affluent
individuals in developing nations have similar impacts, on

average. However, as in developed nations, a large number of them will have a far greater impact than the average. Indeed, globally the amount of greenhouse gas pollution from one person can vary by a factor of one thousand, depending on that person's level of consumption.[26]

Comparing average per capita greenhouse gas emissions among nations, consumption in the United States reveals the problem: with less than 5 percent of the world's population, it produces about one-fifth of global emissions.[27] Average per capita emissions of carbon dioxide in the United States exceed 20 metric tons, but the IPCC has determined that a "relatively safe level of carbon dioxide emissions" is closer to 2 metric tons per person globally.[28] On a per capita basis, consumption of fossil fuels and consequently emissions of CO_2 in North America are ten times the levels in developing nations.[29] Thus, it is not the number of Americans per se that has con-tributed so much to the climate change problem. Far more important is their extraordinarily high level of individual con-sumption and the North American economies' heavy reliance on the profligate use of fossil fuels. If people in the United States alone were to continue using so much fossil fuel energy and maintaining their high levels of material consumption in the future, achieving global sustainability would require the US population, now over 300 million, to drop to 50 million.[30]

It is not quite so bad in Europe, but bad nonetheless: in a given year, "by the time a typical British family sits down to its evening meal on 3 January, they will already have been responsible for a volume of greenhouse gases being pumped into the global commons of the atmosphere equivalent to that produced by a similar-sized Tanzanian family in a year."[31] This brings into sharp focus the consumption and pollution of people in affluent nations who have, for a very long time, contributed far more to climate change than have people in developing countries. Indeed, pollution from people in the developed countries is in the order of 100 times that of those living in the world's poorest ones.[32]

One method for calculating the environmental effects of population is to use a simple formula given the acronym IPAT: environmental *impact* equals *population* size multiplied by per capita *affluence* multiplied by the impact of *technologies* used to achieve that level of affluence.[33] The assumption here is that, while the number of people does matter for the environment, what can matter more is how wealthy they are and what technologies they (and society) use, or more specifically how much and what they consume. But the IPAT formula, while portraying the general relationship between population and the multiplying effect of consumption, underestimates the full impact of population. It fails to account for key thresholds. For example, we may be quickly reaching a point (if we have not already reached it) where positive feedback loops, such as methane and carbon emissions from melting permafrost, could greatly accelerate global warming.[34] Nevertheless, the IPAT formula exposes the key role of affluence: a smaller population with higher material affluence is no solution to climate change.

Technologies that truly reduce per capita and thus overall environmental impacts are beneficial, whereas those that increase these impacts, such as "greener" technologies that are much more widely adopted than their predecessors, can make things worse. If population increases, material affluence and technology must be adjusted to reduce environmental impacts. If population falls *alongside* favorable changes in material consumption and pollution from affluence or technology, environmental impacts could be reduced quite substantially. This is what will be needed to combat climate change.

What this reveals, as Clive Hamilton points out, is that "it makes no sense to single out population growth without linking people to their expected consumption . . . it is affluence rather than population growth that is mainly responsible for the climate crisis."[35] Because material consumption will inevitably increase among the world's poorer individuals if they escape poverty (as they should), far less consumption among the world's affluent people, combined with a widespread shift to alternative, carbon-free energy sources, will be essential quite soon.

Capitalism, modernity, and growth

Population matters: all things being equal, more people mean more greenhouse gas emissions. However, the formula we must consider more carefully is population multiplied by consumption. If the multiplication factor is too high, no amount of population control will be enough to ensure that humanity does not exceed the long-term carrying capacity of the earth. This is especially true because consumption is so closely connected to the burning of fossil-fuels: most of the things that people consume, including the energy to produce and transport it, requires fossil fuel energy. This creates problems for climate politics: much of what individuals and societies do will have to change, but change is always resisted by those with an interest in business as usual. Importantly, much of global consumption, and an enormous proportion of it in economically developed societies, is not a result of meeting people's needs. It is caused by consumption of modern luxuries. Thus modernity and affluence, and an associated addiction to unnecessary material consumption, are among the most important sources of global environmental problems, climate change especially. This forces us to think about how people live in the modern world. Do they consume and pollute to fulfill personal needs, or do they consume and pollute because they are caught up in modern social and economic systems that leave them with few alternative ways of living? The latter points to the role played by modern lifestyle, capitalism, and economic globalization.

Inge Ropke has summed up several significant features of the modern lifestyle: individual economic independence, the ease and practice of greater mobility, diets comprising more meat and foods from around the world, much greater convenience and comfort in daily life (from mechanization, air conditioning, and the like), intensified use of time (with relaxation discouraged), and greater variation and novelty across all aspects of life (novel experiences, novel products, and a greater emphasis on excitement).[36] A feature of this modern lifestyle is that people seldom see or make the connection between their consumption behaviors and the associated use of natural resources and the waste produced. They consume for perfectly normal reasons – to provide for families, establish their status, find meaning, and so forth – which means that changing behaviors is very difficult. Nevertheless, as Ropke argues, if we are to address climate change effectively, the "ever-growing consumption of the affluent must be brought on to the agenda."[37]

The modern capitalist system that now describes the majority of the world's economic activity has positive attributes. It has arguably lifted millions out of extreme poverty (although some might say it has doomed as many to it). It has also made millions of people truly affluent in material terms, with widespread luxuries hardly dreamed of not long ago. But this has come at great cost to the natural environment. Orthodox economic growth has reduced the prices of many essential commodities and foods, but in the process it has often come at the expense of local ecosystems and the earth's climate system.[38]

James Gustave Speth lays the blame for global environmental problems squarely on modern capitalism (the world's current system of political economy, not an idealized notion of capitalism):

An unquestioning society-wide commitment to economic growth at almost any cost; enormous investment in technologies designed with little regard for the environment; powerful corporate interests whose overriding objective is to grow by generating profit, including profit from avoiding the environmental costs they create; markets that systematically fail to recognize environmental costs unless corrected by government; government that is subservient to corporate interests and the growth imperative; rampant consumerism spurred by a worshipping of novelty and by sophisticated advertising; economic activity so large in scale that its impacts alter the fundamental biophysical operations of the planet – all combine to deliver an ever-growing world economy that is undermining the planet's ability to sustain life.[39]

John Barry joins Speth and a growing number of scholars who argue that capitalism itself is at the root of the climate crisis: "Carbon-fueled capitalism is destroying the planet's life-support systems and is systematically liquidating them and calling it 'economic growth.'"[40]

The significance of growth for modern capitalism and for climate change is important to emphasize. As Speth points out, for governments, businesses, and many people, growth "is modern capitalism's principle and most prized product," and for most economists the notion that "there are or should be limits to growth is typically met with derision."[41] Hamilton argues that "the obsession with economic growth has been the principal obstacle to effective global warming policies."[42] It blinds officials and citizens to the long-term ailments of climate politics. Bill McKibben is among those who criticize the role of "relentless economic expansion" in contributing to climate change: "Global warming literally threatens the underpinnings of our civilization, and it's caused, quite directly, by the endless growth of material economies."[43] Hamilton describes this as "growth fetishism," whereby people "internalize the discourse" of economic growth so that "in our consumption behavior we conduct ourselves in ways that perpetuate the system."[44] This is exacerbated by the tendency of political leaders to be those people "who have internalized the goals of the system most faithfully and are therefore most immune to arguments and evidence that might challenge it. The state itself, which once represented the interests of the people ... has been reshaped since the 1970s to serve the interests of the Economy."[45]

Thus it seems impossible to explain the world's impact on the environment, and the causes and responses to climate change in particular, without emphasizing the practices of the global capitalist system.[46] Fundamental to this system almost everywhere is that national economies are "healthy" only when they are experiencing economic growth. Such systems have been shown to be environmentally damaging because economic growth is now largely premised on increasing material throughput, characterized by the growing use of resources and the increasing production of waste and pollution. But societies cannot continue to overconsume the planet's resources and pollute the environment in search of limitless economic growth. For Tim Jackson, the "simplistic assumptions that capitalism's propensity for efficiency will allow us to stabilize the climate or protect against resource scarcity are nothing short of delusional."[47] He argues that it is "entirely fanciful" to assume that the cuts in pollution and resource use necessary to reverse climate change can be realized without "confronting the structure of market economies."[48] As Barry observes, an environmental critique of economic growth would view its *"infinite continuation as a permanent objective of public policy* as both socially and ecologically irrational."[49] While underdeveloped communities still require growth to escape hardship, this no longer applies to all but the poorest parts of developed nations and to those localities in the developing world where affluence dominates.

Governments are of course addicted to material affluence – or, more specifically, to economic growth, which is often seen as synonymous with development.[50] The consequence for the environment is that it almost always falls lower on the list of priorities, or is seen as something to address in the future or which must be "balanced" with economic growth. Scientists have warned for decades that there are *limits* to growth.[51] For just as long, they have been pilloried by economists for being wrong, the assumption among the economists being that markets and innovation will perpetually find ways around the limits.[52] Incredibly by today's standards (although they are still given credence by climate deniers), some of these same critics predicted less than a generation ago that "the world in 2000 [would] be less crowded (though more populated), less polluted, more stable ecologically, and less vulnerable to resource-supply disruption than the world we live in now."[53] As Susan George puts it, "despite incontrovertible proof of impending climate crisis and ecological disaster, mainstream economists and most politicians still don't see things that way" because they continue to assume that extraction of natural resources and material production and consumption have no boundaries, with nature viewed by them as "a mere subsystem" from which humanity obtains materials and into which it dumps its wastes.[54]

However, it is becoming clearer that predictions of environmental limits to growth are likely to be realized later this century, short of major changes in the way the world's growing population consumes and pollutes.[55] The key scarcity is not so much a lack of resources, for which substitutes can usually be found, at least by those wealthy enough to afford them. The real scarcity is the lack of environmental "sinks" to absorb the pollution and other environmental consequences of human activity.[56] Emissions of greenhouse gases into the atmosphere are the most widespread and profound example of this phenomenon. In a long-term sense, we are already beyond the limits. In Jackson's formulation, "the climate may turn out to be the mother of all limits."[57]

Because of climate change, we are facing what Paul Gilding calls "the Great Disruption."[58] He believes that an end to economic growth is inevitable as natural resources become less widely available and the global ecosystem reaches its physical limits. As growth quickens, the limits to growth approach ever faster, and the more the world economy grows, the harsher will be the inevitable collision with natural limits: "So ironically, our obsession with economic growth will force the end of economic growth."[59] As Gilding sees it, "while we appear to be getting rich because we have more stuff, we are spending all sorts of hidden capital to get that stuff, so our actual real new wealth is going down, not up."[60] In Jackson's portrayal of the problem, the notion of social progress, based on ever-expanding material desires and consumption, is fundamentally unsustainable: "In pursuit of the good life today, we are systematically eroding the basis of wellbeing tomorrow."[61]

The combined environmental and economic crises afflicting the world are intimately tied up with, and arguably caused by, the way that consumption has come to define modern society and the way that it has become the aspiration of people almost everywhere.[62] What is clear is that the practice of capitalism, without major change, is no longer compatible with global environmental sustainability.[63] In spite of this, that practice is being globalized, spreading beyond the West to almost every corner of the globe.

Affluenza and the globalization of consumption

This section briefly explores some of the hedonistic features of the modern world economy, describing the addiction of "affluenza" and the spread of material consumption from developed to developing nations.[64] Most of the developed world already suffers from affluenza, defined as "a painful, contagious, socially transmitted condition of overload, debt, anxiety, and waste resulting from dogged pursuit of endless more."[65] Andrew Brennan and Y. S. Lo argue that affluenza is a disease "suffered by the affluent in their addictive pursuit of capital and consumption, at the cost of destroying welfare, the environment, and individual health."[66] Juliet Schor describes what she calls "new consumerism": "an upscaling of lifestyle norms; the pervasiveness of conspicuous, status goods and of competition for acquiring them; and the growing disconnect between consumer desires and incomes."[67]

Very importantly for global climate politics, this affliction of consumerism is increasingly being imitated around the world as "the American lifestyle" grows in popularity and becomes achievable for more people.[68] If it continues to spread, the epidemic of affluenza "threatens to exhaust the earth itself."[69] One tragic irony is that the more affluent people destroy nature, the more they turn to forms of satisfaction that cause the destruction – such as shopping in malls. It is highly questionable whether this behavior serves any truly useful purpose. Again, a distinction must be made between fulfillment of human needs and environmentally reasonable aspirations, which too many people around the world have not yet realized, and the "affluenza" of material consumption and energy use that characterizes the lives of most of the world's relatively affluent people (and of course the rich).

The affluenza of consumption can arise from the desire to keep up with one's peer group, and from powerful social influences, cultural norms, and advertising.[70] To a great extent, people's connections to society in economically developed communities are defined by their consumer activities: lives revolve around consumption.[71] By William Marsden's reckoning, in today's society, people share "the desire to pursue individual material wealth," while society at large "remains unflagging in its almost pathological pursuit of material self interest."[72] People in the developed world are enmeshed in a busy cycle of work to earn more money that will enable them to consume more, which in turn requires working harder to earn more money to consume yet more. Because people work so hard to do this, they tend to think that they ought to enjoy the fruits of their labor. But too few people in the United States and similar nations do that through relaxation, enjoying free time, devoting attention to family activities or working in the community. Instead they undertake further material consumption – they shop – thereby feeding the cycle. The long hours required to achieve the so-called American dream results for many in nightmares of work that they do not enjoy but which pays the most, weakened family relationships, personal debt, isolation from communities, homes full of possessions they do not need, a lack of meaning in their lives, obesity, and depression.[73]

Too many people want more material goods even when their material needs are fully met. One reason is that material things are used to convey messages to other people, such as to send signals about supposed social status or to help individuals to fit into groups they want to be part of.[74] What seems to matter most is not how much income people have or how many possessions they can buy with it in absolute terms, but rather how much they have relative to others. In short, people tend to want more than those around them, more than their parents had and more than they themselves had in the past. This is especially the case in unequal societies where having more money and more things equates to status and power. It is especially problematic because, as societies become more affluent, the appetite for more income and more material things increases as everyone competes to have just that much more than those around them.[75] It is a never-ending cycle of consumption that is occurring in most western societies and in cities across the developing world.

While individuals who have more than others may feel better off, society as a whole is not. Indeed, studies on relative happiness and life satisfaction in different nations and cultures repeatedly show that, once people's basic needs have been met, quality of life overall does not increase significantly with an overall growth in wealth.[76] As more people become wealthier, wellbeing remains more or less static. This helps to explain why many developed societies that experience economic growth and indeed growth in individual wealth do not see analogous increases in citizens' feelings of wellbeing.

Consumption by a large number of already affluent people on the planet, especially in the developed nations, exacerbated by the official obsession with economic growth and widespread affluenza, is a fundamental driving force behind greenhouse gas emissions causing climate change. Alas, things are set to get much worse. This is because western modernity and affluenza have gone global. Expanding global consumption is encouraged by the globalization of American culture, which is spread through trade, advertising, modern communications, and travel.[77] The problem is that the American lifestyle is extremely energy-intensive and environmentally destructive. As people's incomes increase around the world, demand for products and services grows, with all the attendant environmental consequences. If everyone were to live like Americans, the world would require ten times the energy it is using today.[78] Indeed, if all of the 9 billion people who will be alive around mid-century were to enjoy the average level of affluence in developed nations today (which is well below the US average), the global economy would be 15 times the size that it is now, and 75 times its size in the middle of the twentieth century.[79] This would be impossible to realize from an environmental perspective, at least if the size of economies four decades hence is measured as they are today.

As economies of the developing world grow, governments and people there are making the same environmentally unsustainable mistakes made in the global North: developing a love for material consumption, private automobiles, air travel, and consumption of meat and processed foods made from imported commodities. Norman Myers and Jennifer Kent have dubbed the growing class of consumers in the developing world the "new consumers."[80] They define these new consumers as people in a four-person household with purchasing power of more than US$10,000 (purchasing power parity) per year (over $2,500 per person per year, purchasing power parity).[81] This threshold is a starting point, with most of the new consumers that Myers and Kent examined having much higher purchasing power. They set the threshold at this level because they see it as roughly the point at which people "start to engage in a distinctly middle-class lifestyle."[82] It is where people "choose what they will consume, rather than being driven by the necessities of life."[83] With roughly this income, people begin to purchase cars, televisions, computers and other electronics, washing machines and modern kitchen appliances, and it is a point where people shift to a diet high in grain-fed meat and their lifestyles consume larger quantities of water.[84] As Myers and Kent point out, these new consumers are simply following a well-beaten path laid down by people in the developed nations.[85]

The rise of the new consumers is a relatively new phenomenon, starting in the 1980s, during which their number reached a few hundred million, followed by a burst in the 1990s.[86] By 2000, the number of new consumers exceeded 1 billion, the majority of them in developing nations, with 40 percent of them in China and India (30 percent in China alone).[87] In 2000, their combined spending power – "the biggest sunburst of affluence the world had ever seen in such a short period"[88] – already approached that of the United States.[89] The number of new consumers continues to grow at an accelerating pace. Myers and Kent predicted that they would easily exceed 1.5 billion by 2010.[90] According to Kharas, the global middle class numbered more than 1.8 billion people in 2009, likely reaching 3.2 billion in 2020 and 4.9 billion in 2030, with 85 percent of these people being in Asia.[91] The spending power of this global middle class has been predicted to increase from over US$20 trillion to US$56 trillion in the two decades up to 2030, with 80 percent of the increase in Asia.[92] Myers and Kent describe these changes as "a consumption boom of a compressed scale beyond the dreams of people in all history."[93]

The impact of the new consumers is highly disproportionate when compared to other people in their own communities, just as the impact of most people in the developed nations is much greater than that of most people in the developing countries. For example, in 2000 new consumers made up only about one-seventh of India's population, but they held two-fifths of the nation's purchasing power and their per capita consumption of energy was 15 times that of other Indians.[94] This is set to become much worse as India's middle class grows by more than 1 billion people over the next two decades.[95]

Nowhere are the growth and impact of new consumers more evident than in China, where many millions of people have very rapidly adopted the consumer habits of the West, increasingly living in large homes, frequenting shopping malls full of luxury goods, joining a nationwide car culture and eating diets full of meat.[96] As Karl Gerth puts it, consumers in China are the new "vanguards of global consumerism."[97] China alone had no fewer than 300 million new consumers by 2000, up from almost none in the 1980s and a few tens of millions around 1990.[98] The size of China's middle class is expected to reach 520 million people by 2025.[99] It is the fastest-growing consumer society in the world, with a quarter of the population being new consumers.[100] Kharas put the number of "middle-class" consumers in China in 2010 at 157 million, exceeded only by the United States.[101] Survey data reveal the eagerness of people in China's new middle class to consume. For example, they spend almost three times as many hours shopping each week as do Americans.[102] Consequently, while China has many good environmental policies and is implementing alternative-energy and energy-efficiency projects, these are greatly outpaced by the environmental impacts of increasing consumption, meaning that the nation's contribution to climate change will continue to grow.[103]

Worryingly, Kharas believes that the rise in Asian new consumers is so rapid that it will "replace the forecast shortfalls in US consumer demand growth" (from the global recession).[104] This trend can go only so far. Certainly, most Chinese can never consume as much as Americans do today. The earth could not sustain it. To understand this reality, Jared Diamond asks us to assume what would happen if the developing world were to reach US levels of consumption.[105] If China alone were to do this, consumption rates worldwide would double. If India were to join China in this achievement, global consumption would triple. If the entire world were to match US consumption rates, consumption would be eleven times what it is today. Diamond puts this into stark perspective:

> It would be as if the world population ballooned to 72 billion people (retaining present consumption rates). Some optimists claim that we could support a world with nine billion people. But I haven't met anyone crazy enough to claim that we could support 72 billion. Yet we often promise developing countries that [they] will be able to enjoy a first-world lifestyle. This promise is impossible, a cruel hoax.[106]

A profound manifestation of new consumerism is the automobile. By 2000, the new consumers alone were driving 125 million cars, double the number ten years earlier.[107] Just during the 1990s, the number of cars in China grew by 400 percent, and by over 200 percent in India.[108] In 2000, China comprised a mere 1 percent of global car sales; by 2010, it accounted for 13 percent.[109] As Myers and Kent put it, in developing countries the car culture is entering "high gear."[110] Worldwide carbon emissions from cars have been increasing much faster than emissions from other sources, and they are likely to be the fastest-growing type of energy use for quite some time.[111] If per capita car use in China were ever to reach that in the United States, CO_2 emissions from China's cars alone would be about equal to the *entire* world's current emissions from transportation.[112]

But cars do more than add greatly to global carbon emissions; they also create smog, which contributes to adverse health consequences (including death) and acid rain, which affects agriculture, forests, and waterways. The millions of new consumers who are purchasing and driving their own automobiles, and especially the millions more who aspire to do so (not to mention their governments), would do well to consider the adverse effects that the car culture has had in the West, ranging from traffic congestion and diversion of national resources away from public transport, to the health effects of air pollution and, of course, the enormous amount of greenhouse gas pollution that cars produce.[113]

One of the biggest contributions of new consumers to climate change is their growing consumption of meat, especially that from grain-fed livestock. Demand for meat in developing countries has been projected to grow by 90 percent between 1997 and 2020, with the new-consumer nations leading this increase. For example, in China, meat consumption doubled in the 1990s, reaching 28 percent of global consumption (despite its population being only 20 percent of the world's), making China by far the largest consumer.[114] At 50 kilograms per person, its average per capita meat consumption is less than half that of the United States. However, within this average are hundreds of millions of new Chinese consumers eating much larger amounts of meat even while roughly one billion of them rarely consume it.[115] Production of meat uses vast tracts of land for growing feed and for grazing, consumes enormous amounts of water to produce food for livestock and to flush away their waste, and requires very large amounts of energy for processing and transportation. What is more, livestock animals, notably cattle and sheep, are major sources of greenhouse gas emissions because, as ruminants, they produce methane, a greenhouse gas that is 20 times more powerful than CO_2. Production of meat for consumption results in more greenhouse gas pollution than the world's entire transport sector.[116] Depending on the studies and statistics one uses, livestock already account for anywhere from one-fifth to over one-half of global greenhouse gas emissions.[117]

In many respects, the growing global consumption of meat emulates the United States, where most meals include some form of meat, with well-known adverse effects on health, notably heart disease and obesity.[118] What is more, feeding livestock raises the cost of food and diverts grains away from feeding the world's hungriest people. It will be necessary to *double* global food production by 2050 to meet growing demands for meat and western-style foods as the world's population increases, but it may be impossible to do this sustainably.[119]

Conclusion

The world's population cannot continue to increase indefinitely if we are to have any real hope of preventing the worst effects of climate change. But more vital than population is the worldwide growth in consumption. What we have is a world with more people consuming well beyond their needs – while simultaneously too many people consume too little to meet theirs – and rapidly growing numbers of new consumers suc-cumbing to the affluenza that has long been entrenched in the developed nations. Consumption and affluenza largely created the problem of climate change, and their spread is making it far worse. The world's population is expected to peak later this century. Without a change in how billions of people live, con-sumption will increase even if population falls. Currently, the global economic crisis does not seem to have greatly under-mined enthusiasm for consumption. Consequently, ways must be found to limit its environmental effects while also actively helping individuals to find ways of living that do not involve overconsumption (see chapter 7). We need an alterna-tive to capitalism as currently practiced. For Speth, the most fundamental question facing the world is this: "How can the operating instructions for the modern world economy be changed so that economic activity both protects and restores the natural world?"[120]

The large and growing human population is vitally sig-nificant in driving climate change (and other adverse environmental changes). When coupled with material con-sumption and the spread of modern lifestyles, it becomes a force that will, without interventions, send climatic changes running wild. The spread of material consumption around the world is not only accelerating emissions of greenhouse gases; it is also changing the political calculus for the world's responses to climate change. As more nations and more people adopt the lifestyles of the West, change becomes that much more difficult. Just like other addictions, addictions to modernity will be hard to break.

Summarizing the ailments of climate politics described in Part I, among the most harmful and intractable are: (1) the cancerous influence of state-centric Westphalian norms that encourage nations to fight for their narrow, short-term interests and which make truly effective international cooperation on climate change extraordinarily difficult; (2) the most malignant polluters, the United States and China, which together already produce well over one-third of global greenhouse gas emissions even as they refuse to act in the interests of the world and the long-term interests of their own people; and (3) what are described here as addictions of modernity, especially affluenza and the spread of material consumption typical of the West to the developing world, resulting in growing greenhouse gas emissions globally (even as they stabilize, or in some cases fall, in the developed nations) and increasing political resistance to change.

These diagnoses of what ails climate politics suggest certain treatments, which are the subject of Part II. While skeptics may call these treatments unrealistic, they are not intended to appear as such. Together they are an attempt to find a middle path between, on one hand, failed climate politics and, on the other hand, a radical overhaul of the current world economic and political systems to create an environmentally benign future, which may be desirable but which would take far too long to realize. A fundamental assumption is that continuing on our current path is the *least* realistic way to fix what is wrong with climate politics.

Part II

Treatments

CHAPTER FIVE

People-Centered Diplomacy: Human Rights and Globalized Justice

This chapter and the two that follow conceptualize some treatments for key ailments of climate politics described in Part I. There is extensive debate about whether nations are capable of guiding the world toward environmental sustainability: some argue that nations themselves are the problem, while others argue that they are the only solution.[1] While this debate will and should continue, the discussions in this and succeeding chapters have an underlying assumption: nation-states are not the only or necessarily the most important actors, but they will not be going away anytime soon (if ever), requiring that their power be harnessed to simultaneously promote human interests and environmental protection, and specifically to respond far more effectively to climate change. Some people will say that nations and other actors can continue with business as usual.[2] These people are deluded or immorally selfish, or both. Others will say that it is probably too late, that humanity might not be up to the enormous task of changing course in time.[3] They may well be right, but they could also be too pessimistic. The world has no choice but to work hard to combat climate change because its consequences have the potential to be catastrophic. There is no shortage of proposals for acting much more robustly toward this end.[4] The treatments here for what is wrong with climate politics should be viewed as supplementing them.

We can begin by addressing possibly the most damaging ailment of climate politics: the cancer of Westphalia. Chapter 2

described how this cancer of interstate norms pervades international relations, including in the context of climate change.
This chapter proposes a category of treatments that, while
accepting the reality and even preeminence of nation-states,
involve redirecting attention toward the fundamental causes
and victims of climate change: human beings.[5] The fundamental drivers of climate pollution are people, especially the
world's affluent people. It is their lifestyles that are harming the planet. More specifically, climate change is a global
problem that is caused by billions of individual actions and
choices.[6] What is more, those who will suffer the most from
climate change are not nations or governments per se – the
usual recipients of sympathy and increasingly of aid (albeit
too little) related to climate change – but people, especially the
world's poor. The world's affluent consumers are essentially
taking away the right of all people to a sustainable and livable
environment. People have obligations based on their contributions to climate change (through their pollution), their
responsibility for it (through their consumption choices and
connections to those affected) and their capabilities (to act and
to aid). Affluent individuals are not entitled to behave frivo-
lously in ways that violate the fundamental rights of others,
including people far away, to enjoy a stable climate.

Given these obligations, and the failure of state-centric
policies to stem global greenhouse gas emissions, climate
politics, and policies should be aimed at helping responsible
and capable people (and other actors) behave in ways that
do not exacerbate climate change. Climate politics ought
to be aimed at preventing people from becoming victims of
climate change, aiding those who are victims to cope with it,
and helping those in poverty to rise above it in ways that do
not unnecessarily make the problem worse. If climate politics are to be treated effectively, "doses" of human rights and
human security need to be absorbed into the fabric of climate

diplomacy and policy. The recognized role of climate justice among nations needs to be supplemented by a clear recognition of the need for realizing climate justice among and for people. In short, one treatment for climate politics is directing attention away from state-centric responses to the problem toward a globalization of climate justice – from thinking mostly in terms of nations' rights toward thinking and acting much more in terms of human rights.

Human rights and human security

As we saw in chapter 1 and especially in chapter 4, individual human beings are at the root of climate change. Mary Robinson, former United Nations High Commissioner for Human Rights, reminds us of something that many diplomats and governments seem to forget: in the case of climate change, "immediate causes are generally found in private acts."[7] This imposes some significant obligations upon individuals (see chapters 6 and 7). But people are not just causes of climate change; they are also the *victims* of it. One can routinely read about particular nations suffering from climate change. Attention is often directed at the poorest nations that are most vulnerable to it. But nation-states per se (the legal entities) do not and cannot suffer; it is the people living within them that do. That we seldom hear much said of the potentially climate-related suffering of, say, Russia or the United States, despite an unfortunate number of Russians and Americans suffering and even dying most years from "natural" disasters – hurricanes, tornadoes, floods, avalanches, wildfires, and so forth – shows how our attention is most often directed at nations rather than individuals. This section introduces two approaches to the problem that redirect our attention away from nations as victims of climate change and toward individuals. These approaches focus on human rights and human security. The next section develops this move toward the individual by considering a global justice perspective on climate change.

According to the Global Humanitarian Forum, climate change harms people in many ways, particularly in the following areas:

- Food security: More poor people, especially children, suffer from hunger due to reduced agricultural yield, livestock and fish supplies as a result of environmental degradation.
- Health: Health threats like diarrhea, malaria, asthma, and stroke affect more people when temperatures rise.
- Poverty: Livelihoods are destroyed when income from agriculture, livestock, tourism, and fishing is lost due to weather-related disasters and desertification.
- Water: Increased water scarcity results from a decline in the overall supply of clean water and more frequent and severe floods and droughts.
- Displacement: More climate-displaced people are expected due to sea-level rise, desertification, and floods.
- Security: More people live under the continuous threat of potential conflict and institutional breakdown due to migration, weather-related disaster, and water scarcity.[8]

Every year, climate change results in more than 300,000–400,000 deaths (climbing to about 500,000 by 2030), seriously affects 325 million people (660 million by 2030), causes health problems for several hundred million people, and leaves one-third of the world's population physically vulnerable and half a billion at extreme risk.[9] By mid-century, 250 million people could become "climate refugees," forced to permanently flee their homes and communities due to floods, droughts, hurricanes, and famines related to climate change.[10] The World Health Organization reports that 150,000 people, 85 percent of them children, already die each year in developing nations due to just some of the effects of climate change (crop failure, malnutrition, diarrhea, malaria, and flooding).[11]

Climate change will greatly exacerbate global poverty. It already contributes to economic losses of almost US$125 billion annually, pushing about 12 million additional people into poverty (reaching 20 million by 2020) and, by 2030, will likely leave 75 million people hungry.[12] According to the African Development Bank and its sister institutions, climate change puts poverty eradication programs at "serious risk," and it "threatens to undo decades of development efforts."[13] The United Nations Development Program has predicted that climate change will lock hundreds of millions of people into poverty, subjecting them to malnutrition, loss of livelihoods, water scarcity, and other ecological threats.[14] As such, the connections between human rights, human security, and climate change are very close: it is the human rights of the poor that will be violated most systematically by climate change, and thus indirectly by those who cause it.[15]

Stephen Humphreys observes that climate change will most adversely affect people and communities whose rights are "already precarious."[16] These people are by definition less able to prepare for and adapt to the impacts of climate change. Significantly from both practical and moral perspectives, climate change is not about violating just any rights; it is about violating the most *basic* ones, those that precede and are prerequisites for all others, such as physical security, subsistence, health, and life itself.[17] Simon Caney describes how climate change violates several very fundamental human rights.[18] It violates the human right to life because severe weather events, landslides, floods, heat waves, and the like will lead to widespread loss of life. It violates the human right to health by exacerbating health threats, such as injuries from severe storms and wildfires, spread of mosquitoes that carry malaria and dengue fever into new areas, and increased frequency of diarrheal diseases. Climate change also violates the human right to subsistence because temperature increases will contribute to starvation due to loss of crops from more widespread droughts, loss of agricultural land to rising seas, crop failures from increased flooding and extreme weather events, and increasing prices for staple foods that will put them beyond the reach of the world's poor.[19]

Climate change has many adverse implications that go beyond what some might see as the most fundamental human rights. For example, temperature changes, extreme weather events, threats to ecosystems, changes in precipitation and water distribution, threats to biodiversity, sea-level rise, storm surges, flooding, and other impacts of climate change will undermine people's rights to self-determination, indigenous ways of life, safe childhoods, property, and adequate housing, in the process violating a number of existing international human rights conventions including: the 1945 United Nations Universal Declaration of Human Rights; the 1966 International Covenant on Economic, Social and Cultural Rights; the 1966 International Covenant on Civil and Political Rights; the 1979 Convention on the Elimination of All Forms of Discrimination against Women; and the 1989 Convention on the Rights of the Child, among others.[20] Policies for adaptation to climate change, if successful, can help to avoid climate-related human rights abuses, while others may serve as compensation for undermining human rights, but some adaptation policies may themselves involve rights violations, as might happen if people were forced to move from flood-prone areas.[21]

In the last decade, human rights have started to receive some attention in debates about climate change, in part due to the belief that the impacts on "individual people and communities around the world" deserve more attention.[22] The United Nations highlighted the impacts of climate change on human rights in its 2007/8 *Human Development Report*, noting that climate change is a human tragedy that "represents a systematic violation of the human rights of the world's poor and future generations, and a step back from universal values."[23] The International Council on Human Rights Policy has been forthright in declaring that, "as a matter of simple fact, climate change is already undermining the realization of a broad range of internationally protected human rights: rights to health and even life; rights to food, water, shelter and property; rights associated with livelihood and culture; with migration and resettlement; and with personal security in the event of conflict."[24] In 2007, Deputy UN Human Rights Commissioner Kyung-wha Kang told the 2007 conference of the parties to the climate change convention in Bali that "any strategy to deal with climate change, whether in terms of adaptation or mitigation, must incorporate the consequences for humans, as individuals and communities, and the human rights framework is the most effective way to do so."[25]

A human rights framework can help to direct attention toward both the human causes of climate change and the human suffering that results.[26] As Mary Robinson has noted, looking at the problem in this way highlights "the human misery that results directly from the damage we are doing to nature" and draws greater attention to "who is at risk and how we should act to protect them."[27] In addition to focusing attention on how individuals' lives are impacted, a human rights perspective can highlight the importance of listening to the views of those who will be most affected by climate change, notably the poorest and most vulnerable people of the world.[28] According to Kang, the human rights perspective requires that the needs of these affected people be integrated into climate change policies and programs.[29] As Philippe Cullet points out, bringing the human rights dimension to climate politics can "completely change the way in which law and policy are conceived in this area. Indeed, the human rights consequences of climate change are potentially so severe that, if taken seriously, they must prevail over economic and related considerations."[30]

The climatic changes that undermine human rights also undermine human *security*. The United Nations Security Council acknowledged this connection in 2007 and again in 2011 when it debated the relationships between climate change and human security.[31] According to the Commission on Human Security, human security is about "freedoms that are the essence of life. It means protecting people from critical (severe) and pervasive (widespread) threats and situations."[32] The concept of human security assumes "the intrinsic value of dignity of all human beings in a holistic way that includes their dependency on and their relations with the natural environment, and it holds that the basic needs of any individual are neither to be sacrificed nor discounted."[33] Like the notion of human rights, as a concept human security is focused on people rather than on nations.[34] It is about "prioritizing the needs of people above the needs of the nation-state."[35] The idea of human security shifts the objective of security away from the state and toward people, redefining it as being much more about sustainable human development.[36] Put more simply, human security is about everyone's right to a healthy environment.[37]

Thus an important treatment for what ails climate politics, particularly its state-centric orientation, is to do far more to recognize the connections between climate change and the rights and security of people, both as individuals and as communities. Global justice, and indeed practicality, requires that people be made explicit, first-order objects and priorities of climate politics.

Globalizing climate justice

Climate change and justice are intimately linked. As we saw in chapter 2, justice among *nations* has been an important basis of climate negotiations, albeit with limited implementation. The climate change agreements are permeated with considerations of justice and related principles of equity and fairness.[38] Stephen Gardiner describes several associated domains of justice, including some that go well beyond nations.[39] At the international level, focus has been on the greenhouse gas emissions of the greatest national polluters, until recently the United States but increasingly China. Related to this has been focus on the relatively (very) high per capita emissions of Americans and citizens of other western nations. The perception is that it is unjust for some nations and their citizens to pollute the atmosphere disproportionately. At the domestic level, there is increasing interest in looking at the differences in emissions of individuals within nations (which happen to coincide with other kinds of injustices associated with wealth, class, race, and gender). Gardiner points out, for example, that in India the emissions of the top 10 percent of urban residents is over 24 times that of the bottom 10 percent of rural residents, that China's relatively low per capita emissions mask the very high emissions of the nation's affluent millions, and that in many developing countries poor women disproportionately suffer the effects of climate change.[40] Climate change also raises questions about justice between present and future generations, both in terms of causes and impacts.[41] Furthermore, climate change is about "ecological justice" – justice between humans and other species – because it will harm ecosystems and nonhuman species.

In a relatively rare examination of climate-related human rights, Humphreys summarizes four associated justice claims.[42] First are claims for corrective justice by those who have been harmed by the greenhouse gas pollution of others. Those who cause the harm should stop doing so and compensate those who have been injured. Second are claims for substantive justice associated with the loss of future potential or capacity that arises from responses to climate change. For example, efforts to reduce carbon emissions will likely result in higher costs for energy, making life difficult for many people and increasing the costs of economic development. Third are claims for procedural justice. Those affected by climate change are entitled to have a say in what is to be done, who is to pay (and how much), and who is to be compensated (and how much). A fourth justice claim is that associated with the expectations of those who became accustomed to polluting due to no fault of their own, for example due to ignorance about climate change before the science became clear. For example, we ought not to expect the worst polluters – most people in developed nations – to reduce their pollution to safe levels overnight. From this perspective, they should be allowed a reasonable amount of time to bring their pollution down.

These justice claims, while often applied only to nations and certainly subject to much debate, supplement human rights perspectives in helping to highlight the role of human beings in climate politics. Various obligations and entitlements arise because people are both the causes and victims of climate change. If it is to be effective (and just), climate policy should account for this. The failure of *international* climate justice – the failure to implement common but differentiated responsibilities among *nations* – suggests that alternative thinking is required. Gardiner's observations are again helpful: "climate change involves issues which current political institutions and theories do not seem designed for, nor obviously well equipped to handle. . . . Most prominently, climate change is one of a number of contemporary global problems that casts doubt on the traditional philosophical strategy of constructing basic justice on the model of a single self-sufficient nation-state."[43] Thus one potential antidote to state-centric responses to climate change may be found in globalized conceptions of justice that focus on *people* as well as states.[44] These perspectives are often characterized as "cosmopolitan."[45] Cosmopolitan and cosmopolitan-like approaches can help us to frame, visualize, and talk about climate politics, and to formulate and implement related policies, in new ways. Doing so pushes us to think more globally.

Such "globalized" thinking is helpful because it recognizes, and indeed is premised upon, the rights, obligations, and duties of individuals, regardless of nationality. Inter*national* justice – the kind of justice that has guided the climate change regime and resulting national policies – considers national borders to be the practical and ethical foundations for justice. In contrast, *global* (or cosmopolitan) justice, while accepting the practical reality and significance of nations and their borders, views the nation-state as an inadequate basis for deciding what is right and just in world affairs.[46] As David Held has argued, cosmopolitans want to "disclose the ethical, cultural, and legal basis of political order in a world where political communities and states matter, but not only and exclusively. In circumstances where the trajectories of each and every country are tightly entwined, the partiality, one-sidedness and limitedness of 'reasons of state' need to be recognized."[47] Indeed, in the context of climate change, our preoccupation with the nation-state might be seen as precisely the problem. For example, Derek Heater critiques what he calls the "traditional linear model of the individual having a political relationship with the world at large only via his state" because, at least if we are concerned about "the integrity of all planetary life, the institution of the state is relegated to relative insignificance – if not, indeed, viewed as a harmful device."[48]

Scholars often disagree on the fundamental tenets of global (cosmopolitan) thought. Nevertheless, Thomas Pogge sums up three commonly recognized core elements that can help us to think about climate politics from a more global perspective. These elements include:

> First, *individualism*: the ultimate units of concern are *human beings*, or *persons* – rather than, say, family lines, tribes, ethnic, cultural, or religious communities, nations, or states. The latter may be units of concern only indirectly, in virtue of their individual members or citizens. Second, *universality*: the status of ultimate unit of concern attaches to *every* living human being *equally* – not merely to some sub-set, such as men, aristocrats, Aryans, whites, or Muslims. Third, *generality*: this special status has global force. Persons are ultimate units of concern for *everyone* – not only for their compatriots, fellow religionists, or such like.[49]

At the most basic level, from this global perspective "the world is *one* domain in which there are some *universal* values and *global* responsibilities."[50] Such a perspective is a better way to think about the realities of who or what is most responsible, in a practical sense, for climate change, and for finding and implementing solutions to it.

Why might such a perspective be appropriate for better understanding and responding to climate change? Generally speaking, environmental harms crossing borders "extend the bounds of those with whom we are connected, against whom we might claim rights and to whom we owe obligations within the moral community."[51] Lorraine Elliott describes this as a "cosmopolitan morality of distance" that effectively creates "a cosmopolitan community of duties as well as rights."[52] She argues that this is true because "the lives of 'others-beyond-borders' are shaped without their participation and consent [and] environmental harm deterritorializes (or at least trans-nationalizes) the cosmopolitan community. In environmental terms, the bio-physical complexities of the planetary eco-system inscribe it as a global commons of a public good, constituting humanity as an ecological community of fate."[53] Robin Attfield believes that criticisms of state-centric responses to environmental problems will inevitably be based on cosmopolitanism because "the selective ethics of nation states are liable to prioritize some territories, environments, and ecosystems over others. If this meant nothing but leaving the other environments alone, this might not be too perni-cious. [But] it often means not leaving alone the others but polluting or degrading them."[54]

One reason that climate change is a matter of global jus-tice is that millions of people who are far from the sources of greenhouse gas pollution, whether in space or time (or both), suffer from its consequences. Steve Vanderheiden points out that all people "depend on a stable climate for their wellbeing, all are potentially affected by the actions or policies of others, and none can fully opt out of the cooperative scheme, even if they eschew its necessary limits on action. Climate change mitigation therefore becomes an issue of cosmopolitan jus-tice by its very nature as an essential public good."[55] Climate change is a global justice concern because greenhouse gas emissions do not remain within national borders. Regardless of their source, these emissions cause harm globally, includ-ing to people far away. What is more, the economic growth that has driven so much climate change has brought the least benefit to those most affected – the world's poor.[56]

Another reason that climate change is really a matter of *global* justice is that people presently causing future climate change do not live only within the nations that have his-torically caused it. Until quite recently, we could reasonably conceive of climate change as a problem caused by the world's developed nations and their citizens. They were the primary sources of greenhouse gas pollution and therefore the logical bearers of responsibility to end it and to assist those who will suffer from it. The climate change agreements acknowledge this responsibility and are premised on the belief that developed nations, and indirectly their people and corporations, have primary responsibility. However, the relatively affluent people of the world living in the developed nations are no longer the sole or even the predominant causes of climate change. Increasingly, greenhouse gas pollution comes from affluent people in developing nations – from the new consumers.

Given the developing nations' lower (often much lower) per capita greenhouse gas emissions, this new reality does not greatly alter the inter*national* moral calculus. What has changed is the growing number of affluent people in the developing world who are living lifestyles like those of people in developed nations. Indeed, many of these new consumers are living more like the wealthiest classes in the industrialized world. As we saw in chapter 4, these people already number in the hundreds of millions. In China, a few hundred million people, and in India many tens of millions, have higher standards of living – and higher levels of pollution – than do millions of people in the developed nations. They produce greenhouse gases through voluntary consumption at a pace and scale never experienced in human history. The consequences for the atmospheric commons will be severe indeed. Yet these new consumers are not adequately encompassed by the mostly state-centric responses to climate change. This raises quite profound questions about the responsibilities of nations and the responsibilities of individuals for dealing with climate change, in turn having profound implications for climate politics at all levels.

Prioritizing people in climate diplomacy

This section briefly introduces some potential ways in which human beings can be brought toward the center of climate diplomacy. Thinking about a world where individuals are given much higher priority relative to nation-states and their interests can inform practical responses to climate change in the near future.[57] Governments are currently failing adequately to recognize the role of people both as causes and victims of climate change. A less state-centric and more global perspective points to a corollary (or supplement) to the international governance of climate change that can diminish this failure.[58] Such a corollary would acknowledge the responsibilities of developed nations while also explicitly acknowledging and acting upon human rights and the responsibilities of all affluent people, regardless of their nationality. It offers an alternative to a climate regime that is premised on the rights and duties of nations and mostly ignores the rights and duties of individuals. It points toward converting a global justice perspective into a different kind of climate politics and diplomacy that regulate and coordinate the actions of both nations and people. Climate politics, from this perspective, should be premised on the understanding that "the demands of justice must be decoupled, at least to some degree, from the territorial bounds of the state."[59] While governments will inevitably retain a central role, a global corollary to prevailing climate politics would have governments facilitating the implementation of global obligations and entitlements related to climate change.

Philippe Cullet argues that fundamental human rights should be the primary objective of climate policy: "realization of the human rights of life, health, food, water and environment for the majority of the poor should be put at the center of climate change policies. In other words, any shift away from a carbon-based economy must be conceived with the priority of realization of human rights in mind."[60] The International Council on Human Rights Policy points to several benefits that come from doing this: it would prioritize harms to actual persons, requiring that policies for mitigation and adaptation be referenced to human rights thresholds (and specifically to not exceeding those thresholds); help to translate ethical demands into legal obligations (admittedly difficult to actualize, but necessary to attempt); promote accountability (by determining who is accountable for environmental changes that undermine human rights and how that accountability is to be attributed to them); and facilitate procedural guarantees (by requiring that individuals whose rights are harmed by climate change have a say in policy responses).[61]

The United Nations has officially recognized the relationship between human rights and climate change, most vividly perhaps in the context of the Human Rights Council, which has passed several resolutions on the matter, starting in 2008.[62] As the Human Rights Council affirmed, "human rights obligations, standards and principles have the potential to inform and strengthen international and national policymaking in the area of climate change, promoting policy coherence, legitimacy and sustainable outcomes."[63] The connections between climate change and human rights are apparent, but for the United Nations and governments to consider them seriously in these terms is quite unusual, and indeed official recognition of such connections was opposed by major oil-producing and -consuming nations.[64]

Marc Limon identifies several policy-related advantages of thinking about climate change in terms of human rights.[65] First, a "human rights lens" focuses the international climate debate on "individuals and the effects of climate change on their lives."[66] This helps to overcome the failure so far to "humanize" climate change.[67] If the object of climate policy is

severe human suffering rather than environmental phenom-
ena, such as melting icecaps or the withering of coral reefs, it
may become more difficult for governments to avoid action.
Second, framing climate change in terms of human rights
"helps amplify the voices of those who are disproportionately
affected," notably the poor and vulnerable.[68] Third, debating
climate change in terms of individual people "has the potential to 'level the playing field' in international negotiations,
which have to date been dominated by large states involved in
largely economically motivated power plays and tradeoffs."[69]
Fourth, framing climate change in terms of human rights
provides a well-established set of principles, set out in international agreements related to human rights, which can serve
as the basis for international responses, thereby potentially
contributing qualitatively to formulation of national and international policies.[70] This would include access to information,
decision-making, and legal remedies. Fifth, a human rights
framework may help to encourage international cooperation
because actions by nations are necessary to protect and realize
human rights in the context of climate change.[71]

Somewhat paradoxically, taking a human rights perspective
also draws attention to the need for policies that do not undermine the rights of people to statehood: it reminds us that for
people in the most vulnerable nations, specifically low-lying
small-island states most vulnerable to rising seas, climate
change has the potential to make them stateless.[72]

What does this mean on a practical level internationally?
Diplomats should devote large amounts of time at each climate change conference to discussing human rights very
seriously and to finding ways to protect those rights through
the international agreements they negotiate. Limon believes
that what is needed is the "organic integration and evolution"
of human rights principles into the climate regime.[73] This
is akin to the global corollary proposed above.[74] This would

entail including specific wording in future climate change agreements (both formal and informal) "recognizing that climate change has significant negative implications on the lives and livelihoods of individual people (especially vulnerable people) around the world, that climate change policy must therefore be premised on the need to protect and rehabilitate such individuals, and that human rights policy offers an important way of understanding the former and informing and facilitating the latter."[75] This should of course be followed by concrete policies for implementation to achieve these aims, but the step of making human rights – and more generally human beings – a central object of climate diplomacy is likely to be an essential prerequisite for doing so.

Several frameworks have been proposed to make people more explicit objects of climate diplomacy.[76] For example, Aubrey Meyer's concept of "contraction and convergence" effectively calls for setting an equal per capita allowance of greenhouse gas emissions, followed by a gradual contraction of emissions in nations where they are above the allowance and an increase in emissions for those below the allowance, to the point where emissions converge.[77] While it is developed nations that are expected to contract and developing nations that will converge, what is unusual here is that the fundamental measure of which nations must do what is directly related to per capita emissions. Human beings are a bigger part of this proposal than in the standard approaches discussed in most of the climate change negotiations among nations. Some form of contraction and convergence is essential if the world's responses to climate change are to be fair over the long term. While there may be instances where some people are entitled to pollute the atmosphere more than others – for example, if they live in circumstances that require doing this as a means of survival – making such exceptions will require justification.

One problem with the contraction and convergence approach, however, is that, insofar as it is directed at nations, it neglects differences within them. For example, it does not pay enough attention to the new consumers in the developing world. Affluent high polluters in poor countries can hide behind their nation's low per capita emissions.

An idea that can move us toward overcoming this drawback is that of "greenhouse development rights" (GDRs) as proposed by Paul Baer and others.[78] Underlying the GDR framework is a crucial and very realistic premise:

> So constrained is the global carbon budget . . . that it is too late to talk of emissions reductions in [developed] countries alone. It is now necessary to secure significant cuts in emissions in the growing nations of the developing world. And yet, even in the burgeoning Chinese and Indian economies, there is still huge poverty. This is the crux of the current climate impasse. [GDR] argues that while people remain poor, it is unacceptable and unrealistic to expect them to focus their valuable resources on the climate change crisis. And it draws the necessary conclusion – that others who are wealthier and have enjoyed higher levels of emissions already must take on their fair share of the effort.[79]

The GDR framework takes a global approach to burden sharing based on both capacity and responsibility. It uses income distribution within nations to quantify obligations so that in principle an individual "with the same income and historical emissions would bear the same proportional share of global obligations, regardless of the country in which he or she lives."[80] The GDR approach takes account of intra-national distributional equity by allocating "obligations to pay for climate policies (both mitigation and adaptation) on the basis of an individually quantified metric of capacity (ability to pay) and responsibility (prior emissions)."[81] What is special about the GDR framework, apart from its important focus on people as the basis for allocating rights and obligations, is that it allocates the latter to both rich *and* poor nations based on their proportions of affluent (middle- and upper-class) people.[82]

The GDR plan sets a national per capita income of US$7,500 (based on purchasing power parity) as the point above which nations should be responsible for lowering greenhouse gas emissions and paying into some kind of system, such as an international climate fund for both mitigation and adaptation, that would promote development in nations below this level.[83] The advantage of such an approach is that it accounts for global poverty – people who are very poor are not expected to take action on climate change – while also accounting for the new consumers in the developing world, appropriately allocating full rights to their poor compatriots, but in principle not requiring the poor in affluent nations to pay the costs of climate policies. The focus on "development rights" is a proxy for ensuring that basic human needs are met in the context of determining international (and national) responses to climate change. Importantly, this approach looks at disparities in wealth within nations to identify which of them should be acting on climate change and compensating those people who are likely to be most harmed by it. It determines the capabilities and responsibilities of nations in a way that in effect accounts for the new consumers while avoiding imposing burdens on people who have not yet achieved a "decent standard of welfare" (a level of income "modestly above a global poverty line").[84] However, like contraction and convergence, the GDR approach is based on national per capita emissions. It ultimately sets national responsibilities and capabilities. Depending on their governments' policies, it also leaves open the possibility that the poor in developed nations will have to take difficult action even while the affluent in poor countries are able to avoid doing so. Again, the affluent can potentially hide behind their poor compatriots.

Shoibal Chakravarty and colleagues have developed the so-called Princeton Proposal, a framework for allocating carbon emissions among the world's one billion high-emitting individuals.[85] Their innovative approach takes a global perspective, allocating emissions targets based on common but differentiated responsibilities of individuals, in turn using that allocation to derive national responsibilities. Their approach treats everyone with the same emissions equally, focusing on the obligations of the one billion high emitters, while allowing for increased emissions among the lowest emitters. Those above an agreed "universal individual emission cap" needed to meet global reduction targets would be required to reduce emissions; those below this threshold would be allowed to increase them.[86] The individual cap is fair and equitable because nations with a larger proportion of people who pollute more are required to do more, and those nations with similar emissions profiles have similar obligations.[87] Very importantly, in this proposal "individuals who emit similar amounts of CO_2, regardless of where they live, are expected to contribute to fossil fuel CO_2 emission reductions in similar ways. In principle, no country gets a pass, because even in the poorest countries some individuals have CO_2 emissions above the universal emission cap."[88]

In contrast to the GDR framework, which is premised on individual income (using this as a proxy for emissions, with the advantage that it also implies capability), the Princeton Proposal relies on individual emissions. It places the same obligations on high emitters *regardless of where they live*, in the process replacing (or at least supplementing) the common but differentiated responsibilities of nations with those of individuals. As Chakravarty et al. point out, "It is important to develop more refined tools that reveal the high emitters in developing countries now hidden in the tails of the distribution."[89]

Having said this, like the GDR framework, this high-emitters approach is ultimately about determining national obligations, specifically targets for limiting greenhouse gas emissions. It is up to national governments to decide how to implement these obligations. As such, this approach provides the right framework for deciding nations' international obligations to limit greenhouse gas emissions by deriving those obligations from what individuals are doing, but it only implies that *national* policies must also be based on individuals.

Contraction and convergence, greenhouse development rights, the Princeton Proposal, and other alternative ways of thinking about climate politics highlight the importance of the rights and obligations of persons rather than those of nation-states alone. By shifting climate policies fully toward individual persons, leaving governments more as conduits for acting on rights and obligations, these types of approaches can provide the basis for new, more effective, and more just climate politics and diplomacy. What comes from these approaches is the need for hybrid frameworks that capture both emissions and affluence when assigning responsibilities for action, while ensuring that the world's poor (including the high-emitting poor) are not harmed by climate-related policies. Rather than being appendages of climate politics, therefore, people – their rights, needs, capabilities, and obligations – ought to be at the center of climate politics and the objects of related international agreements and policies. This means recognizing that people, not nations per se, create climate change and suffer from it, and therefore that people, not nations alone, should bear the burdens and enjoy the benefits associated with actions to mitigate greenhouse gas pollution.

Conclusion

Climate politics has been overwhelmingly an arena for nations, especially in the context of policies to address the problem's causes. Hence, as we saw in chapter 2, diplomats have been involved in a near-constant series of international negotiations to arrive at agreements designed to guide national policies, often clearly aimed at regulating industry at the national level. During those negotiations, discussions routinely revolve around which nations have caused climate change, the focus of course falling, in historical terms, on the United States and other affluent western countries. From this came agreement on common but differentiated responsibilities, whereby developed nations were to act first to reduce their greenhouse gas pollution and to help developing nations cope with climate change, with the latter countries allowed to develop and presumably take action in the future when they are more economically developed. The discourse is mostly about nation-states (and to a lesser extent industries) as the causes of climate change and bearers of rights and obligations.

Unsurprisingly for students of introductory international politics, the response has been one of governments digging in their heels to protect their nations' perceived interests and indeed the interests of influential industries, most prominently those with the most to lose from reductions in greenhouse gas emissions (especially those emissions from fossil fuels). Chapter 1 described the result of this approach to climate politics: global emissions of greenhouse gases continue to *increase.*

This chapter has proposed a different approach to climate diplomacy. Rather than being only a process for promoting the narrowly perceived interests of nation-states, it should also be about promoting the interests of people. People should be *at the center* of climate change discourse and politics, and they ought to be viewed as the primary *ends* of climate diplomacy and policy (see chapter 8). Global conceptions of justice point us toward understanding why this matters, and they help to direct us toward the kinds of diplomacy and policies that will be needed in the future: diplomacy that makes people the primary objects of international negotiations and agreements, and government policies that are focused on those who pollute and those who are affected by that pollution (see chapter 6). Practical advantages for nations and governments can come from reframing climate change in terms of human rights and human security, rather than in terms of states' rights and national security. Human rights and security are violated by the impacts of climate change. It is in the interests of nations and indeed of their governments to protect people and to meet their needs. That is supposedly why nation-states exist, and that is what governments are supposed to achieve.

As the consequences of climate change become more widespread and more severe, it may be a matter of time before people start to realize that they have more in common with people in other nations than they do with governments intent on avoiding action. If we extend the focus on the United States and China that was the subject of chapter 3, there is much to the argument that a growing number of Americans harmed by climate change impacts have more in common with many poor Chinese people than they do with US politicians who downplay the problem. Indeed, as noted in chapter 3, the most important manifestation of the state-centric preoccupation of climate politics is the deadlock between the United States and China. Make no mistake (as many observers in the West tend to do): all of the praiseworthy policies and programs being implemented in China to limit its greenhouse gas pollution will not be enough to reverse the tide. Far more will need to be done to end the growing Chinese threat to the earth's climate system. And the United States must reduce its emissions very substantially in the very near future – eventually bringing them close to zero – thereby meeting its long-standing international obligations. This will not be possible in the current international diplomatic milieu, which will at best result in agreements and policies that do far too little, consistent with decades of climate diplomacy and related national policymaking.

The failure of both the United States and China to act much more aggressively to combat climate change looms large over the international relations of climate change. This in turn limits initiatives at the national level around the world to limit greenhouse gas pollution. What is needed is a way to break free from the US–China deadlock as a first step toward far more robust international and domestic policy responses. Building on this chapter's discussion, and addressing the ailments examined in chapter 3, the next one proposes a way of doing that. It argues that people can and should be at the center of American and Chinese foreign and domestic policies on climate change. It suggests that China may have a vital role to play given long-standing US incompetence in this issue area, and that the Chinese could quickly become leaders in responding to climate change – but only if people are given the priority in climate diplomacy and policy that they deserve. Broadly speaking, this entails a move away from Westphalian notions toward more globally responsible conceptions of climate politics. Doing this offers a politically viable way to break free from the you-go-first syndrome that characterizes climate change negotiations, specifically between the United States and China but also more broadly between the developed and developing worlds.

CHAPTER SIX

Differentiated Responsibility: National and Individual

Global economic development and growth around the world have changed the practical and ethical calculus of climate politics. It is increasingly difficult to talk in terms of developed and developing nations because many of those that are classified as developing in the climate convention, such as South Korea and Singapore, are now affluent, and a number of others are hardly poor. They must be contrasted with the truly poor nations, and their very poor majorities. One of the anomalies is China, which is "developing" in many respects, with millions of people still living in poverty. But it is also a new center of economic growth and wealth, with some of the most developed cities in the world populated by millions of affluent people. Meanwhile, a number of developed nations, including several European countries and to some extent even the United States, are experiencing economic stagnation and serious poverty, and indeed decline relative to China and some other major developing countries. In the case of the United States, this hardly diminishes its moral failures with respect to climate change, but it does make it more difficult to persuade US officials and the American public to correct those failures.

A growing rejection of traditional definitions of "developed" and "developing" nations has been a central feature of recent international climate change negotiations, with diplomats from both wealthy and very poor countries calling for recognition that China has developed greatly since the principle of common but differentiated responsibilities was first agreed in the 1990s.[1] What is more, the shift of affluence and consumption toward the developing nations reveals a fundamental flaw in the international response to climate change: the developing nations, where by far most consumers and polluters will reside in coming decades, are not obligated by treaties to limit their greenhouse gas emissions. If these nations, and more specifically the new consumers in them, continue to avoid limiting and eventually reducing the greenhouse gas pollution that they cause, there will be little hope of making climate politics sufficiently effective to avert a widening and irreversible catastrophe – even if the developed nations and their citizens live up to all legal and ethical commitments to reduce their own emissions.

Part of this problem was illustrated in chapter 3, which identified one of the primary ailments of climate politics as the malignancy of the world's largest national polluters of the global atmosphere: the United States and China. A way must be found to break the deadlock between them (and like-minded nations). This chapter proposes a way of thinking about treatments for this malignancy that focuses on individuals, this time as crucial distractions from the counterproductive obsessions with national interests that prevail in Beijing and Washington (and other capitals). Building on the more human-centered approach to climate politics described in the previous chapter, this one uses the US–China relationship to highlight important distinctions between the common but differentiated responsibilities of nations, which are well established in the international politics of climate change (at least in principle), and the common but differentiated responsibilities of individuals, which have received very little official attention. The US–China relationship is used here as a case study both for examining issues that arise widely in international climate politics and to look further at the most important international relationship in this context. If the United States and China can transform their relationship and their actions, climate politics among and within other nations would likely be transformed as well.

Short of a major change in American politics sometime soon, the greatest hope for new international leadership in climate politics may have to come from China. From traditional perspectives, this may sound like an unfair prospect. The United States is more obligated to show leadership. But if the United States will not lead, someone has to. And China's obligations, and more precisely the obligations of many Chinese people, may be greater than they are often portrayed to be. More attention being given to the hundreds of millions of new consumers in China helps to make this evident. Global conceptions of justice, as introduced in the previous chapter, tell us that the pollution of an affluent person in China is just as wrong as pollution of an affluent person in the United States, even while China *as a nation-state* continues to be less obligated (in terms of historical pollution) to respond to climate change than is the United States. Treatments for climate politics, and specifically for the deadlock between the United States and China, cannot be found in attempts to persuade China as a nation-state to take on climate-related burdens alongside the United States. It will not do this, certainly not anywhere near enough to deal with the problem head on. Instead, we would be better advised to persuade the Chinese government that affluent Chinese individuals ought to act alongside most Americans. This will not be easy, but at least it has much better prospects than ongoing demands for China to accept sovereign burdens alongside developed nations.

Of course, it would not be enough even if China were to take the lead in this way. Other nations will have to follow, in the process struggling through their individual domestic political systems to formulate and implement a range of policies that help people and other actors break free from traditional models of measuring, promoting, and realizing human well-being – which is, after all, the reason that governments and nation-states exist. As a proposal for additional treatments for climate politics, this chapter presents some ideas related to these policies. The fundamental message is that a nation's government, in addition to acting on the common but differentiated responsibilities of nations for climate change, needs to be an enabler to assist and encourage action on the common but differentiated responsibilities of individuals, too.

National and individual responsibilities for climate change

The traditional approach to climate politics, especially at the international level, has been to ascribe blame to developed nations and to view developing nations as victims. It is hard not to agree with this approach. A problem is that it has not got us very far. Ascribing blame in this way, while logical and even ethical from a statist perspective (which governments and most observers adopt), may be preventing us from seeing the full picture of who and what cause climate change, and who and what are responsible for doing something about it. Causes and responsibilities are more widely distributed than most governments would have us believe. What we need to do is to think about the causes of climate change from both national *and* individual perspectives. To be sure, the United States is the primary historical cause of climate change. However, many Americans, chiefly the poorest ones, are not. They may pollute relatively little or have no choice but to pollute, due to lack of capability. If China is not the principal cause of climate change historically, many Chinese people today, including millions of affluent ones who consume and pollute at very high levels, are causing climate change that will be felt in the future.

Furthermore, while per capita emissions of greenhouse gases in the developing world remain below those in the developed world, collectively the nations of the latter now produce more than half of all greenhouse pollution. Ninety percent of energy demand from 2010 to 2035 will come from the world's developing countries.[2] Kevin Rafferty has observed that this will not change under existing policies, with the possible resulting increase in global temperature, exceeding 6° Celsius, "bringing prospects of a traditional fiery hell to life on earth."[3] As a practical matter, this will have to be addressed by climate politics.

It is widely assumed, and often repeated by the Chinese government, that climate change is being caused by the historical emissions of the world's rich nations, which began polluting the atmosphere with the advent of the industrial revolution and have since enjoyed over two centuries of economic growth as a consequence. In particular, the United States is singled out for contributing the most to the problem. The argument is that China and other large developing countries have only recently started contributing to the greenhouse gas emissions causing climate change. Consequently, their cumulative historical contribution to the problem is low relative to developed nations.

However, Tom Holland questions the Chinese assumption that the West is all to blame for climate change.[4] He points out that China's historical emissions are hardly negligible. Due to its dirty coal-fired industries, even at the start of its economic opening to the world in the 1980s, China was emitting more CO_2 than Germany – despite having a far smaller economy. Since then, China's CO_2 emissions have ballooned – from 1.5 billion tons in 1980 to 8.3 billion tons in 2010, one-third more than US emissions.[5] Consequently, China's total historical emissions are now second only to the United States, exceeding those of Russia, Germany, Britain, Japan, France, and other developed nations.[6] This becomes truer if we add cumulative CO_2 emissions from deforestation and agriculture to those from burning fossil fuels.[7]

The United States remains the largest historical contributor to climate change, so arguments blaming it for the problem today still make sense. But (if we focus on nations only) the argument using historical pollution to reach the conclusion that other developed nations should take action before China does so is empirically incorrect. With the exception of the United States, China is by far the largest historical national source of greenhouse gas pollution.

Given its very large historical emissions, the only way to give China's argument much weight is to consider population – per capita emissions – and thereby to bring people into the debate about which nations are more or less responsible for the problem. Even those who accept that China's emissions were considerable in the past, and that those emissions are now very high by any standard, may acknowledge that this is not especially important because China's population is so large – four times that of the United States. This focus on China's *per capita* emissions reveals the problem with the statist view of climate change: it utilizes people to reduce the responsibility of the whole nation, thereby making progress in climate politics difficult both internationally and domestically. In contrast, people are not considered fully when doing so pushes the calculation in the other direction. Yet a large proportion of greenhouse pollution arises from the consumption behaviors of individuals, including affluent people in China.[8]

The point is that we need to do more to connect people's responsibilities to people's actions, rather than routinely attributing them to nations. Doing the latter allows the most affluent and most polluting individuals to hide behind national per capita averages. This is unfair to those individuals who pollute less and who make up part of that average, and it is most unfair to the poor who may pollute very little and whose pollution is nevertheless a necessity for meeting their most basic needs.

One might argue that young Americans living today did not cause today's climate change, but that they are nevertheless enjoying the fruits of past emissions. This makes them indirectly responsible for climate change, albeit due to no fault of their own. If one follows this logic, which makes some sense, then it follows that many Chinese – millions of them, at least – are similarly responsible for climate change. They are enjoying the fruits of development in the West that enables westerners to buy exports from China that have helped millions of Chinese to become affluent. What comes from this is that all affluent people who enjoy the fruits of past greenhouse gas pollution may have some responsibility for acting on climate change right now. One cannot apply this "fruits of the past" argument against Americans (and most people in other developed nations) but ignore it when the same applies to Chinese (and affluent people in other developing nations). The Chinese who invoke the historical emissions argument officially cannot have it both ways, at least not if they are to maintain logical coherence.

Of course, the argument that those people enjoying the fruits of past pollution have more responsibility than those who do not still applies. Thus, most people in developed nations have more responsibility than most people in developing nations. But what comes from this kind of "per capita" historical argument, given globalization and the way it has spread economic fruits around the world, is that increasing numbers of people in developing nations are becoming more and more responsible, in line with their growing affluence – at the very least insofar as that growing affluence is helped along by past and present development in the developed world.

The point here is that historical arguments, which normally attribute blame to the United States (and rightly so), reveal distinctions between national and individual responsibilities. Recognizing and accepting this reality has practical and ethical significance for climate politics, specifically the US–China deadlock, because it means that millions of Chinese should be doing what China says most Americans should be doing: reducing their greenhouse gas pollution, and indeed helping poor nations and people respond to climate change.

Related to the historical argument is one of capabilities. Economic globalization has made more people around the world, including more people in China (to continue with the crucial US–China case), more affluent and thus more capable of acting to address climate change. About 15 percent of Chinese people – roughly 200 million of them – have salaries comparable to average wages in Europe.[9] According to some studies looking at national income distribution and greenhouse gas emissions from personal consumption, per capita emissions seen of the most affluent 10 percent of Chinese people, who together receive one-third of the nation's income, are considerably above those of the poorest 10 percent of Americans, putting these Chinese people at the level of per capita emissions in some European nations.[10] As a result of continued economic growth, from 2010 to 2020, 100 million new Chinese households will join the "middle- and affluent-class," about the same number of households in this class as in the whole of the United States.[11] The number of US dollar millionaires in China now certainly exceeds one million.[12]

Those who want to attribute the expansion in China's greenhouse gas emissions to exports to the West – much of it does come from export industries – must also consider the benefits and specifically the wealth generated by those exports inside China. The United States, for example, sees its national greenhouse gas emissions lowered because much of the pollution from American consumption occurs in China. But the associated transfer of wealth enables many millions of Chinese to consume and pollute just like Americans. Thus things are more complicated than we are often encouraged to believe. The focus on nations hides the realities of what people are doing.

Thus the notion of equal per capita rights to emissions makes absolute sense from the perspective of individual persons. However, when put in terms of per capita emissions of the United States or China, which by definition are averages *of nations*, the idea loses sight of who has rights and responsibilities. Human rights and responsibilities become hidden by those of nations. As Matthew Paterson and Johannes Stripple describe it, when the idea of "equal per capita emissions" is converted by diplomats into actual policy proposals, they become "mediated by the Southern state's right to negotiate on behalf of 'its' people through the principle of nonintervention which means that [for example] the Indian state can conceivably argue for equal per capita emissions in international politics while rejecting a right of the international community to question the distribution of emissions within India."[13] Paterson and Stripple argue that the per capita arguments used by nations, "while being instinctively cosmopolitan and working in ethical terms alongside the scientific constructions of climate change as 'global,' in fact get drawn back to the statist account of rights. In the climate negotiations, the principle of 'sovereign equality' is underpinning the agreed protocols for emission reductions."[14] Consequently, the entire population of (in this example) India is averaged out, with the vast majority of Indians (the poor) potentially forced to subsidize the lifestyles of a minority (affluent Indians). The latter are able to hide behind the former, rather than take action to reduce their greenhouse gas-polluting behaviors and help those who suffer from climate change.[15]

What all of this tells us is that nations are not the only causes of climate change, and therefore that they are not the only actors bearing responsibility for taking action to address it.[16] Consequently, climate politics should be much less about the per capita emissions *of nations* and much more about per capita emissions per se – that is, *individual* emissions. Affluent individuals, including the world's middle-class consumers in both developed and developing nations, are among the real culprits because they often consume and pollute for nonessential reasons. As such, they should be asked to take on much or even most of the burden of mitigating the causes of climate change and helping those people and communities most adversely affected.

The European Union has tried to act on such principles with expansion of its emissions trading scheme to all airlines flying to and from member nations. It is hard to argue that flying on airliners is a necessity; it almost never is.[17] A number of governments, notably those of China and the United States, have opposed the EU scheme. They argue that it discriminates against their airline companies. But this criticism reflects a failure to recognize how the world is changing – not to mention a continued failure to put the global interest in averting dangerous climate change before the interests of corporations. It fails to acknowledge that responsibility for preventing climate change is no longer restricted to sovereign nations. As Connie Hedegaard, EU commissioner for climate action, described the scheme: "All we are doing is treating everybody who can afford a long-haul flight ticket equally, irrespective of their nationality. It's hard to see how anyone can be against this principle in the world of the twenty-first century."[18]

It is difficult for governments to accept alternatives to state-centric thinking about climate change. Nevertheless, this distinction between national and individual causes and responsibilities offers a potential way for breaking free of the deadlock in international climate politics. It could help to end the you-go-first relationship between the world's two largest national polluters. The upshot is that, as time passes, this problem is less about the United States and China, and much more about Americans and Chinese.

Reconciling the responsibilities of nations and individuals

If we start to think carefully about the sources of climate pollution, it quickly becomes less a problem of what nations are doing than one of what individuals are doing. To illustrate what is happening, and how this relates to climate politics, it can help to imagine several different maps of the world.[19] We can start with a political map, which effectively reflects the international politics and diplomacy of climate change. This map would be a typical depiction of sovereign nation-states, each within generally well-defined political boundaries. (On most such maps, each nation is colored to distinguish it from its neighbors.) We can imagine a second world map with *current* greenhouse gas emissions layered on top of the political map. Imagine that on this second map nations with high annual greenhouse gas emissions are colored red, those with moderate emissions are yellow, and those with low emissions are green.

On such a map, China and the United States would be red because they are the largest national sources of greenhouse gas pollution, as would be some European nations and Japan, while middle-income countries, such as those in Latin America, would be largely yellow, and nearly all African and many South Asian nations would be green. Imagine also a third map of the world. This one would depict total *historical* greenhouse gas emissions. On this map, China's color might change from red to yellow (or at least a paler shade of red) because its historical emissions are, according to most calculations, relatively modest compared to those of the United States, whereas India might change from yellow to green, and most African nations would remain solidly green to depict low historical contributions to climate change.

These three maps would provide most of the information one needs to understand what we might call the *political geography* of climate change. The maps would show us national boundaries coinciding with the participants in climate change negotiations. They would depict which nations are contributing the most (and the least) to the climate change problem, thereby revealing which among them are most important for global solutions to it. These maps would also show which nations are historically at fault for causing the problem, thereby carrying the most responsibility, and which nations are least at fault. It would be unjust for international negotiations around climate change to expect the latter nations to bear many of the burdens of addressing the problem. This depiction of climate politics is, for the most part, how climate change has been viewed so far, both officially and popularly: a picture of the common but differentiated responsibilities of nation-states.

There is, however, another way of looking at responsibilities related to climate change. It is the common but differentiated responsibilities of individual persons. To get a picture of this kind of responsibility, we can replace our political map of the world, with its layers of greenhouse gas emissions on top of national boundaries, with that of a physical map of the earth that shows no political boundaries whatsoever, with all land surfaces colored, say, brown and oceans colored blue. Imagine one billion tiny red dots – one for each of the one billion most affluent people on the planet – spread across this borderless map. Hundreds of millions of those tiny dots would be clustered in North America, Europe, Japan, and Australia. Large splotches of red, comprising millions of dots, would overlay New York, London, Tokyo, and Sydney. Smaller but still very prominent collections of these red dots would be spread, sometimes in waves, throughout the developed world. These splotches and waves of red would correspond to something in the order of one-quarter to one-third of current global greenhouse gas emissions.[20]

In contrast, much of the developing world would have relatively few red dots, and the poorest parts of the world would have large areas devoid of them. However, many locations in the developing world would contain large and expanding spots and splotches of red. This would be especially true in areas that correspond to major cities in the world's newly industrialized nations, for example Bangkok, Beijing, Jakarta, Mexico City, Rio de Janeiro, and Shanghai. This map would also reveal waves of red dots along the coastal areas of China and in the suburbs of major cities of many developing nations. These red spots in the developing world would correspond to perhaps (roughly speaking) something approaching a quarter of the world's current greenhouse gas emissions, with the relative size of these emissions growing rapidly compared to emissions from the activities of people in the developed nations.[21]

The remainder of global greenhouse gas emissions can be attributed to those people who contribute relatively fewer emissions per capita. While some responsibility lies with many of these people, most of the responsibility for climate change can be attributed to the most affluent (and usually the most polluting) people. Some of the people in the middle, and all of those at the bottom (one billion or more people), should not be expected to bear any burden. Indeed, it would be the responsibility of those in the top billion or so to help those in the bottom one or two billion to increase their use of energy, if needed, to help them meet their basic needs and to escape poverty (at least until alternative energies are widely available and affordable).

If we now compare the physical map of greenhouse gas emissions with the political map of the world, climate politics start to look quite different. We can see that the diplomacy of climate change does not correspond to the *environmental geography* of climate change. It is largely divorced from many of the actual persons who pollute the atmosphere. While the political map, and possibly the one overlaid with national historical emissions of greenhouse gases, would suggest that China has a right to sit on the sidelines and wait for the United States (and other affluent nations) to take the lead in responding to climate change, the map depicting the world's individual affluent polluters would reveal that hundreds of millions of people who contribute to climate change live outside the developed world, many of them in China. This puts China's new status as the world's largest *national* source of greenhouse pollution in a new light.

If we focus on political boundaries, this new status does not yet put much responsibility on China. It remains a developing nation, after all, and developing nations generally are not to blame for greenhouse pollution today. However, if we focus on who is actually polluting, we see that many millions of people in China, along with many people in other developing nations, are in fact to blame, along with the usual suspects in developed nations, notably most Americans, Australians, and Europeans.

Considering the geographical map again, if we ask ourselves where the red dots are located (for the most part corresponding to both western consumers and the new consumers described in chapter 4), we can see that the red splotches of the western world have spread across parts of the developing world. We can see that the international politics of climate change, which

have focused on sovereign nations and their political boundaries and which mostly view developing nations and all people
in them as beyond the bounds of mandatory greenhouse gas
limitations, fail to encompass a large proportion of the red.
This is not very surprising, given the long-standing focus of
climate diplomacy on sovereign nations and their roles and
responsibilities. It was the case only two or three decades ago
that the individual sources of climate change were more or
less enclosed within the borders of developed nations; the red
splotches depicting individual greenhouse gas emissions in
developing nations were much smaller than they are now.

However, circumstances have changed quite radically
in recent decades. As hundreds of millions of people in the
developing nations have joined the global consumer class, the
splotches of red showing the greenhouse gas emissions of
affluent people in those nations have quickly expanded. This
trend will become even more pronounced in coming decades.
The question is how much responsibility will be attributed to
this growing class of consumers and polluters. One implication is that solutions to climate change, if they are to capture
as many of the sources of greenhouse gas pollution as will be
required to mitigate future impacts significantly, will have to
include hundreds of millions of affluent people in the developing nations, alongside most people in the developed ones.

As we saw in chapter 2, at the heart of this problem are
national interests, or, more accurately, how they are perceived by governments, politicians, and diplomats, and
how those perceptions are influenced by special interests.
The narrowly perceived national interests that have guided
climate diplomacy are inconsistent with the wider global
interest and arguably the long-term interests of most nations.
This has contributed to the tragedy of the atmospheric commons. How can the world address this tragedy? One way is to
shift away from mostly statist conceptions of who or what is

most responsible for climate change – the common but differentiated responsibilities of nations – to more globalized
conceptions of responsibility – the common but differentiated
responsibilities of individuals.

Doing this would focus attention on the world's affluent
consumers as being among the fundamental causes of climate
change. It would also help to highlight alternative politics and
new policy solutions that include these people as actors that
ought to respond if they have the capability to do so. It would
direct more attention to the red spots described above. Doing
this would mean that individual consumers and polluters in
the developed world would receive necessary scrutiny, but it
would also mean that more attention would be given to the
developing world's new consumers. This would include the
hundreds of millions of newly affluent polluters in China and
other developing nations who are now living and polluting in
ways very similar to those of people in the developed world.

What is very significant about such a more global approach
to climate-related responsibility is that it would, paradoxically,
allow a major developing country to lead the world in combating climate change, in the process possibly breaking the
international political deadlock. This leadership role could be
taken up by China, partly because the United States seems to
be politically incapable of doing so, partly because China has
the capacity (wealth) to take on such a role (unlike India, for
example) and partly – or even largely – because China *must* do
far more than it is planning to do, and very soon, if the world
is to avoid the worst effects of climate change. Just because the
United States and indeed most Americans will not act on their
responsibility does not mean that China, and especially affluent and capable Chinese people, should also fail to do so (any
more than it is acceptable for a capable bystander to ignore a
great harm he sees being inflicted on another person).

China could take on this leadership role by explicitly

placing climate-related restrictions on its most affluent citizens. The Chinese government could start doing this by, for example, heavily taxing luxury goods and using the resulting funds to help its poorest citizens escape poverty and cope with the effects of climate change. It could outlaw polluting automobiles and all luxury and sports cars. More broadly, it could regulate the pollution of its affluent citizens by implementing not just national emissions trading, as it is planning to do, but also *personal* emissions trading, or some other mechanisms to increase the costs of personal greenhouse gas pollution, using revenue that is generated to offset costs for the poor and to aid them in escaping poverty. Importantly, in taking these and other leading steps, sovereign China would not be taking on any new *national* obligations. It would not be undermining the principle of common but differentiated responsibilities among nations at all. Obligations would apply to affluent *people* in China, not to China itself.

This sort of Chinese leadership could have profound positive effects on climate politics. Developed-nation governments have for years been demanding that China and other large developing countries do more to limit their greenhouse gas emissions. By taking on this leadership role, China would in effect constrain greenhouse gases from within its borders for climate-related reasons without having to take on new state-to-state obligations (which its government absolutely refuses to do for good reasons, including international justice). Developed-world governments, and indeed most people in the West, would be left with no place to hide, politically and morally. They could no longer complain that the Chinese are failing to act on climate change. Leaders, politicians, and officials in the developed nations could then point their voters to what is happening in China and ask why people in developing countries are taking the lead while people in the West continue to pollute much as they have done for many decades.

The political implications could be very significant because the primary excuse for inaction given by diplomats and politicians in the developed nations would be gone.

To propose that one logical extension of the common but differentiated responsibilities of individuals for climate change would be for China to take the lead in climate politics – for it to take a bold step that would shake up climate diplomacy and force a reassessment of the world's responses to climate change – is undoubtedly controversial. Many people, Chinese among them, may argue that even to suggest that China take the lead is unfair and possibly preposterous, especially when it is commonly argued (rightly so) that the United States should do so first. But Chinese leadership could be read as an illustration of how we might think about the US–China relationship differently, at least in the context of climate change, while focusing on human rights and responsibilities – and potentially treating, at least partly, the long-standing cancer of Westphalia.

Globalized justice tells us that the pollution of an affluent person in China is just as wrong as pollution of an affluent person in the United States, despite China as a nation being much less obligated than is the United States. Thus a remedy is not found in attempts to persuade China (as a sovereign nation-state per se) to act alongside the United States, but instead to persuade the Chinese government that affluent Chinese ought to act alongside most Americans. This might allow the two governments to work around their state-centered arguments, interests, and conceptions of justice.

From the perspective of the Chinese government and the Chinese Communist Party, depending on how it acts and the kinds of policies it implements, working to fulfill the climate-related responsibilities of affluent Chinese citizens could provide it with significant political benefits. Policies to limit and even reduce greenhouse gas pollution caused by the most affluent Chinese would generate financial resources that could be transferred to the wider community, the poor in particular, while visibly reducing the increasingly perverse behaviors of the wealthy that have been undermining social stability in recent years. The government would be seen as helping the wider population and cracking down on many of the excesses of a wealthy minority, thereby enhancing its legitimacy in the eyes of most Chinese. And there is the argument that China's authoritarian political system, resulting so far in horrendous environmental pollution (including greenhouse gas pollution), might be more capable of acting to address climate change than are many democratic societies.[22] Insofar as doing so helps to limit local pollution in China, the government would bolster its power.

In what is otherwise an excellent summary of the growing consumerism in China, Clive Hamilton argues that the government has little choice but to continue supporting consumption:

> The fact that the large part of the country remains impoverished while another large part has come to define itself by its access to western consumer goods vitiates any attempt to reduce carbon emissions that may jeopardize growth. Despite the government's recognition of the dangers of global warming, it would sacrifice its political legitimacy if it pushed through the sorts of measures required by the science.[23]

Naturally, development that lifts the poor of the country out of poverty is crucial, but to say that every Chinese consumer needs her or his desires fulfilled, as happens in the West, misjudges the domestic political circumstances facing the government. Indeed, one can reach the opposite conclusion to Hamilton's: it is only through visibly acting to restrain the excessive consumption of its affluent citizens that the Chinese government, and specifically the Chinese Communist Party, can hope to alleviate growing social unrest that might undermine its rule.

Put another way, the government's interest in remaining in power is actually consistent with restraining the worst excesses of Chinese consumerism. If the Chinese government recognizes this, it has an opportunity to take the lead in climate politics internationally while doing so at home *and* while achieving its other goals, including maintaining its legitimacy, reducing national pollution, and lowering the nation's contribution to climate change.

Of course, even if China were to take such a lead, others must follow. National policies in most nations will have to reflect the new reality of living within the carrying capacity of the planet to protect human rights and promote human wellbeing. Climate policy at the national level, like the international politics of climate change, will have to be centered on people – their rights, needs, obligations, and capabilities.

People-centered climate policy

How might the United States and China, and indeed other capable nations, act to reconcile their responsibilities and those of their citizens? In general, climate-related policies, while aiming to do what they can to transform economies and societies away from nonessential material growth, ought to be directed at connecting individual needs and responsibilities related to climate change back to individuals as well as to nations. Governments will have to use both carrots and sticks to push people to behave in ways that are good for them and for the environment.

Economic libertarians will likely view this notion with contempt, but state measures need not be draconian. (Having said this, if the world's affluent people do not change their ways quite soon and help the developing world avoid repeating the excesses of western fossil fuel consumption, harsh policies will probably become necessary sometime this century.) Rather, what is needed are changes in infrastructure, alterations in the way prosperity is measured, new education programs at all levels geared toward climate-appropriate behaviors, tax measures to discourage unnecessary pollution, changes in subsidies so that "clean" energy benefits and dirty energy does not, and regulations to help make all of this happen while promoting equity, community, and freedom. Doing this enough to put the brakes on climate change is only possible if everyone able to do so joins in. This will mean putting systems in place to make it as easy as possible for people to behave in environmentally responsible ways.

Ian Gough and James Meadowcroft have summarized a number of methods for "decarbonizing" modern developed societies, in the process highlighting two possible sets of climate policies at the national level: technological innovation to enable a decoupling of economic growth and carbon emissions while also decarbonizing the modern welfare state; and a move away from growth to a "steady-state economy" while simultaneously transforming the meaning of welfare.[24] The first scenario would likely include green taxes (for example, a carbon tax), development of eco-social investments (such as carbon-neutral housing), decarbonization of social services (for example, procurement of low-carbon materials by governments), changes in consumer behavior (particularly in housing, transport, and food) and synergies between climate-related policies and other national policies (for example, health benefits that come from shifting away from car transport to cycling and walking, and from subsidized livestock production to lowering the consumption of meat).[25]

These sorts of policies should be implemented, but they would be unlikely to achieve the degree of cuts in greenhouse gas emissions required to address climate change adequately.

The modern "growth state" is unsustainable, at least if people in developing nations are going to enjoy improved standards of living alongside continued high-carbon lifestyles in the West. Thus the second set of scenarios, what Gough and Meadowcroft call "rethinking the welfare state" for "zero growth and radical transformation," takes on great importance.[26]

This latter approach could involve policies such as redistribution of carbon through personal carbon trading; redistribution of work and time, in part to "break the habit of working to earn to consume" but also to allow people to have a better balance between work and other activities; redistributing income and wealth to ensure that changes in the economy do not harm the less well-off and, in the process, to discourage conspicuous material consumption among the most affluent people in society (which has perverse consequences, including driving consumption trends up among the less well-off); and, very likely, family planning geared toward reducing population.[27] As part of these kinds of policies, the way that we think about and measure human wellbeing should be "progressively dissociated" from wealth and material consumption.[28] Gough and Meadowcroft are not sanguine about whether these policies can be realized to the degree that is necessary unless elite interests and social movements can combine to enable the transformation of domestic institutions.

One way that individuals can be brought directly into the policy sphere is through market-based mechanisms, such as personal emissions trading or, more narrowly, personal carbon trading and related policies that allocate rights and responsibilities for CO_2 and other greenhouse gas emissions resulting from household and personal activities, notably energy use, "at the individual level."[29] Personal carbon trading effectively involves everyone in the redistribution of "environmental property rights" through imagining "a different relationship between citizens and the state in terms of who is responsible for reducing personal carbon emissions. It embodies specific and explicit ideas about equity – the issue at the heart of international carbon negotiations."[30] Ideally, personal emissions/carbon trading schemes would be global in scope: they would not be conditioned on national citizenship or a person's place of residence. A global cap on allowable emissions could be set, and each individual would be entitled to her or his share at no cost.

Even if such a scheme or schemes were to be implemented only at the national or the subnational level, obligations should be based on global calculations of environmental sustainability – how much greenhouse gas pollution that each person can safely produce without bringing about dangerous climate change – and on individuals' rights to assistance for adaptation to climate change. Allowances would have to be made for individuals' circumstances, to be sure; every person must be given a greenhouse gas allowance that permits a minimum standard of living in his or her particular local circumstances, which would mean higher limits for some people. Such schemes would require individuals who exceed their emissions allowances to purchase credits from those who have a surplus. Nobody would be allowed to sell unused emissions below the minimum required to meet basic needs, thus preventing exploitation of the poor and the weak by the affluent and the powerful. Surpluses that come from such schemes would ideally be paid into a global fund for redistribution to those in need around the world. Barring that, the schemes could be operated at national levels with oversight by a credible global agency or nongovernmental organization.

Technical obstacles to such a scheme would be significant in some of the world's poorest areas, but these could be overcome as part of larger programs to aid sustainable development in the context of climate change. A key to implementation of personal emissions/carbon trading schemes would be their acceptability. While there would certainly be opposition, particularly from entrenched interests and publics resistant to change, this would be true of most policies related to climate change, and at least people find personal carbon trading preferable to carbon taxes (both direct and indirect) and they believe it to be effective and fair.[31] In addition to being fairer to everyone, such individualized schemes have practical and political advantages. For example, it is likely that it would be far easier (politically) to finance the Green Climate Fund (see chapter 2) or something similar if the sources of funds came from *all* countries – that is, if affluent individuals (some people) in developing nations are paying into the fund alongside affluent individuals (most people) in developed nations because many (poorer) people in the latter countries would be far less likely to oppose, and might even support, such a scheme. The practical result would be both reductions in greenhouse gas emissions and more financial resources to aid the most vulnerable communities in preparing for and adapting to climate change. In other words, if the climate fund is financed by national governments *and* individuals (and industries), it is more likely to address climate change while spreading the benefits and burdens more widely and more equitably.

What else might it take to get consumers to behave in ways that produce much lower carbon footprints? At least in the case of the United States (but this probably applies in varying degrees elsewhere, at least in developed nations), Andrew Szasz argues that several conditions will have to be met: consumers will have to believe that climate change is real and urgent, there will have to be affordable and attractive lower carbon footprint alternatives; people must be motivated to behave responsibly (instead of following alternative motivations to consume, for example); they must trust that doing so will have a positive impact; and, if people are to be committed to low-carbon lifestyles, they would ideally feel that doing so is part of being a good citizen and worth continuing.[32]

To be sure, global justice requires that everyone capable of doing so limits her or his impact on the environment simply because that impact harms others. As Andy Dobson puts it, "the duty of the environmental citizen is to live sustainably so that others may live well."[33] Looked at from this perspective, living more sustainably is driven by a sense of environmental justice, including at the global level, which is an attitudinal shift that is more likely to last when compared to effects of the normal fiscal incentives of many environmental policies.

A big challenge is that encouraging people to think like (and be) environmental citizens is more difficult than implementing fiscal incentives. Interventions might therefore include extensive education, historical stories, and propaganda akin to what has proved successful (some might say too successful) in developing powerful feelings of loyalty to specific nationalities and nation-states (even to the point where many people become willing, even eager, to die for those ideas). Shaping people's thinking in these ways would not be simple or easy, to be sure. Certainly, it is important for people to see environmentally responsible behavior as being in their individual interest. This may not be as improbable an outcome as some might at first imagine. As discussed in the next chapter, *not* overconsuming is in people's best interest; it is likely to make them happier and healthier. It is the role of institutions to help and encourage people to move toward this realization as quickly as possible.

Conclusion

In an era of globalized consumption, reconciling the common but differentiated responsibilities of nations requires much

more attention to the common but differentiated responsibilities of individuals. Nations bear responsibility, but in
a globalized world they should not absolve individuals of it.
Thus the world's affluent people, and specifically individual
affluent consumers and producers of greenhouse gas emissions, have responsibilities to take action alongside the
responsibilities of nations, especially the developed ones.
Government policies on climate change should reflect this
by being people-centered – by being focused on affecting the
roles that people play in the climate context – to bring the
greenhouse gas emissions down while meeting the needs of
the least well-off everywhere.

This chapter has highlighted some of the implications for
climate politics and policy of considering both national and
individual responsibilities for climate change. These implications point to alternative interpretations of how the United
States and China might respond to the problem. For example,
the American failure to take robust action to cut its greenhouse gas emissions, least of all to lead the world in doing
likewise, does not imply that China should also do nothing.
Instead, just the opposite is required. It may not seem right
to demand that China take the lead, but the American failure
leaves little choice. The consequences of climate change are
so deeply unjust for millions, possibly billions, of people in
the future that they outweigh China's rightful demands *as a
sovereign state* for action to come first from the United States.

On a very practical level, now that China is the largest single
national source of greenhouse gas pollution, no solution is
possible without it taking major steps. Thankfully, there are
good reasons from the perspective of the Chinese government for it to take the lead: it is capable of doing so and such a
response would raise its stature internationally and among its
own people (who are increasingly critical of visible affluence
among Chinese elites). What is more, if the United States is

primarily responsible for climate change, many Americans, chiefly the poorest ones, are much less so. If China is not principally responsible for climate change from an historical perspective, many Chinese, including millions of affluent ones, do have responsibility.

This raises the question of what individuals everywhere should do, and why they should do it. Thankfully, doing what is necessary to address climate change is also what is necessary to maximize overall human happiness and wellbeing. Chapter 8 draws on these conceptions of the problem to propose some steps for responding to climate change in ways that make human beings the central players, in keeping with their roles in causing the problem to begin with. In the meantime, the next chapter examines in greater detail how and why a robust global response to climate change would make people happier and enhance their wellbeing, rather than – as climate skeptics, liberal economists, and vested interests like to argue – make them worse off. One thing seems certain: the longer we wait to get climate politics and policies right, the more likely it becomes that people living today will be required to make radical changes to their lives. This would likely still improve their wellbeing, but the transition would be more trying. It is the role of governments to help people make this transition sooner and with as little hardship and difficulty as possible.

CHAPTER SEVEN

Consumption of Happiness: Sustainability and Wellbeing

Chapter 5 explored some approaches to treating what is wrong with climate politics at the international level, and chapter 6 introduced some potential responses to the you-go-first stalemate between the world's largest national polluters. Those treatments have people and the protection of their rights and security as primary objects. Chapter 4 located the failures of climate politics in addictions of modernity, manifested in growing affluence and material overconsumption spreading from developed nations to the developing world. This chapter is concerned both with what individuals can do about this, why they ought to do it in their self-interest, and specifically how doing so will help to promote their happiness, health, and overall wellbeing while reducing their impact on the earth's climate system. Contrary to popular belief, and especially diverging from what we hear and see in most media, affluence beyond a point of sufficiency does not bring overall happiness. In particular, increasing wealth and material overconsumption as practiced in the western world for generations generally does not increase people's wellbeing. Societies with the highest levels of wealth and material consumption are not the happiest. This is because affluence is routinely manifested in consumption of "goods" that people do not need, rather than through consumption of experiences that make them happy.

Everyone should be free from poverty, and everyone needs and deserves material possessions to meet her or his needs and to bring some comfort. But, to be happy, each of us does not need to consume much beyond meeting our needs. Put another way, many of the activities that result in growing greenhouse gas emissions do not simultaneously increase human wellbeing or happiness. Indeed, excessive consumption can and does bring unhappiness and can reduce human health and wellbeing. In the process of damaging the earth's climate system, we are routinely harming ourselves. It is extremely important to emphasize these points because some of the most fundamental questions about how to address climate change are about human actions: How do we persuade people that they are better off getting out of their cars, avoiding jetting off to far-away destinations, and not indulging in the temptations of material consumption that the modern world makes almost irresistible? Answering this sort of question and making the answers reality is very difficult; it would be fatuous to suggest otherwise. At the very least, this chapter will attempt to reiterate why *not* changing behavior is doing people more harm than good. Recognizing and accepting this reality is the first step to behavior change. Even that first step will be difficult.

In contrast to behavior as usual, happiness and wellbeing are increased by behaviors and practices that coincidentally are less harmful to the environment. Replacing unnecessary material consumption with consumption of additional time with family and friends, relaxing pastimes and community activities, among other behaviors that are increasingly neglected in the modern western way of life, is more likely to bring happiness.[1] A life of sufficiency rather than excess can be not only environmentally sustainable, even with a larger global population, but also one that brings fulfillment to those who adopt it.[2] Doing what is *actually* in our self-interest, rather than what marketers encourage us to do, is more sustainable. In other words, human happiness and wellbeing are consistent with a healthy climate system – but achieving them is possible only if we are more conscious of what really makes us happy.

This chapter describes how consuming sustainably and living simply can reduce climate pollution while simultaneously *increasing* human happiness and wellbeing. What is important here is that we need *not* ask people to be highly virtuous or to undermine their own genuine interests. Quite the opposite: to discourage greenhouse gas emissions, what is needed is to encourage people to behave in ways that will enhance their interests. As part of this process, the world will have to move away from traditional models of economic growth toward alternative forms of development that focus on growth in human happiness and wellbeing, with environmental sustainability – including a stable climate system – among the factors that are essential for doing so. By doing this, we can move toward overcoming the addictions of modernity.

Consumption vs. happiness

As we saw in chapter 4, growth in material overconsumption and the associated affliction of affluenza have been rooted in the developed world for generations. They are now taking root and growing rapidly in the developing world. Affluenza is a pathology, an influenza of consumption that harms those who suffer from it. There is little evidence that the increasing wealth and consumption have resulted in greater happiness for those people whose needs are already met. Social surveys of happiness show the opposite: by seeking wealth and possessions, people end up shortchanging family life and health, in the process reducing their happiness.[3] Having more money and possessions often adds to stress and takes time away from enjoyable aspects of life.[4] As Norman Myers and Jennifer Kent observe, many people in developed nations have come to realize that "the good life does not lie with piling up ever-more goodies."[5] Tim Jackson puts it succinctly: "Having more stuff doesn't always make us happy. Material aspirations don't necessarily deliver wellbeing. And a society dedicated to materialist values sometimes undermines the conditions on which wellbeing depends."[6] For most of the world's affluent people, consumption presents a multiple tragedy: it results in doing harm to ourselves and to the environment, and to those people most vulnerable to climate change. Stephen Gardiner argues that this behavior is irrational because it seriously harms "ourselves, the poor, the future, and nature through behavior that on reflection seems seriously absurd," suggesting that affluent people have a collective problem that is "a bizarre (and arguably vaguely stupid) superficiality. This is genuinely tragic – but might also be seen as somewhat pathetic."[7]

Jagdish Sheth, Nirmal Sethia, and Shanthi Srinivas summarize some of the scholarly findings on the adverse impacts of unnecessary consumption: consumption can bring immediate gratification but harms long-term wellbeing; people who want income and possessions are usually less happy, lower in self-esteem, higher in anxiety, and have poorer social relationships; lifestyles dominated by consumption undermine satisfaction with life; overconsumption results in stress and makes finding a proper work–life balance more difficult; at best, rising consumption can lead to a stagnation in people's happiness, and at worst it can cause people to be less happy; overspending is often associated with overconsumption, contributing to financial stress.[8] These symptoms of consumption are most evident in Europe and the United States, but one can expect them to spread to China, India, and other parts of the developing world where high-consumption lifestyles accompany increasing prosperity.[9]

Why does consumption often fail to bring the happiness we are promised by advertisers? Social and psychological studies show that, for most people, the more they have, the more they want; people never seem to have enough. Most new luxuries are rapidly seen to be requisites of life (examples being televisions, microwave ovens, and mobile telephones), and yet newer luxuries are sought to replace these new necessities (an example might be the iPhone, which many people seem unable to live without for even a few minutes – until a newer gadget comes along).[10] Alan Durning has pointed to the hedonistic nature of consumption as well as the tendency for people to become habituated to affluence. People garner pleasure from material consumption, but generally speaking they become accustomed to having what they consume, leaving more consumption as the (perceived) essential source of more pleasure.[11] Worse still, each generation wants to consume more than the last, so that things that did not exist in the recent past have become "necessities," the mobile telephone perhaps being the most obvious example today.

Even upper-class people, who say that they are more satisfied, are no more satisfied than were upper-class people living in much less affluent times. Instead, what seems to matter most is how much people consume relative to those around them: people want to consume more than others (and often to be seen to be doing so). Wealthy people report higher levels of happiness because they are relatively wealthier than those around them, not because of their absolute wealth or possessions per se. This creates an obvious problem: if people want to consume more than other people, and those other people also want to do the same, most people can never be satisfied. Consumption becomes a means to achieving something that is unattainable as long as there are other people with more possessions and more visible wealth, which in most societies there always will be. This tells us that it is not affluence (beyond a baseline) that matters for promoting happiness.

Andrew Brennan and Y. S. Lo portray this failure of

consumption to bring lasting happiness as "an everlast-
ing cycle that runs from discontent through to desire, hope,
belief, and then back to discontent. For many people, the cycle
of yo-yoing emotions from the low ends of disappointment
and boredom to the high ends of excitement, hopefulness,
and optimism is a psychological equivalent to physical addiction resulting from drug abuse."[12] A consequence of this
addiction to consumption (affluenza) is that it replaces other
sources of pleasure and happiness, with people increasingly
unable to garner enjoyment from what were traditionally the
simple pleasures of life.[13] Further undermining wellbeing,
the desire to consume pushes people to work longer hours,
in the process robbing those afflicted of ability to see that
their lives have ironically become consumed by consumption. People work more to consume more, contributing to
stressful lives that people attempt to relieve through yet more
consumption.[14]

Mirroring the effects of increasing material consumption,
increasing *wealth* also does not bring the happiness that is routinely expected from it. It often leads to the opposite. People
in modern societies believe that they require more money
to purchase things that they "need," but what they end up
buying with additional income are more conspicuous goods
that help to establish their status in society.[15] Evidence shows
that what we sometimes hear but perhaps believe less often is
actually true: among the already affluent, money cannot buy
happiness.[16]

The United States is a case in point. Despite the average
American household possessing things that were barely imagined even half a century ago – such as computers, widescreen
televisions, mobile "smart" telephones, microwave ovens, cars
with satellite navigation systems, and other novel gadgets –
Americans are no happier than they were then. Indeed, during
the last half-century, levels of overall economic prosperity

have increased greatly in the United States, yet indicators of happiness there have remained stable while those of unhappiness (such as rates of depression, divorce, violent crime, suicides among teenagers) have increased.[17] Most places that are currently underdeveloped need more material growth, but the "overdeveloped world," as Bill McKibben describes it, needs less because "the tie between more stuff and more happiness has broken down – that economic growth is now more likely to yield isolation . . . and disconnection."[18] Indeed, in the developed nations, majorities of people say that they favor *reducing* consumption, with one-third of people in developing countries saying likewise.[19]

For very poor nations, rising national income can result in greater satisfaction among people who are able to escape poverty, showing that growth in parts of the developing world remains important. To be sure, consumption to meet one's basic needs and to provide some simple luxuries is important for wellbeing. But social science research generally shows that, with the exception of the poor, a person's income or socioeconomic status does not affect his contentment significantly, and even economic growth does not have a significant effect on happiness.[20] Diener and Seligman show that wellbeing and income lose their importance above an annual income of about US$10,000.[21] Jackson reports that after reaching about US$15,000, people's sense of "life satisfaction" is barely correlated to even large increases in national GDP, with many countries reporting higher levels of satisfaction even though their GDPs are not the highest (for example, people in Denmark, Sweden, and New Zealand are more satisfied than are Americans),[22] and even some nations with fractions of that wealth show high levels of "flourishing" (physical, psychological, and social wellbeing).[23] Some of the happiest people in the world live in relatively poor countries – and some of the least happy live in some of the wealthiest ones.[24]

Although the income of Americans, Japanese, and many others in the developed nations has multiplied in recent decades, the number of them saying that they are very happy has fallen.[25] More often than not, according to analysts, wealthy people and their children (at least in the United States) suffer more psychiatric pathologies and greater amounts of stress than do people with modest incomes.[26] Psychological analyses have shown that the more people concern themselves with financial success, the less likely they are to experience self-actualization and the more likely they are to feel depressed or anxious.[27] This seems to be because the more one earns, the more one expects or wants to earn; one's expectations keep increasing with one's income. The desire for more income and "psychological investment in ever-higher levels of consumption has an addictive quality. People seek to purchase and amass ever more goods whether they need them (in any sense of the term) or not."[28]

As Gardiner points out, psychological research confirms that, beyond a threshold, happiness is "largely insensitive to income," suggesting that promoting happiness need not be focused so much on increasing people's income.[29] This is an important message for people in the developed nations, but it is also a warning to the world's expanding class of new consumers: in joining the world's middle class, they ought not expect that more wealth or more possessions will make them happier (especially if they live in an unequal society).

Incredibly, even in China, which has experienced enormous economic growth in recent decades, self-reported feelings of satisfaction with life have trended slightly *downward*.[30] How is this possible, given a fourfold increase in per capita income in China? In answering this question, Richard Easterlin and his colleagues note that "relative income comparisons and rising material aspirations" in China have a tendency to counteract the expected impact of rising incomes.[31] They point out that this is consistent with the wide literature on human happiness: "growth in aspirations induced by rising income undercuts the increase in life satisfaction related to rising income itself."[32] One possible and tragic conclusion may be that the increased life satisfaction of China's most affluent people can be largely attributed to them being surrounded by many other people who are much less well off. The message to take away is that growth can be good for some people in poor countries, but it is unnecessary in affluent ones and even for many people in the developing world. The world would be much better off if growth were focused on lifting the world's poor out of poverty rather than making the well-off even better off materially and financially.[33]

Things may be even worse than this. John Barry notes that there is a link between *in*security, economic growth, and well-being: feelings of "personal insecurity and vulnerability" have increased because people are not consuming to add to their quality of life; instead they are consuming simply to maintain the material standard of living they currently experience – "to run to stand still" – with the end result being *reduced* wellbeing.[34] The inability of material consumption and growing financial wealth to make people much happier overall should come as no surprise. As Clive Hamilton observes, consumer capitalism relies on "a constant feeling of dissatisfaction to sustain spending."[35] The tragic irony is that in consumption societies economic growth does not bring human happiness; "*unhappiness sustains economic growth.*"[36]

Apparently confirming that traditional economic growth is not as important for human happiness as its advocates believe, despite four years of global economic stagnation, by early 2012 the level of self-described happiness in nations around the world was largely unchanged. The happiest people were often found in developing nations (for example, India, Indonesia, and Mexico), people in some of the world's wealthiest nations (such as Britain, Canada, and the United States) were only in the middle of the happiness scale, with others from highly developed societies (for example, French, Germans, Italians, and South Koreans) falling at the low end of the scale.[37]

This does not mean that weak economies promote happiness or that stronger ones necessarily harm it. Rather, it shows that promoting consumption and economic growth is not the key to human happiness. To put it in Durning's words, "the consumer society fails to deliver on its promise of fulfillment through material comforts because human wants are insatiable, human needs are socially defined, and the real sources of personal happiness are elsewhere."[38] The real sources of human happiness are found in social relations and quality leisure time, but these are the very things that are undermined in consumer societies. In effect, "the consumer society, it seems, has impoverished us by raising our income."[39]

Thus a key question is how people can break free of affluenza – how they can be made to realize and assisted to act upon the reality that consumption contributes greatly to climate change while also harming them collectively and individually. This is where government and other institutions can help, and indeed should.

Sources of wellbeing

Overconsumption by the world's affluent people is largely responsible for driving up global greenhouse gas emissions. It is tragic that enormous environmental harm results from unnecessary material consumption that does not generally increase the wellbeing of those doing the consuming. But there is reason to believe that this ongoing tragedy can be brought to an end. People can live in ways that contribute far less to climate change by doing more of the things that *genuinely* make them happy, and by acting in their *genuine* self-interest to improve their lifelong wellbeing. As Barry notes, after a person has reached a "decent standard of living," human flourishing is possible with much reduced use of natural resources and far lower environmental impact but without reducing people's wellbeing.[40] People can (and should), for both selfish and environmental reasons, work to promote their *genuine long-term self-interest* by consuming more happiness and less "stuff."[41]

What would it mean to consume more happiness? Material security is essential; everyone requires adequate food, shelter, and physical security. But having these things and having more than one needs of them does not make a person *prosperous*.[42] Prosperity is about much more than material pleasures and concerns.[43] It requires happiness which, if one is not materially poor, does not equate to having more things or more money. Instead, the "things" that make people happy are generally not things at all. They are relationships with other people – partners, friends, family, neighbors, and favorite co-workers – and spending more time pursuing one's interests, whether at work or during leisure time.[44] In short, once people's basic needs have been adequately provided for, that which brings happiness is "belonging with other people" and participating fully in society.[45]

The notion of economic growth is especially problematic, in large part because it is focused on traditional measures of GDP.[46] Gross domestic product, whether nationally or on a per capita basis, is a poor measure of wellbeing. Despite many economists still believing that "you can keep adding another unit of growth or another ton of CO_2 forever and the graph will always show a nice straight ascending line," Susan George argues that "no rational person should believe them."[47] The current view of GDP and growth needs to be replaced by alternative measures that capture human wellbeing and environmental sustainability. We need measures that recognize the environmental limits to growth while meeting people's needs.

One move toward such measures has been the United Nations' "human development index." First developed two decades ago in an effort to reveal true indicators of human wellbeing and successful national development, this approach now focuses on both equity and environmental sustainability.[48] In 2012, the United Nations introduced a new measure, the "inclusive wealth index," which builds on human development indicators by incorporating the status of natural resources, ecological conditions, and the long-term environmental sustainability of national policies.[49]

Scholars and creative economists have proposed other alternatives to traditional measures of material growth, such as the "genuine progress indicator," which shows that more economic growth can contribute to a *decline* in human welfare.[50] Similarly, the "Happy Planet Index" provides evidence that "wellbeing in terms of long, happy and meaningful lives" does not require environmentally unsustainable material consumption.[51] This index and similar measures reveal that "long and happy lives" can be realized through modest living that has relatively little impact on the environment.[52] The New Economics Foundation, which compiles the Happy Planet Index, has argued that if most of the last century was about material consumption and a focus on economic growth, this one should be characterized by "the pursuit of good lives that do not cost the Earth."[53] But in abandoning traditional growth, we ought not abandon growth in what is good. We need *de-*growth in material consumption but *more* growth in human wellbeing and environmental health.

Quality of life can be maintained and even improved while lowering material consumption, but this will require persuading young people in affluent communities to focus more on happiness than on consumption, and pushing older people (those that are already overconsuming) to make significant changes to their lives. The latter will be especially challenging. One has to admit that the message to consume less, to lower greenhouse gas emissions, and to redefine economic growth is not a "rabble-rousing mantra for change."[54] To deal with this, the negative discourse that puts people off doing what will make them happiest while minimizing their contributions to climate change should be changed. For example, the usual discourse about responding to the problem on an individual level is about *sacrifice* (in the pejorative sense), the assumption being that doing enough to address climate change requires giving up that which is dear to us.[55] This "rhetoric of sacrifice" undermines positive conceptions of doing with less and undervalues everyday ways of living that have brought people happiness for millennia while encouraging people to sacrifice their wellbeing for the good of the free-market economy.[56]

Putting aside the real meaning of sacrifice – giving up something for the sake of something more important – this typical way of portraying the problem diverts us away from the involuntary and unavoidable harmful sacrifices that we already make as we contribute to climate change, for example through consumerism that undermines our happiness. It also diverts us from the alternatives, the things that are worthy of sacrifice, such as living lives that are far less damaging to the earth's climate system and much more likely to be fulfilling and to bring happiness to the most people. For example, the use of automobiles, which puts drivers and their passengers in more danger than they would be if using mass transit, is correlated with poor health and weight gain but is often a requirement for getting around in places where there is a lack of public transportation – the United States being perhaps the most profound example of this.[57]

Paul Wapner points out that many observers of the human–environment relationship have made the case for "environmental sacrifice."[58] The sacrifice to which they refer is about *gaining* more in life: "more ecological health, greater spiritual enrichment, enhanced appreciation for others, deeper relationships, and more fun."[59] Paul Gilding believes that if enough people could be helped to realize that overconsumption does not improve their wellbeing but instead locks them into "time-poor lives, unsatisfying work, and endless debt, they might stop."[60] The effects might cascade across the global economy as demand for material goods falls and those that rely upon selling them move to alternatives. To ensure that this happens, people will of course have to find happiness somewhere other than in what Gilding calls "the emotional drug of materialism."[61] They can do this by devoting more time and energy to their families, friends, relationships, and communities. And by consuming less, people would find that they do not need to work and earn as much, giving them greater freedom in choosing jobs and the amount of time that they devote to them. Indeed, survey data show that those who choose to live "simpler" lives become happier.[62]

The message that comes from this is that by *truly* acting in their self-interest, individuals will also be living more in keeping with the limits of environmental sustainability and in ways that will contribute far less to climate change. A major objective of climate policy should be to foster, cultivate, support, nurture, encourage, and push such thinking and behavior. It should do so in a way that helps people to realize what the experts know: that there is a happier life to be had from living more simply and more sustainably. The realization that overconsumption and unnecessary wealth do not equate to happiness and improved wellbeing will have to become widespread, not just in the West but among the expanding middle (and upper) classes of the developing world. The next section explores some of the options for achieving this.

Realizing wellbeing *and* sustainability

John Urry has described the "sedimented high carbon social practices" that were cemented in place around the world during the twentieth century as what he calls the "carbon military–industrial complex."[63] He warns that fossil fuel-centered patterns of life are "locked in" and indeed spreading around the world, creating an enormous burden for politicians, policymakers, and officials.[64] Although Urry's concern with systemic forces that often dictate people's lives cannot be underestimated, he may overstate the problem in some ways. Climate politics should be aimed at reducing material overconsumption, to be sure, but what is required is lower consumption of material things *that people do not need* and those that *undermine people's own wellbeing*. Going against people's individual interests is *not* what is needed for climate politics to be successful. On the contrary, what is needed is much more attention to doing what is best for people and their individual long-term wellbeing.

Societies should not use more natural resources than the earth can sustainably provide, and they should not produce more waste and pollution than the environment can safely absorb. At present, these limits are being exceeded. Thus what we need is to move toward *sufficiency*. Living a life of sufficiency would not mean an end to consumption in the literal sense. It would instead involve less unnecessary material consumption and more consumption of experiences, knowledge, and time with other people or with nature.[65] To be sure, for people whose needs are not met, who are already living *too* simply and not consuming enough to meet their needs, more material consumption is necessary to achieve sufficiency. To a great extent, what is most important about future climate politics is that it should help to avert the environmental conditions that make it more difficult for these people to meet their basic needs.

Climate politics is thus about helping people to live happy and full lives that are environmentally sustainable. It should be geared toward lifting the world's poor out of poverty, but not so far beyond it (in the material economic sense) that they, too, become sources of the problem, while ending the overconsumption of the world's affluent so that everyone is living well but without undermining the earth's climate system. This can be characterized as contraction and convergence toward sufficiency at the individual level. By addressing climate change, we can create opportunities for more people to have much improved lives, for example by diverting the environmental resources used to feed the consumerism of affluent people toward the needs of the world's poor, without reducing the wellbeing of currently affluent people.[66]

There is plenty of evidence that people who choose to live more simply are happier and more fulfilled than people who do not.[67] As an alternative to lives of destructive consumerism, Duane Elgin has proposed what he calls "voluntary simplicity."[68] Voluntary simplicity enables realization that true satisfaction can come from *intentionally avoiding* unnecessary material consumption and wealth.[69] As Jackson points out, contrary to conventional wisdom, voluntarily consuming less can improve people's subjective wellbeing.[70] Far from being a sacrifice, voluntary simplicity supports a higher quality of life because it is more harmonious with the environment; promotes fairness and equity among people, including future generations; avoids needless busyness and clutter; brings people closer to nature and saves other species from extinction; responds to shortages of petroleum, water, and other resources; helps people to focus on what matters most in their lives, notably relationships, family, friends, and community; brings greater satisfaction than consumerism; and connects people more closely to others.[71]

Sheth, Sethia, and Srinivas advocate an alternative to

the mostly mindless consumption that is practiced by most affluent people today: "mindful consumption." Mindful consumption involves developing "a sense of *caring* about the implications and consequences of one's consumption."[72] This much more conscious approach to consumption is aimed at reducing "self-defeating excesses" that come with "acquisitive, repetitive, and aspirational consumption."[73] Overconsumption is bad for the environment and a major contributor to climate change, but it also involves disregarding the wellbeing of oneself and one's community as a consequence of "ignorance, indifference, or denial."[74] In contrast to this self-harming attitude, mindful consumption involves consuming in a way that consciously aims to care for oneself, for one's community and indeed for nature.[75]

From this perspective, to promote their own wellbeing people should aim to accumulate only what they need, to avoid the "cycle of buying, discarding, and buying again," and to work toward overcoming the desire to consume conspicuously.[76] The sort of temperance implied by mindful consumption is not about asking people to end consumption altogether, but rather to direct people's attention toward consuming in ways that maximize their own wellbeing and that of others.[77]

Motivation for living more simply is not widespread and will probably not become so – certainly not in time to cut greenhouse gases as much and as quickly as is needed to avert the worst effects of climate change – without reframing it in the mind of the public. Many people, particularly in affluent communities, will balk at the idea of consuming less. They may believe that decades of surveys and social science research are false; they will often assume that consumption will make them happy. In reality, the opposite is more likely to be true, and it is very important to make everyone aware of this. It is also very important to make people aware that it is possible to be happy and even to flourish while living simpler lives.

A key variable here is how sufficiency, simplicity, and sustainability are *sold* to people. It is vital for sustainable lives to be characterized in government policies, educational systems, and marketing campaigns as means to promote people's own interests, needs, and wellbeing. Rather than idealistically trying to do away with people's selfishness (which may be impossible), what is needed is a concerted effort to help people realize what decades of research has shown: material consumption (at least in the developed world and in expanding pockets of development elsewhere) is both unsustainable *and* a dead-end path to happiness and wellbeing.

Some people have already got the message. Especially in the West, they find "escaping the rat race" of modern life a great relief. To them, living "simply" is a source of greater happiness and wellbeing. Acting "selfishly" in this way is not a problem because it means wanting and trying to obtain that which truly enhances people's lives rather than those things that harm the planet and other people.

Putting sufficiency and sustainability into practice will also require abandonment of both official and personal preoccupations with economic growth in its traditional form, at least outside poor nations. Jackson questions the whole idea of economic growth as being compatible with environmental limits.[78] As he puts it, "the myth of growth has failed us."[79] To address climate change, Barry proposes replacing the current global focus on economic growth with "economic security," comprising basic social security (basic needs related to health, education, housing, social protection, and the like), job (or income) security, and democracy and equality.[80] He argues that achieving these objectives, along with sustainability, will involve implementing principles of sufficiency, such as frugality and thrift.[81] This means measuring the success of economies not by how much they grow materially but rather by how well they provide meaningful and secure work and how well they meet basic human needs within environmental limits. The aim of maximizing profit and growth is replaced by one of creating "the most human wellbeing from the least resources whilst living within the thresholds of tolerance of the ecosystems we depend on."[82]

In contrast, today governments and corporations encourage consumerism at the individual level and growth at the national level. That is, they encourage long-term unhappiness for many and unsustainability for the planet. Government's role should instead be simultaneously to help people overcome forms of selfishness encouraged by modernity, particularly material-ism, while taking advantage of people's tendency to promote their own self-interest. To do this, the modern culture of material consumption should be reimagined and rebranded as what it really is: something dirty and harmful.

This will not be easy, but governments could require, at the very least, that advertising sell products instead of lifestyles, and that it be honest about the known environmental and human impacts of consuming. Every effort must be made to reduce inequalities within nations (and among them), not only for reasons of social justice but also because inequality encourages material consumption even after people's needs are met. Education should, from preschool through univer-sity, be focused on cultivating among pupils understanding and appreciation of living a truly good and healthy life, rather than encouraging them to aspire to wealth and endless consumption.

Insofar as self-interest dictates wider social interests, it is the consumption of happiness – consuming more time with friends, giving one's labor to community groups, being involved in fulfilling work that helps others, and so forth – that should be encouraged. The key is for government and other institutions to do what they can to redirect selfishness toward true happiness rather than, as now, toward overconsumption.

By doing this, governments would be doing what they are supposed to do: promoting the long-term interests of their citizens, in the process mitigating emissions of greenhouse gas pollution.

To diminish doubt about the ability of governments to change people's motivations and behaviors, with dramatic widespread effect in a short space of time, one need only look at the role of nationalism and related propaganda. Extreme examples include Nazi Germany, where millions of people tolerated and often participated in the worst sorts of widespread brutality, and Maoist China, where millions more did extraordinarily bad things, even harming close family members, in the name of a particular view of socialism. But now Germany is the model of a peaceful society and Chinese passion has shifted to consumption and wealth. In the latter case, the nation went from communist penury to capitalist excess in less than a generation. Starting in the late 1970s, the message of government propaganda became "getting rich is glorious."[83] That message was hugely successful from the standpoint of economic growth, so much so that by getting rich Chinese are undermining the good of the whole planet. Or consider the way that people are apparently willing to commit the ultimate sacrifice – to give their lives – in time of war for nations, even those that are quite new. (An example may be Singapore, which became a nation only in the 1960s but has a very strong sense of public loyalty to the state.) If people are willing to die for powerful ideas, surely they can be persuaded to see overconsumption for what it really is, and to behave accordingly.

The message we can take from these examples is that governments can utterly transform people's thinking if that is their objective. If governments were to put as much effort into encouraging their citizens to live in ways that are both environmentally responsible and good for people as they put into encouraging patriotism, material consumption, and economic growth, we might quickly get on the path toward global sustainability. What may be needed is a sort of new "nationalism of sustainability" whereby governments use their considerable resources and influence to transform people's thinking, albeit this time toward doing what is truly good for them and for the earth. With such support from governments, the big cuts in greenhouse gas emissions that are required to avert the worst effects of climate change would not be so daunting after all.

Material consumption will never disappear, so what consumption there is must be sustainable. One potentially useful step toward sufficiency is "sustainable" consumption, which involves consuming "green" products that are much less environmentally harmful than typical ones.[84] In the view of Myers and Kent, sustainable consumption is about using energy and resources in ways that enhance people's quality of life today without causing "protests from our grandchildren that we have cut the environmental ground from under their feet."[85] Sustainable consumption may help to overcome many of the injustices associated with climate change, but it does not address the fundamental problem of consumption itself. It could encourage a righteous sense of consumption on one level – by drinking sustainably grown "fair trade" coffee, one may feel he is helping the poor in underdeveloped nations[86] – while failing to address the question of whether that consumption is appropriate in the context of climate change.

The sustainable consumption movement capitalizes (often literally) on consumerism to promote environmental sustainability, although in the process it may not prevent unnecessary consumption.[87] Marketing departments adopt the idea to encourage yet more purchases of apparently less-polluting products by affluent consumers around the world or, worse, use "greenwashing" to mislead people into believing that their products are not environmentally harmful.[88] Thus campaigns for sustainable consumption related to climate change should be explicitly geared toward reducing overall global consumption, rather than making overconsumption "greener."

Societies will have to stop burning fossil fuels almost completely, starting with coal, if the world is to avoid very dangerous climate change in the future.[89] This will require new policies. Lester Brown has called for a restructured world economy fueled by carbon-free sources of energy and full-cost pricing of resources to reflect their environmental impact. His plan would include a tax on carbon commensurate with the harm it does, using the resulting funds to reduce income taxes. At the same time, fossil fuel subsidies would have to be eliminated. This final step alone, if done by 2020, would cut carbon emissions globally by almost 6 percent.[90] Some of the government funds currently spent on these subsidies could be directed toward the development of alternative energies. In such a plan, all coal-fired power plants would be closed as soon as possible.

Similarly, as part of efforts to shift away from fossil fuels, James Hansen proposes a "fee-and-dividend" approach to carbon pricing that is consistent with human rights, needs, and obligations.[91] Under this approach, all fossil fuels would be taxed at source – at the mines where they are extracted or where they enter a nation's territory. This tax would raise the cost of carbon-based fuels and discourage their use, although in Hansen's plan the fee would rise gradually to allow people time to adjust.[92] To compensate for the rising costs of polluting energy, all of the fees collected would be directly transferred to citizens in the form of dividends paid into individual bank accounts or debit cards. People who reduce their carbon footprints more than the average would receive larger payments, thus encouraging the move away from fossil fuels. Under this plan, the bureaucracy involved would be very limited; money would be transferred on a monthly basis almost directly from fossil fuel companies to the public. Nations that refuse to implement such fees would be subject to import duties, which would likely give them an incentive to do so.

On the individual level, a vital objective for both wellbeing and sustainability is to break free of the desire to consume beyond one's needs. If enough people were to do this, climate change would be mitigated *and* human happiness and well-being would increase. This may be easier than it seems. The example of meat consumption shows how simple it could be to reduce climate-changing behaviors while improving people's wellbeing.

A study of more than 100,000 people in the United States found that consumption of red meat is associated with sub-stantial increases in mortality from cardiovascular diseases and cancer, with the opposite likely to result if meat were to be replaced by healthy sources of protein (for example, whole grains, legumes, and nuts).[93] Meanwhile, livestock for human consumption accounts for 20–50 percent of the world's green-house gas emissions.[94] One study found that changing from an average American diet, which is high in meat (27 percent of daily calories), to a vegan diet (free of meat) would reduce personal annual carbon emissions by 1.5 tons.[95] Another study concluded that if people in Britain were to adopt vegetarian diets, the reduction in the nation's greenhouse gas emissions would be 22 percent, and even more (26 percent) if everyone adopted a vegan diet.[96] Thus, ending meat consumption would be one of the easiest and fastest ways for affluent people to reduce their impact on the earth's climate *while also greatly improving their long-term health*.[97] Alas, the current global trend is for more people to adopt diets increasingly heavy in meat, akin to the typical American diet, contributing to growth in western diseases *and* greenhouse gas emissions.

Conclusion

Politics involve people. The choices and behaviors of individuals can determine how the distribution of power and resources shape the world around us. This chapter has sought to highlight the detrimental impact that our behaviors can have on the environment *and* ourselves, and to point to some alternatives. People who devote more time to family, friends, exercise, sleep, and "restorative activities," and those who consume inconspicuously, are happier and live longer and healthier lives, whereas those who seek material possessions and conspicuous consumption generally experience less happiness and report less satisfaction with their lives.[98] What is more, for the majority of people who indulge in it, excessive consumption lowers their economic wellbeing – their financial health – often because they spend beyond their means, go into debt, or reduce their savings in doing so.[99] This can harm the wider economy, as the financial crisis and resulting recession in the West have revealed.

As with the other treatments for climate politics, this one will not go down easily. We cannot deny that millions of people garner a sense of personal identity from material consumption. Indeed, this is precisely the sentiment that is assiduously cultivated by advertisers. A vital element in pushing back against this environmentally harmful formulation of personal identity is to recognize that it is not the best source of wellbeing, and very likely undermines it. The world's current approach to material consumption, which contributes greatly to climate change, is the *opposite* of what is best for people's wellbeing. It makes no sense from the perspective of long-term human happiness and environmental sustainability. Personal climate politics, and wider politics that involve individual behaviors, should be premised on this reality rather than on the fictions that consumption is good for everyone, even those who are already affluent, and that there is a trade-off between people's wellbeing and combating climate change. To mitigate the causes of climate change is instead to *increase* people's wellbeing. It is easier to say this than to get people to realize it and act accordingly, but surely saying it and spreading the notion is a prerequisite for positive change.

People living in developed societies should ask what material consumption and long hours on the job are for. If people are working to meet their essential needs, what they do can be justified as being in their interest. The task then becomes one of doing all that is possible to limit how this activity contributes to climate change. But if people's behaviors are for something else – for keeping up with those around them or seeking long-term happiness in shopping and possessing material "goods" – they would be better off making a change.[100] Certainly, people should start by individually discarding the notion that more stuff and more money will make them better off. It might do the opposite, even while it exacerbates climate change. What comes from this is that *to act in one's best interest is to reduce material consumption toward the level of one's needs while increasing consumption of those things that all the evidence shows make people happy*: time with friends and family, leisure activities, rewarding avocations, and the like.

To be effective in combating climate change, individual behaviors and climate change policies intended to maximize long-term human wellbeing should aim to make it possible and even easy for people to live happily *and* sustainably. This means encouraging and enabling people to be more "selfish" about promoting their true wellbeing, rather than contributing to the balance sheets of corporations. Some argue that moving in this direction may require abandoning capitalism, while others maintain that the best approach is to use capitalism, albeit in a highly managed way, to achieve major cuts in greenhouse gases.[101]

While this debate continues, the prevailing way of doing things at the global, national, and corporate levels (enthusiasm for "corporate social responsibility" notwithstanding) is probably too ingrained and powerful to avert climate catastrophe, given the trajectory of greenhouse gas emissions and the accelerating globalization of consumption. What is necessary, therefore, is to get to the heart of the problem – self-interest – and to use it for promoting and realizing both human welfare and climate protection. This requires action by individuals in the near future. That action needs all the help and encouragement that governments can muster. This will not provide an instant cure for the addictions of modernity, but it is an essential part of the overall remedy.

The next chapter brings some of these and related ideas together with those from previous chapters, in the process suggesting the sorts of treatments – the kinds of steps that diplomats, governments, and individuals should take – to start overcoming the ills of climate politics internationally, nationally, and individually.

CHAPTER EIGHT

Conclusion

Diagnosing a patient with complex cancers often poses major challenges for physicians, sometimes requiring innovative and even radical treatments. The same is true of climate politics. This book is mostly about identifying some of the most serious problems with climate politics and proposing ways of thinking about how "treatments" for them can be found and administered. This chapter proposes some policies and actions that should help to move us in the right direction. As noted at the outset, some of these prescriptions are aspirational. It will not be easy to persuade governments, industry, and individuals to accept all of the diagnoses and to "take their medicine." There is genuine disagreement about how best to perceive what is wrong with climate politics and how to fix it. But continuing to do what we are doing now is no solution. That would make the problem much worse.

Continuing the medical analogy, if there is a realistic chance of curing a patient's cancer, it would be wrong to tell him to do nothing or to continue the behaviors that have made him ill. Nevertheless, the advice that most governments are giving their citizens, and indeed what many people seem to be telling themselves, is that we do not need to change the way we live, at least no more than a tiny bit, and that we should continue to consume and seek wealth for the good of a growing economy. Such counterproductive thinking needs to be confronted head on. Thankfully, there are many ongoing efforts around the world to reverse the rising tide of greenhouse gas emissions

– although those efforts are grossly inadequate relative to the scale of the problem. Much more needs to be done. In short, the main objectives of nations, governments, and individuals should be doing everything they can to limit climate change, thereby protecting and promoting the security and wellbeing of as many people as possible.

To help do that, this chapter briefly revisits the diagnoses of what is wrong with climate politics (identified in Part I). It proposes several treatments at the international, national, and individual levels to illustrate how prescriptions for what is wrong with climate politics (discussed in the three preceding chapters) might be administered. These are suggestions rather than well-developed policy proposals (each of which would require its own book, at least). They are only some of the kinds of treatments that should be attempted. Most of them can help to remedy more than one of the key ailments.

While these treatments are likely to be essential in some form, they will not be enough. Neither the diagnoses nor the remedies described here should be considered or administered in isolation. They are intended to supplement what many other scholars, scientists, and experts have proposed.[1] Additional policies and actions that are consistent with the diagnoses and prescriptions of what is wrong with climate politics (and how to fix it) that follow should be welcomed. Indeed, they are almost certainly essential.

How to fix the cancer of Westphalia

Fundamental to what is wrong with climate politics is the state-centered foundation of the world's responses to greenhouse gas pollution and the environmental and other consequences that result – what was dubbed the "cancer of Westphalia" in chapter 1. For too long, the assumption has been that nation-states are the causes of climate change, when of course that is literally impossible: states are sets of legal institutions and ideas around which people and other actors coalesce. They cannot, of themselves, pollute. More importantly, the real causes of climate change – corporations and individuals for the most part – have had their responsibilities attributed to nations. The rights of these actors have also been attributed to nations. As such, the world's responses to climate change have been monopolized to a very great extent by national governments. It has been negotiations and agreements among them that have been the focus of attention for a generation. The results have been weak agreements that move *on paper* in the right direction, both in terms of action and fairness, but which in fact have utterly failed to prevent global *increases* in greenhouse gas pollution, let alone the massive *reductions* that are required.

Therefore, what is most wrong with climate politics at the international level is the continuing preoccupation with the nation-state, indeed with traditions and ways of thinking and responding to "international" and global problems that were codified in the seventeenth century. Addressing climate change effectively will require a new, or at least reformulated, international politics that is more suited to the twenty-first century.

Fundamental to the treatments of what is wrong with climate politics are global conceptions of, and approaches to, the problem. These approaches need to do a better job of bringing people, including their rights, needs, and responsibilities, much closer to the center of climate diplomacy, in the process integrating human rights and obligations more routinely and explicitly into the climate change regime and the policies that result from it. The objective of international climate politics should focus on the reason that nations negotiate at all: to protect and promote the interests and wellbeing of their citizens, which are now and forever connected to the interests and wellbeing of citizens of other nations, due to climate change.[2] Put another way, the current practice of focusing on abstract perceived "national interests" is an inadequate guide to how the world should respond to climate change. It is often not consistent with the actual interests of a nation's people and can lead to policies and actions that undermine their wellbeing (most obviously in wealthy nations) or even destroy their lives (especially in very poor nations). This is proved by the lack of fit between climate science – the realities of what causes climate change, the magnitude of those causes and related trends, and what will result from them in practical terms – and the international negotiations and diplomacy for dealing with the problem.

To be sure, governments have smartly come together, and their diplomats and officials have worked hard to address climate change. This has resulted in international agreements and annual climate conferences, including ongoing efforts to produce a new global agreement for implementation by 2020. However, without a major rethink, international climate politics will continue to be predictable. There will be more agreements, and great progress will be announced and celebrated by diplomats after major climate conferences. But future agreements will be more of the same in most respects: baby steps in the right direction, more or less, resulting in policies and actions that are essentially too little, too late. Far more aggressive responses to climate change are urgently needed. These responses should go beyond *national* interests to focus much more on agreements that promote and protect *people's* interests.

What would prescriptions for the cancer of Westphalia look like? The overriding aim should be to raise the priority of human rights and needs. With this in mind, treatments might include the following kinds of approaches and policies (but, again, this is only a suggestive sample of possible treatments):

End the fixation on "national interests" by putting people at center of the climate change negotiations, thereby making human rights and security the primary aims of climate diplomacy.[3] This might include concrete action on recommendations of the UN Human Rights Council and other bodies that have advocated a human rights approach to climate change. It would involve diplomats and their superiors thinking more explicitly and more often about what their work means for people. Doing this will not be easy, not least because diplomats, when pressed by humanitarians, will claim that they already put people first. But the results of climate conferences suggest very much otherwise: the interests of powerful actors within individual powerful nations, combined with the assumed need for perpetual economic growth, almost always take priority.

To start breaking the fixation on Westphalian norms, the whole approach to the problem needs to change – the rhetoric should be shifted in favor of people. This will probably never happen completely; that is not the point. Rather, the point is to give people who are affected by climate change and ultimately cause it a much higher status in climate diplomacy. One first step might be to learn from the title of the first global environmental conference, which was held in Stockholm in 1972. It was officially called the United Nations Conference on the *Human Environment*. At the very least, climate diplomacy should do more to explicitly embrace and work toward protecting the intimate connections between people and the earth's climate system.

Devote the plurality of time at all international climate conferences to discussions of the rights, needs, capabilities, and obligations of people. There will always be debate about whether officials, diplomats, and national leaders believe what they say. Nevertheless, rhetoric can matter. If discussion of the needs and obligations of people, including individuals, becomes a much greater focus of international negotiations on climate change, diplomats and governments are likely to be more educated about their importance and they are more likely actually to make people a greater priority in the agreements and policies that emanate from climate conferences. This will not be a panacea, but it will help to shift attention toward people's interests and away from narrowly defined supposed national interests.

A lesson can be learned from the *non*governmental conferences that are held nearby official conferences of the parties and other international negotiations around climate change. These side conferences, usually comprising representatives of environmental, developmental, and human rights organizations from around the world, routinely focus their attention – and try to get the official negotiators to focus *their* attention – on the relationships between people and climate change, including the human suffering related to it. Combined with greater participation of these and other nongovernmental actors in the official deliberation, this would help to shift the focus somewhat, perhaps greatly, away from perceived interests of sovereign nations and toward the real interests of people.

Explicitly address the long-term needs and wellbeing of people in the wording of climate change agreements, and ensure that those agreements are predominantly devoted to realizing human rights and security in the context of climate change. In addition to trying consciously to put people at the center of climate talks and actively devoting more time to them than anything else in those deliberations, the formal and informal agreements among nations that emanate from climate negotiations should put the people-centered orientation down on paper. Thinking more about the needs of people relative to nations is important, as is orienting discussion toward that end, but it is also important that the agreements themselves be about putting this into practice. Including people in the international agreements is no cure-all, but at least it provides support for those groups and activists who are working to promote people's interests through climate action. It gives them more ammunition to fight for the causes of those people most affected by climate change.

To be sure, many climate change agreements are weak and often implemented in the breach. This is quite often the nature of diplomacy and is unlikely to change radically anytime soon. Nevertheless, this treatment is akin to writing a more correct prescription. A prescription will not of itself put the cancer of Westphalia into remission, but a prescription is normally a prerequisite for a cure.

Place the common but differentiated responsibilities of people alongside the common but differentiated responsibilities of nation-states in the international politics of climate change. An important development in the international politics of climate change has been agreement, at least in nominal terms, that nations have common but differentiated responsibilities to respond to the problem, but that this responsibility is differentiated – some nations are more responsible than others. In practice, this allows affluent people to effectively hide behind the relative responsibilities of the nations in which they live. Consequently, it is important that diplomatic discussions and resulting agreements be devoted in significant part to the common but differentiated responsibilities of individuals – to affirming and establishing the basis for policies acknowledging that some people are more responsible for taking action, whether because they are polluting too much or simply because they are capable of doing something, whereas others are less responsible, or not responsible at all, given their low pollution or their poverty.

In other words, climate change negotiations and agreements need to be about the rights and needs of all people *and* about the obligations and responsibilities of those who are capable of acting on those obligations and responsibilities. Putting this into practice would end the obvious and unrealistic hypocrisy of well-off individuals who are heavy polluters being absolved of any legal responsibility simply because all responsibility is attributed to the sovereign nations in which they happen to live.

Include democratically chosen representatives of people most affected by climate change in international deliberations. People should be the central objects of climate politics. This means more than talking about them and integrating their rights and obligations into international agreements. It also means letting them be involved in making those agreements. Consequently, future international negotiations should do much more to bring people's representatives into the conference halls and the "back rooms" where deals are done so that they can at least fight on their fellows' behalf. This is necessary because diplomats represent nation-states, not people. Again, taking such a step would not be a panacea; one assumes that most diplomats would not hand over very much power to people. But having people's representatives in the room, and giving them official status to speak and to deliberate, would be an important step in the right direction. At the very least, this would make it harder to hide cynical deals made between governments. Some of this happens already; some national delegations take direct input from representatives of nongovernmental organizations. More movement in this direction is needed.

How the people who will be involved in official negotiations are chosen, and who they actually represent, will be contentious – there is already some debate about whether many nongovernmental organizations truly represent people's interests – but this is the nature of politics. Making climate diplomacy more democratic and responsive to the needs of people is a worthwhile and important goal, despite the difficulty of doing it.

How to fix the malignancy of the great polluters

The failure of governments to take climate change seriously enough, both domestically and in their relations with one another, is typified most profoundly in the policies and actions of the United States and China. What they do, and what they fail to do, is vital to climate politics. These nations are especially important because they epitomize the actions and relationships among most nations, notably the continuing (if increasingly unrealistic) developed–developing nation dichotomy in perceptions of how to respond to climate change. If the deadlock between the United States and China can be broken, it likely portends progress in ending the broader international deadlock on climate change. More generally, the rest of the world looks to them for leadership, for better or worse. Just as importantly, China and the United States are crucial simply because they are the largest national sources of greenhouse gas pollution. Without robust action from within their borders, the problem cannot be addressed adequately. Both of them are already implementing climate-related policies, but this is far too little and it is happening far too slowly. Each of these nations essentially blames the other for the problem and demands that the other effectively go first in responding to it. The two of them are playing a game of chicken with the planet and its inhabitants.

How might the world break free from this you-go-first stalemate between the United States and China? To start with, there should be much greater focus on what really matters, both practically and ethically, in causing and responding to climate change: the excessive greenhouse gas pollution of both countries' affluent residents. Put another way, there need not be any rivalry between China and the United States *as nation-states*. They generally agree that responsibilities and obligations between them are "common but differentiated." China is rightly entitled to continue developing economically and the United States is obligated to be among the national leaders in cutting greenhouse gas emissions and in helping developing countries to cope with climate change.

But, at the same time, there is lack of agreement on the role that the citizens of these two nations ought to have in all of this. Indeed, there is very little discussion of citizens per se. This is extremely important because the role of people has changed dramatically in recent decades and will continue to do so for decades to come. To put it simply, from an environmental perspective at least, many millions of Chinese are becoming just like Americans, consuming and polluting at increasingly prodigious rates as they aim to enjoy the lifestyle that has been commonplace in the West for half a century at least. Chapter 3 argued that China's new consumers and affluent classes have the same obligations as do most Americans: to do all that they can to live well without adding to the problem of climate change. Most Americans today are obligated, at least ethically, to behave differently than Americans did in past decades; that is a given. But so too are millions of Chinese.

More generally, climate politics between China and the United States highlights actions that are required by other nations to stem greenhouse gas pollution and otherwise respond to climate change. For the poorest nations, contin-ued economic growth is probably required to lift people out of poverty, but growth should not reach a point where afflu-enza takes hold. For already affluent nations, the focus on growth must stop and be diverted to promoting people's wellbeing and happiness; the focus must be on curing affluenza and replacing it with genuine human wellbeing. For newly industrialized countries, the key is to avoid too many people catching affluenza, helping them to realize that the enormous economic growth in the West has not been accompanied by a concomitant growth in happiness and wellbeing. These nations have the potential to enjoy a "sweet spot" of economic vitality short of affluenza, thereby avoiding sending climate change even further out of control.

The upshot is that the world cannot and must not deny the right of the world's poor to meet their needs and enjoy good lives, but more people must not be encouraged to live like Americans. This means that governments should officially acknowledge the globalization of affluence and act accordingly, starting with the United States and China. One bold (and no doubt controversial) recommendation from chapter 3 is that China could take the lead in this respect. If the United States will not start the process of saving the world, China can and should do so.

What would prescriptions for the malignancy of the great polluters look like? A key objective should be to accept officially and act upon the globalization of individual affluence. Treatments might include the following sorts of strategies and policies (to repeat: this is only a partial and suggestive list):

Convene an ongoing summit between the United States and China aimed at breaking the deadlock between them. The United States and China need to confront their differences head on. One way to do this would be a series of frequent bilateral climate summits, ideally taking the approach to climate politics suggested by the treatments outlined above. The objective during discussions would be to find creative ways of breaking free of the you-go-first mentality that characterizes their relationship. Because it will be very difficult to overcome their *national* positions – which would require rather profound changes in US domestic politics and overcoming deep-seated Chinese feelings of international injustice, neither of which is likely to happen – these should be put to one side as the two nations' officials focus on alternative solutions, notably those that consider the rights and obligations of individuals in the two nations. They might start by agreeing that individuals in *both* nations who have wealth equal to, say, 25 percent above the US poverty level should be considered responsible for acting (or starting to act) to limit their contributions to climate change. To be sure, such summits would be met with great skepticism and indeed would worry many nations, not least the poorest among them. No effort should be spared to reassure those nations that the China–US climate summits will not become a great-power alliance to do nothing in perpetuity, and of course every effort is required to ensure that such a reassurance reflects reality.

These summits would no doubt be testy and very difficult affairs, but the underlying difficulty is precisely why such meetings are needed. Ultimately, the people of both nations face growing threats from climate change. That should be sufficient motivation to justify such talks and get them started.

In future negotiations and in resulting policies, act upon the reality of growing affluence in China and other developing nations. Both China and the United States, including their citizens, can gain from accepting that climate politics must now be based in large part on the growing new-consumer classes in China. The United States benefits because this effectively means bringing Chinese (if not China as a sovereign nation-state per se) into more global solutions to climate change, solutions that benefit Americans. China benefits because it will be helping to address a problem that will bring great hardship to its people in the future, in the process garnering international prestige for its action and praise from the majority of its own people.

Associated policies and regulations will (as outlined in chapter 6) strengthen the Chinese government (and specifically the ruling Chinese Communist Party) by addressing growing inequalities and injustices in society. This requires escaping the assumption that Chinese people will be better off repeating the development path followed by the West. Barring unlikely leadership from other quarters, China could take the lead by visibly implementing policies aimed at its most affluent citizens, including expanding the government's current plans for new taxes on luxury goods.

End the fixation on economic growth (as conceived today) as the main objective of national economics and politics. This applies to the United States, China and indeed all nations, at the very least those that are no longer poor – and even for poor countries it applies to affluent segments of their populations. To say that this is among the most difficult treatments for climate politics would be an understatement, but pretending that it is not necessary would mean a future of unimaginable climate change resulting in widespread human suffering. Traditional economic growth has limits in its capacity to promote human wellbeing. After a point, the fixation on growth becomes counterproductive from a human and social perspective, making its impact on climate change all the more tragic.

The idea that growth is harmful is slowly taking hold among scholars and even a few governments. Alternative measures of human progress are being officially explored in nations as diverse as Bhutan and the United Kingdom.

Such experiments should be encouraged, including in the context of international and national responses to climate change. The United States would find that addressing climate change instead of focusing only on growth would be good for bolstering the wellbeing of its population, and China would find that encouraging excessive wealth and consumption is unnecessary for its long-term development. This should aid cooperation between them.

Tax carbon at source and end fossil fuel subsidies. The coming climate crisis can only be averted if the world moves quickly to transition away from carbon-based fuels. We need to find ways to convince people in the West to drive less, to fly on holidays less often (or not at all), and to consume less. And we need to find ways of persuading the world's growing middle classes from adopting behaviors that exacerbate climate change. One strategy for making this happen is to increase the cost of carbon substantially, thereby making coal, oil, and gas less attractive while making alternative fuels (for example, wind, solar, geothermal, tidal, and biomass) more attractive.[4] Taxing carbon fuels at source, as described in chapter 6, would generate enormous financial resources that could be transferred *directly* to people to help them cope with the transition to a post-carbon world. Ending existing gargantuan subsidies for fossil fuels would in turn provide funds that could be partly returned to the public (possibly through lower taxes) and partly used to subsidize cleaner, alternative fuels, and to build public transport and to advance social programs that improve people's lives. The beneficiaries of government policies would be citizens instead of big corporations, with greenhouse gas pollution falling at the same time.

When people realize that most of them will be better off financially with such steps, there may be enough political support to overcome entrenched interests, especially the coal and petroleum industries that have become accustomed to subsidies over many decades. This is a potential vote winner for politicians able to articulate the benefits for citizens. Once such changes and financial transfers are in place, it would be almost impossible politically to return to the current system of favoring fossil fuels.

Do all that is possible through government policies to empower people to live sustainably. People (and businesses) can be encouraged to live and operate sustainably through taxes and regulations. But it is the job of governments to make this as easy as possible by empowering them with knowledge and the means to live good lives without exacerbating climate change. This treatment would include things like much improved public transport infrastructure, energy codes that result in carbon-neutral buildings (or buildings that produce more energy than they consume), education and research that equip people and industry to transition toward sustainability and adjust to a world impacted by climate change, and foreign aid regimes that enable people in other nations (whether through financial assistance, training, or technology transfer) to cope with climate change and live in ways that minimize individual and societal contributions to it.

This also requires more democracy to enable people to shape their societies rather than having corporations do so. One might counter that democracy is part of the problem: because most people want low energy prices and inexpensive transport, they are unlikely to vote for politicians who support action on climate change. Insofar as this is true, it highlights the importance of government policies, including education policies, that foster people's understanding of how their wellbeing is related to climate change. Until citizens realize that the ways of life they have come to accept, which are heavily reliant on highly subsidized and highly polluting fossil fuels, are doing them more harm than good, many people will indeed vote to support policies that exacerbate climate change. The key is to use government policy to help people realize that doing so is an act of self-harm.

How to fix addictions of modernity

Max Koch believes that "it cannot be excluded that what is today called the 'Western way of life' will earn our generation a place in history books on a par with mass murderers: people who committed a crime against future generations of humanity."[5] Regardless of whether we accept such an indictment, the practical effects of climate change will inevitably violate the fundamental human rights of millions, and possibly billions, of people. From this come obligations for capable individuals. However, as Andrew Simms painfully points out, most people "are still seriously in denial about global warming, both as individuals and as a culture. We are in denial about the changes it demands in our lives. We need psychologists to help us stop rationalizing our self-destructive behavior, as much as we need wind farms for an alternative energy supply."[6] The sort of denial Simms points to might make sense or be easily understood (albeit still condemned) if affluent people generally benefited from the modern way of life and the individual and collective addictions to it. However, to a great extent they do not, and indeed it often makes them worse off. This is one great paradox of climate change: its causes are also causing harms (unrelated to climate impacts) to the very individuals driving those causes.

Material selfishness, whether voluntary or not, is a major cause of climate change. But materialism does not enhance human wellbeing. In contrast, living lives that promote environmental security can simultaneously mitigate greenhouse gas pollution and promote wellbeing. Jon Barnett summarizes what we should be doing as individuals to bolster environmental security: "consuming less, consuming with greater discernment, and being more involved in actions at all scales from local to global for human and ecological causes."[7] Other actions that people can undertake include becoming more self-sufficient where possible, ensuring that any investments they have are "green," using public transport or transporting themselves when possible (by walking and biking), spending far less time shopping and more time with family and friends, eating less energy-intensive foods, avoiding products and companies that are environmentally harmful while supporting those that are the opposite, supporting local businesses and those that focus more on employment than production, getting involved in local politics and communities, and lobbying governments to do what is necessary to protect the environment.[8]

All of this requires that people become more conscious – some would say more mindful – of what they do. Pausing to think about one's behaviors can go a long way.

Ultimately, for individuals it comes down to thinking hard about what will make them happy and what will promote their wellbeing, basing their decisions on rationality and science, and acting accordingly. Everyone should work hard to rewire his or her brain to garner pleasure and satisfaction from doing what will make one happy rather than, like young children and addicts, doing what feels good for the moment but harms oneself over time. At the very least, individuals everywhere need to be helped in understanding that happiness and affluence are not directly linked: affluent people can find greater happiness in consuming fewer things while consuming more of what makes life worth living. The ultimate message is that by trying to maximize the wellbeing and happiness of people, rather than focusing on the narrowly perceived interests of economies, industries, and whole nations as currently perceived, climate politics can help to reverse the growing emissions of greenhouse gases and limit the tragedy of the atmospheric commons.

What would prescriptions for the world's growing addictions of modernity look like? The primary objective should be the realization of human wellbeing through sustainability, and vice versa. Treatments might include the following types of government policies and individual actions:

Do all that is possible to end the individual focus on growth in material consumption and wealth as perceived sources of happiness and wellbeing. Much as it is important for whole nations and societies to come to grips with the fixation on economic growth, so must affluent individuals soon come to see that growth in material possessions and wealth are unlikely to translate into happiness and improved wellbeing. For governments of developed nations, this means ending constant references to consumption, growth, and per capita income as positive measures, instead conveying accurate messages about citizens' wellbeing: beyond a point, consumption can be counterproductive for individuals, even as it may continue to be beneficial for businesses and some whole nations. Aspirations for excessive wealth, possessions, and consumption should be treated as harmful, akin to other individual and social harms, such as smoking, use of narcotics, and gambling. This might mean that businesses would no longer be allowed to spend billions of dollars encouraging people to consume things that they do not need, least of all things that serve little useful purpose while doing great environmental harm. At the very least, advertising should convey messages about what products do rather than about the imagined lifestyles they seldom bring. Advertising might even come with warning labels: "Excessive consumption of this product may be hazardous to your wellbeing!"

But it is not enough to tell people that overconsumption will not bring happiness or ensure their long-term wellbeing, or to warn them of the dangers of overconsumption. It is necessary to help them identify and gain access to alternative means of achieving happiness and lasting wellbeing. For example, laws that prevent businesses from requiring employees to work more hours than they desire might be enacted, thereby giving people the option to work less and spend more time with family and friends.

Put in place policies that encourage sustainable living while improving the wellbeing of the majority of people. Combined with policies that encourage people to escape the growth fixation, governments should implement creative and proactive schemes that encourage people to do what is in their best long-term interests and in the best interests of the environment. Examples of the kind of policies that ought to be implemented include personal emissions (or carbon) trading schemes. Such schemes would allocate a science-based greenhouse gas emissions limit for each person, probably of the order of 1–2 tons of carbon equivalent per year.[9] Climate-related pollution ratings could be assigned to all products and services (or more likely categories of them to avoid having to classify each individual product or service) and then modern information technology (likely in the form of individual smart cards) could be used to measure individual emissions from consumption and to assign credits or debits. Individuals that consume below their annual allocation could sell their surplus. They would receive a payment, likely into their personal bank accounts. Those individuals who exceed their entitlement would have to purchase credits from others. These schemes would include both floors in emissions so that the poor would not be asked or coerced to sell off emissions entitlements required to meet their needs, and ceilings so that the wealthy could not purchase unlimited entitlements to pollute, thereby undermining efforts to address climate change.

Such schemes might be very popular with majorities in developing countries because many people would receive payments. Combined with carbon taxes at source that deliver funds into people's bank accounts, potential opposition in developed societies could be averted and even turned into support.

Educate for happiness, wellbeing and global citizenship. This would involve education from pre-school through university to train global citizens who seek good lives of happiness and wellbeing for all within environmental limits. It would also involve public education campaigns to develop understanding among citizens of the consequences of climate change for their wellbeing and the advantages of living more sustainable lives. People need a very good understanding of the role of human beings in ecology and the importance of environmental health for human wellbeing. This would help to overcome the increasingly absurd and utterly destructive climate skepticism and denial that continues in some nations, especially the United States. Environmental education should be combined with education that helps people to understand the true sources of happiness, which tend to be found in environmentally sustainable lifestyles. Such programs would be a contrast to most school curricula and public education programs, which now tend to encourage the attractions of wealth and material consumption, prioritize the present over the future, and perpetuate the fiction that there is a dividing line between people's interests and what is good for the environment – the false notion that one comes at the expense of the other, when in reality they are virtually one and the same.

Education should also be much more about people's practical membership in a wider global community. Climate change has forced everyone into a common global community because the behaviors of people on one side of the planet affect those on the other side. One cannot overstate the importance of education in this context because, without a change in public understanding and values democratic forces will not push for necessary change.

For individuals, live more sustainable and "simpler" lives that simultaneously reduce individual greenhouse gas emissions and enhance wellbeing. This means that each individual should put her or his own happiness and wellbeing, and that of her or his family, before that of businesses and traditional measures of economic growth. It means taking advantage of every opportunity to live more sustainably, in the process finding more time and resources for improving one's physical and mental health.[10] By doing what is actually best for themselves, individuals would do more than anything to reduce greenhouse gas pollution. This would involve each person consuming what he or she needs and that which brings long-term happiness, rather than consuming what media and advertising tell people they ought to consume. For example, people would consume more time with family and less time shopping. They would devote more time to helping their communities, rather than working harder to earn money to buy unnecessary material possessions. For those who are able to do so, it means consuming "green" and "environmentally friendly" products when there is no alternative to consumption. It might mean eating locally grown foods when they are available and affordable, and certainly consuming far less meat, or no meat at all, to limit one's environmental impact. It probably means an end to flying on distant holidays, and driving cars would have to be cut back drastically in places where it is now commonplace (at least until environmentally benign automobiles become prevalent) unless doing so is absolutely necessary.

For people who are so inclined, it might mean not having children.[11] For most people, it would mean having as few children as possible and raising them to have strong environmental and social values and encouraging them to enjoy good lives that do not exacerbate climate change. Teaching kids to want more stuff does them (and the environment) a great disservice.

For individuals, support politicians and political parties that want to create institutions and implement policies designed to enable sustainable living and greater wellbeing. People should vote for politicians who support robust action on climate change and oppose policies that prevent such action.[12] They should support government policies and programs that help them to live more sustainable and happier lives, while opposing those that do not. Not everyone lives in a free society where this can be done easily, but in most nations it is possible for people to either vote for politicians who have the public's real long-term interests in mind or advocate for (or at least support) government policies that do likewise.

Awareness, much of which can come from widespread education, is of course a prerequisite for this sort of voting behavior. This is not a naive proposal (at least it is not intended to be one). People tend to vote to promote their own interests and to promote values they hold dear. Better education can help people to see that policies for environmental sustainability are in their interest, and that such policies are important means to achieving social justice and community wellbeing, both locally and globally.

Again, none of these "treatments" for what is wrong with climate politics will by themselves be sufficient to stop climate change. They are necessary but not sufficient for addressing a problem that the world has waited too long to tackle. However, by earnestly and aggressively applying them, along with other proactive policies and actions, people and governments will be taking important and very significant steps toward finally addressing the problem and all of its harmful consequences for humanity and for the natural world. In contrast, if the world avoids these types of remedies, the future will be a very unhappy one indeed.

None of these proposed treatments will be easy to implement; some may turn out to be too difficult. But politics is seldom easy, at least not if one wishes to bring about major change. And major change is what is needed. At the very least, there must be an end to continuing with business as usual and continuing to live as though the earth's climate system can forever compensate for humanity's growing greenhouse gas pollution.

The human politics of climate change

One assumption made throughout this book is that the actors involved in climate politics are largely self-interested. This is not meant to be critical. It is intended to reflect reality. Of course, there are exceptions. People, government officials, and even nations can sometimes be altruistic, albeit rarely so when their perceived interests, least of all vital ones, are at stake. The question becomes how we can harness this self-interestedness to help solve the climate crisis. The answer is not to simplistically appeal to people's love of nature or their care for future generations. Appeals of this kind are welcome, and there is a very strong case for saying that we should be focusing far more attention on protecting and caring for nonhuman nature because it has intrinsic value quite apart from human beings.[13] However, there is too little time for such appeals to have the necessary impact, not least because they have not worked so far in addressing many tough environmental problems. In contrast, focusing on people and their interests as a means to promote and actualize environmental sustainability is likely to be more effective in the time that may remain to avert the worst effects of climate change – probably a decade or two.

Ultimately, what is most wrong with climate politics is the failure to put the genuine long-term interests and wellbeing of people before the interests of other actors (industrial lobbies, entrenched domestic political interests, oil and coal companies, selfish politicians) in national and international societies, and indeed before those of citizens who, like drug addicts, too often want to behave in ways that are bad for themselves and their grandchildren. This is exacerbated by dangerous ideas, such as conceptions of capitalism and the luster of economic growth premised on material consumption, and a conception of state sovereignty that puts defense of the potentially ill-conceived "national interest" before that of protecting and promoting the actual long-term wellbeing of each nation's citizens while completely ignoring the welfare of people living in other nations and in the future.

The problem is how to strike a realistic balance between selfish interests of nations and governments – determined most often by a constellation of powerful vested interests within each nation – and the global good of a healthy climate system that provides for the needs of everyone. A greater political focus, internationally, nationally, and individually, on genuine *human* interests is a necessary and potentially realistic approach to doing that.

An important step for fixing climate politics is correcting misconceptions of self-interest among publics (and many politicians). The interests of individuals, societies, and nations are the same as the interests of nature.[14] If sovereign nations exist to protect and defend the interests of those who reside within their borders, then to allow climate change, let alone to participate in perpetuating it, is to do the opposite of what nations are supposed to do. It is to deny the *raison d'être* of the nation-state (unless one cynically believes that the state system is all about promoting the interests of powerful narrow interests within nations).[15] If governments govern for the benefit of as many citizens as possible, it makes little sense – especially in the case of the most vulnerable places and peoples – to deny that some people (the affluent) are more responsible for causing climate change and are more capable of doing something about it than are others (the poor), or to continue believing that material growth will perpetually increase the common welfare, regardless of impending environmental limits to that growth.[16] If individuals genuinely want to achieve health, happiness, and long-term wellbeing for themselves, their kin, and their communities, it is counterproductive, and enormously harmful to the environment, to propagate and continue addictions to material consumption and wealth.

Admittedly, preoccupations with national interests, economic growth, and consumerism can bring gratification in the short term. But the realities of climate change mean that this gratification comes at great cost, undermining national, human, and environmental security in the long term.

Climate politics – internationally, nationally, and locally – should be much more about people. It should be about protecting their long-term interests while also protecting the interests of future generations, and about helping people to live healthier and happier lives. It means trying much harder to eliminate poverty and other vulnerabilities to climate change, but also discouraging the excesses of affluence that diminish health and happiness. To be sure, economic and social systems, as well as existing infrastructure, dictate many human behaviors that contribute to climate change. We cannot discount these forces. But we should not surrender to them either. Governments can help people to lower their impact on the earth's climate through regulations, pricing mechanisms, infrastructure development, and education, and especially by ending policies that encourage climate pollution (including fossil-fuel and livestock subsidies).

Those individuals who are capable of acting should do so, regardless of what government does. They ought not to wait for a world to come about in which everyone is living within the carrying capacity of the earth; they should start working hard right now to live sustainably.[17] *Each capable person should do all that he or she can* to reduce his or her contribution to climate change, and indeed to help its victims. This does not mean that everyone can reduce his or her greenhouse gas emissions to a level that the earth can withstand. But each person who is not poor, and especially the world's affluent people, ought to try. They can do this by making their impact on the environment part of their conscious thought – a consciousness upon which they seek to act every day.[18] Ultimately, everyone should be good global citizens for the benefit of others and for themselves. This can be done in a way that broadcasts one's environmentally less harmful behaviors to neighbors, friends, colleagues, and the wider community. Capable individuals also have the obligation to do what they can to encourage a climate politics that is genuinely "pro-climate." They can start by supporting political parties and politicians who want to work toward creating a post-carbon world.

James Gustave Speth believes that "the most fundamental

transition is the transition in culture and consciousness. The change that is needed can be best put as . . . caring, nurturing, and sustaining."[19] He quotes Paul Raskin and others, describing a future where these values prevail:

> Preferred lifestyles combine material sufficiency with qualitative fulfillment. Conspicuous consumption and glitter are viewed as vulgar throwbacks to an earlier era. The pursuit of the well-lived life turns to the quality of existence – creativity, ideas, culture, human relationships and harmonious relationships with nature. . . . The economy is understood as the means to these ends, rather than an end in itself.[20]

This sounds almost utopian by current standards. But when one pauses to think about it, this is precisely the world most of us would want to live in. Certainly, it is better than striving to consume for the sake of consuming when one knows it does us little good – and quite a lot of harm – while also doing immeasurable harm to the global environment upon which all people, present and future, ultimately depend for everything. Surely trying to achieve such a world, however difficult or distant it may be, is far preferable to the path we are on today.

The cure for what ails climate politics is to put people's genuine long-term interests first. By making climate politics much more about human beings and their actual interests – which happen to coincide with the interests of wider humanity, the natural world, and the earth's climate system in particular – leaders, diplomats, executives, and ordinary individuals have a chance to do what is necessary to slow and eventually reverse the pollution that is causing climate change and to free up the resources needed to help the world cope with its unavoidable effects. If in doing this we fail to solve the climate crisis, we will nevertheless be more secure and better off. We have nothing to lose but our obsessions and addictions. What's wrong with climate politics and how to fix it – that's us.

Notes

CHAPTER I INTRODUCTION

1 See, for example, IPCC (2007).
2 This refers to CO_2 emissions from energy use only (International Energy Agency 2011b). In addition to heating the planet, CO_2 emissions are contributing to ocean acidification, with potentially grave consequences for marine ecosystems and fisheries (Garnaut 2011: 13).
3 Record-keeping began in 1880. The 2010 temperature matched that of 2005 (NOAA 2011).
4 World Meteorological Association (2012: 2).
5 See, for example, Global Change Research Program (2009), which highlights ongoing impacts in the United States, and for information on scientists' growing certainty about the relationship between ongoing extreme weather events and human-induced climate change, see Conner (2011) and Schiermeier (2011).
6 Stern (2007).
7 Lipschutz and Peck (2010: 198)
8 Giddens (2008: 5).
9 Throughout the book, the terms "country," "nation," "nation-state," and "state" are used synonymously to refer to sovereign states (for example, Australia, China, India). The term "climate change" refers to anthropogenic (human-caused) climate change.
10 IPCC (2007).
11 See, for example, Hansen et al. (2008), Field et al. (2011), McMullen and Jabbour (2009), and Garnaut (2011).
12 NASA (2011).
13 Baumert, Herzog, and Pershing (2005: 17).
14 Hansen et al. (2008: 15; see also Hansen 2009). The implication is that we must stop all coal burning and find other ways to

reduce atmospheric concentrations of CO_2 very substantially. Brown (2011: 96) proposes cutting CO_2 emissions 80 percent by 2020 to stabilize concentrations at 400 ppm, followed by additional efforts to reduce them to 350 ppm as quickly as possible.

15 Energy Information Administration (2009: 131), International Energy Agency (2011b).
16 See Peters et al. (2012).
17 International Energy Agency (2012).
18 Siegenthaler et al. (2005) and Spahni et al. (2005). Greenhouse gases described were CO_2, methane, and nitrous oxide.
19 IPCC (2007), Jackson (2009: 12, 67).
20 OECD (2012: 72).
21 International Energy Agency (2011a: 1).
22 See Harris (2010c).
23 Compare Hardin (1968).
24 See, for example, Vanderheiden (2008: 186) and Gardiner (2011a: 414–20).
25 Gardiner (2011a).
26 I previously discussed ideas in this and the next paragraph in Harris (2010c: 215–17).
27 Hansen (2009: 184).
28 Hansen (2009: 184).
29 Hansen (2009: 184–5)
30 Compare Tollefson and Gilbert (2012).
31 Grieneison and Zhang (2011).
32 Washington and Cook (2011).
33 Dunlap and McCright (2011).
34 See Pooley (2010).
35 See Yamin and Depledge (2004), Bulkeley and Newell (2010).
36 Bulkeley and Betsill (2003).
37 See Dower (2011).
38 Betsill and Bulkeley (2006), Lipschutz and McKendry (2011).
39 M. Hoffman (2011).
40 M. Hoffman (2011: 19–24). See also Betsill and Bulkeley (2006) and Bulkeley (2011).
41 Peters and Hertwich (2008), Harris and Symons (forthcoming).
42 Roberts and Parks (2007b), Davis and Caldeira (2010), C. Fischer (2011).
43 Launder and Thompson (2010), Hawkins (2010).

44 Pinkse and Kolk (2009), Meckling (2011).

45 Mitchell (2012: 26). See Huesemann and Huesemann (2011).

46 Urry (2011: 152). See Sorrell (2009).

47 Dilworth (2010: 436).

48 On geo-engineering, see, for example, Flannery (2005: 249–57), Fleming (2010: 225–68), Hamilton (2010: 159–67, 174–82), and Gardiner (2011a: 339–96).

49 Ho (2008), Shaffer (2010).

50 For a full discussion of the ocean impacts of climate change, including warming, acidification, and sea-level rise, see Noone, Sumaila, and Diaz (2012).

51 On the psychology of climate denial, see, for example, Norgaard (2011).

52 Kagawa and Selby (2009), Curry (2011: 159–83).

53 News coverage of climate change increased sharply in 2009, probably in response to the Copenhagen climate conference held that year, but dropped sharply in 2010 (D. Fischer 2011).

54 Boykoff and Roberts (2007). See chapter 3.

55 See Russell (2010).

56 Bord, O'Conner, and Fisher (2000).

57 Inglehart (1990).

58 Myers and Kent (2004).

59 Honkonen (2009).

60 Roberts and Parks (2007a), Parks and Roberts (2009: 165).

61 Compare Weiss (2009: 19–48). See Biermann (2006).

62 Olivier et al. (2011: 12).

63 Botzen, Gowdy, and Van Den Bergh (2008), Olivier et al. (2011: 12–15).

64 For a description of what little cooperation there is between the two nations in this context, see Harris (2012).

65 On the relationships between growing rates of obesity and climate change, see Egger and Swinburn (2010).

66 This is not to suggest that nature and indeed other species should not also be the objects of climate politics. But that is another book.

67 This a major argument made in Harris (2010c).

CHAPTER 2 CANCER OF WESTPHALIA: CLIMATE
DIPLOMACY AND THE INTERNATIONAL SYSTEM

1 O'Lear (2010: 34). See Paterson and Stripple (2007).
2 Agnew (1994), Paterson and Stripple (2007: 156), O'Lear (2010: 36).
3 Paterson and Stripple (2007: 157).
4 See Lumsdaine (1993) and Simms and Trimm (2011).
5 On "realism" in international relations, see Smith (1986).
6 Sharman (2012).
7 Roberts (2011).
8 Krasner (1983: 2).
9 On the conflicts between underlying norms and rules for addressing climate change, see Harris and Symons (2013).
10 Clapp and Dauvergne (2011: 23).
11 Compare Rosenau (1990).
12 See Speth (2004: 140–7).
13 For this section, compare Harris (2011b: 109–14) and see Keohane and Victor (2011).
14 Benedick (1998).
15 Young (2011: 83–116). Victor (2011) argues that this is a consequence of following the model of Montreal and other international environmental agreements, which addressed problems that are much easier to solve. For a *defense* of the climate change regime, see Depledge and Yamin (2009).
16 Proving the rule of unintended consequences, the Montreal Protocol has resulted in burgeoning global use of replacements for ozone-destroying chemicals, but these replacements are extremely powerful greenhouse gases. See Rosenthal and Lehren (2012).
17 Bolin (2008).
18 United Nations (1992: Art. 2).
19 United Nations (1992: Preamble).
20 Many additional meetings are held to prepare the way for each conference of the parties. The following summary highlights only the major conferences themselves. For a detailed summary, see Leal-Arcas (2011).
21 See Honkonen (2009).
22 Grubb, Vrolijk, and Brack (1999).

23 Elzen and de Moor (2002). Hansen (2009: 182–3) describes the failure of the Kyoto Protocol.
24 On the evolution toward adaptation policies in the climate agreements and negotiations, see Schipper (2006).
25 Annan (2006).
26 Pew Center (2007b).
27 IISD (2009a).
28 UNFCCC (2009). See IISD (2009b).
29 Falkner, Stephan, and Vogler (2011: 216).
30 IISD (2009b).
31 Monbiot (2006) proposes a potentially feasible way of doing it, but his plan requires reducing CO_2 emissions 90 percent by 2030.
32 IISD (2011: 12–14).
33 UNFCCC (2011).
34 China Daily (2011), Shi (2011).
35 Peters et al. (2012).
36 Harvey and Vidal (2011), Hertsgaard (2012).
37 Vidal and Harvey (2011).
38 Kent (2011).
39 See Nikiforuk (2010) and Marsden (2011).
40 Harris (2010c: 74–95).
41 See Schreurs and Tiberghien (2007) and Harris (2008b). This greater concern in parts of Europe with the wellbeing of others compared to, say, relatively less concern by the United States is consistent with the former nations' domestic welfare principles. In short, nations with more generous domestic welfare systems are more generous in terms of global welfare. See Lumsdaine (1993).
42 See, for example, Fingar (2008), Dalby (2009: 148–52), German Advisory Council on Climate Change (2009), and Moran (2011).
43 Campbell (2008) is such an approach.
44 The serious economic slowdown that began in 2008 does seem to have lowered US greenhouse gas emissions, and new fuel-economy standards may help to perpetuate this trend.
45 Roberts (2011: 776).
46 Kasa, Gullberg, and Heggelund (2008), Hallding, Han, and Olsson (2009: 9, 14), Christoff (2010: 647–8, 652).
47 Hertwich and Peters (2009). See Berners-Lee (2011).

48 See, for example, Energy Information Administration (2010). Of course, if one looks at per capita emissions, developing countries pollute much less per person than do developed ones.

49 See the World Resources Institute, Climate Analysis Indicators Tool, http://cait.wri.org/.

50 M. Hoffman (2011: 16–17).

51 See, for example, Frost (2011).

52 Harris (2008b). See Paterson (2009).

53 Marsden (2011: 287).

54 On the "society of states," see Bull (2002).

55 Dinar (2011: 60), citing the ideas of Stern (1999: 138).

56 See chapter 5 and Harris (2011c).

57 See Schreurs (2008) and M. Hoffman (2011).

58 Young (2011: 83–116). See Harris (2007) and, for another critique of climate diplomacy, Victor (2011: 203–40).

59 See Bodansky (2010: 112–17) and Hulme (2009).

60 Humphreys (2010b: 4–8) explains the "silence on human rights" among scientists, scholars, and others concerned about climate change.

CHAPTER 3 MALIGNANCY OF THE GREAT POLLUTERS: THE UNITED STATES AND CHINA

1 Parts of this chapter build on Harris (2009, 2010a, 2011a, 2012).

2 World Resources Institute, Climate Analysis Indicators Tool, http://cait.wri.org/.

3 On US–China climate-related cooperation, see Harris (2012).

4 Olivier et al. (2011: 25); International Energy Agency (2012).

5 Jamieson (2008: 200), among other scholars, quotes President Bush himself saying this at the summit, and US officials were saying it in advance (see, for example, Elmer-Dewitt 1992).

6 Park (2000: 80–2).

7 Park (2000: 80–2).

8 See Harris (2000, 2001).

9 Harris (2001: 106–10).

10 Betsill (2000: 215).

11 Anderson (2001).

12 Austin and Phoenix (2005).

13 Dunlap and McCright (2010 : 249).

14 Nisbet (2009), McKibben (2010), McCright and Dunlap (2011).
15 See Harris (2009), Carson and Roman (2010).
16 See Pooley (2010), Carson (2012).
17 In June 2012, a federal appeals court upheld the right of the Environmental Protection Agency to regulate greenhouse gas emissions.
18 Christoff (2010: 649–51).
19 See Chatrchyan and Doughman (2008), Schneider et al. (2010: 356–76), Bradley (2011).
20 Brewer and Pease (2008), Desombre (2011).
21 See Pooley (2010).
22 See McCright and Dunlap (2010), Union of Concerned Scientists (2012).
23 Lester (2010), Willman (2010), Boykoff (2011).
24 Oreskes and Conway (2010: 169–215).
25 See Leiserowitz et al. (2012).
26 Netherlands Environmental Assessment Agency (2007, 2008).
27 Friedman and ClimateWire (2012).
28 Netherlands Environmental Assessment Agency (2007, 2008).
29 Boden, Marland, and Andres (2009).
30 Lewis and Gallagher (2011: 259).
31 Pew Center (2007a: 1), Botzen, Gowdy, and Van Den Bergh (2008), Boden, Marland, and Andres (2009).
32 Olivier et al. (2011: 12–15).
33 Botzen, Gowdy and Van Den Bergh (2008), Hallding, Han and Olsson (2009).
34 Minx et al. (2011).
35 Asia Society and Pew Center (2009: 18–20).
36 Gallagher (2006), Miliband (2011: 187).
37 Lewis and Gallagher (2011: 273).
38 Olivier et al. (2011: 11).
39 Asia Society and Pew Center (2009: 19).
40 See Hohne et al. (2011).
41 Holland (2010).
42 Schroeder (2009a: 57).
43 Lewis and Gallagher (2011: 269).
44 See Economy (2010), Watts (2010).
45 Christoff (2010: 644).
46 Miliband (2009).
47 For a brief summary of the long-term costs to China if it were to

participate in a global agreement to limit global warming to 3° C, see Holland (2012b).

48 Lynas (2009) and Miliband (2009). See Christoff (2010: 647–8).
49 Shi (2010).
50 Compare Lewis and Gallagher (2011: 273).
51 Lovbrand, Rindefjall and Nordqvist (2009: 85), Wang and Firestone (2010).
52 See Schroeder (2009b), Shin (2010).
53 Miao and Lang (2010: 410).
54 Harris and Yu (2009: 54–6), Miao and Lang (2010: 411).
55 Miao and Lang (2010: 412).
56 National Development and Reform Commission (2007: 24–5).
57 Richerzhagen and Scholz (2008), Miao and Lang (2010: 405). See Schreurs (2011).
58 Hunt (2011: 115).
59 Xinhua (2010).
60 Shi (2010).
61 Harris (2012).
62 Broder (2011).
63 On socially constructed ideas in international affairs, see Wendt (1999).
64 *Congressional Record*, 25 July 1997, passim, S8113–S8139. I previously described this in Harris (2001: 107).
65 See, for example, Bush (2001a, 2001b, 2002).
66 Giddens (2009: 188).
67 *Congressional Record*, 25 June 2009, S7043–44.
68 *Congressional Record*, 26 June 2009, H7641.
69 Vezirgiannidou (2008).
70 Gallagher (2009: 12), Zhang (2009b), Roozendaal (2009).
71 See Sussman (2004).
72 Fisher (2006: 480).
73 Bang (2011: 70).
74 Compare Harris (2008a: 923).
75 Vezirgiannidou (2008: 48–52).
76 Bodansky (2007: 62). See Claussen and Peace (2007).
77 See Fromkin (1970).
78 See Krugman (2011).
79 Bodansky (2007: 62).
80 National Development and Reform Commission (2007: 24).
81 Kobayashi (2003).

82 Lewis and Gallagher (2011: 269).
83 See Shirk (2007).
84 Drexhage and Murphy (2009: 3)
85 See Zhang (2003).
86 Kaufman (2010).
87 Ladislaw (2010: 1).
88 See Tankersley (2009).
89 Wiener (2008).
90 Lynas (2009).
91 Quoted in Watts, Carrington, and Goldenberg (2010).
92 Christoff (2010: 647–8).
93 Sunstein (2007: 2).
94 Zhang (2009a: 4–5).
95 Falkner, Stephan, and Vogler (2011: 210–11).
96 Falkner, Stephan, and Vogler (2011: 210–11).

CHAPTER 4 ADDICTIONS OF MODERNITY:
AFFLUENCE AND CONSUMPTION

1 Flannery (2005: 77).
2 See Shue (1996).
3 For example, a recent 700-page volume on climate change and
   society contained only one related index entry ("population
   growth") (Dryzek, Norgaard, and Schlosberg 2011: 725). One
   exception is O'Neill, MacKellar, and Lutz (2001).
4 K. O'Neill (2009: 42).
5 Dobkowski and Wallimann (2002: xxii).
6 US Census Bureau (2011).
7 Cohen (2010: 28–30).
8 United Nations Department of Economic and Social Affairs
   (2004, 2010).
9 Tobin (2010: 288).
10 Malthus (1959[1798]: 5).
11 Curry (2011: 199). See Dalby (2009: 16–20).
12 Erlich (1968).
13 Cohen (2010: 33–4).
14 See Royal Society (2012).
15 Flannery (2005: 78).
16 Flannery (2005: 78–9).

17 WWF (2010: 34).
18 WWF (2010: 34).
19 WWF (2010: 8).
20 B. O'Neill (2010).
21 B. O'Neill (2010: 92).
22 Mazur (2010: 1).
23 Cohen (2010: 27).
24 Bryner (2011: 112).
25 Diamond (2008).
26 Hartmann (2011).
27 Tobin (2010: 299).
28 Tobin (2010: 300).
29 Bryner (2011: 113).
30 Tobin (2010: 300).
31 Simms and Smith (2008: 3).
32 Hamilton (2010: 43).
33 See Erlich and Holdren (1971), Harte (2010: 137), Mitchell (2010: 48–52).
34 Heimann and Reichstein (2008).
35 Hamilton (2010: 43).
36 Ropke (2010: 123–4)
37 Ropke (2010: 128).
38 Barry (2012: 134).
39 Speth (2008: 7–8).
40 Barry (2012: 141).
41 Speth (2008: 107).
42 Hamilton (2010: 62).
43 Foreword to Jackson (2009: xiii).
44 Hamilton (2010: 49).
45 Hamilton (2010: 49).
46 See Newell and Paterson (2010) for a detailed discussion of causes and transformations.
47 Jackson (2009: 86).
48 Jackson (2009: 86).
49 Barry (2012: 133), original emphasis.
50 Hamilton (2010: 35). In contrast, Pielke (2010: 59) argues that "climate policies must be made compatible with economic growth as a precondition for their success."
51 See Meadows et al. (1972) and Meadows, Randers, and Meadows (2004).

52 See, for example, Simon (1981).
53 Simon and Kahn (1984: 2).
54 George (2010: 3).
55 See Meadows, Meadows, and Randers (1992), Bardi (2011), and Urry (2011: 165–6).
56 Jackson (2009: 11).
57 Jackson (2009: 13).
58 Gilding (2011).
59 Gilding (2011: 53).
60 Gilding (2011: 189).
61 Jackson (2009: 2).
62 Pelling, Manuel-Navarrete, and Redclift (2012: 2).
63 See Speth (2008), Jackson (2009), Koch (2012).
64 On affluenza, see De Graaf, Wann, and Naylor (2001), Hamilton and Denniss (2006), James (2007).
65 De Graaf, Wann, and Naylor (2001: 2).
66 Brennan and Lo (2011: 127).
67 Schor (1999).
68 De Graaf, Wann, and Naylor (2001: 83).
69 De Graaf, Wann, and Naylor (2001: 3)
70 Speth (2008: 147).
71 Chua (2000: 3).
72 Marsden (2011: 163).
73 See De Graaf, Wann, and Naylor (2001).
74 Jackson (2009: 50–1).
75 Jackson (2009: 52–3).
76 Gilding (2011: 191).
77 Lipschutz and Peck (2010: 190).
78 Ananthaswamy and Le Page (2012).
79 Jackson (2009: 13). "Developed nations" here refers to members of the Organization for Economic Cooperation and Development (OECD).
80 Myers and Kent (2004).
81 Myers and Kent (2004: 8).
82 Myers and Kent (2004: 8).
83 Kharas (2010: 36).
84 Myers and Kent (2004: 8–9).
85 Myers and Kent (2004: 5).
86 Myers and Kent (2004: 13–14).
87 Myers and Kent (2004: 15, 17, 19).

88 Myers and Kent (2004: 15).
89 Myers and Kent (2004: 15).
90 Myers and Kent (2004: 15).
91 Kharas (2010: 16, 27).
92 Kharas (2010: 28).
93 Myers and Kent (2004: 120).
94 Myers and Kent (2004: 19).
95 Kharas (2010: 35).
96 Gerth (2010).
97 Gerth (2010: 36).
98 Myers and Kent (2004: 15).
99 Farrell, Gersch, and Stephenson (2006: 64).
100 Myers and Kent (2004: 67).
101 Kharas (2010: 30). For Kharas, the middle class is defined as
     "those households with daily expenditures between USD10 and
     USD100 per person in purchasing power parity terms" (Kharas
     2010: 12).
102 Kharas (2010: 30).
103 Compare Gerth (2010: 200).
104 Kharas (2010: 8).
105 Diamond (2008).
106 Diamond (2008).
107 Myers and Kent (2004: 25).
108 Myers and Kent (2004: 26).
109 Kharas (2010: 30).
110 Myers and Kent (2004: 28–9).
111 Myers and Kent (2004: 10).
112 Myers and Kent (2004: 81).
113 See Paterson (2007).
114 Myers and Kent (2004: 20, 39).
115 Myers and Kent (2004: 39).
116 Food and Agriculture Organization (2007).
117 Food and Agriculture Organization (2007), Goodland and
     Anhang (2009), Worldwatch Institute (2011).
118 Pan et al. (2012).
119 Foley et al. (2011).
120 Speth (2008: 7).

CHAPTER 5 PEOPLE-CENTERED DIPLOMACY:
HUMAN RIGHTS AND GLOBALIZED JUSTICE

1 On this debate, see, for example, Barry and Eckersley (2005).
2 See the discussion on climate skepticism in chapters 1 and 2.
3 See, for example, Lovelock (2009) and Hamilton (2010).
4 See, for example, Calvin (2008), Stern (2009a), Brown (2009, 2011), Derber (2010), Metz (2010), Gilding (2011), and Blue Planet Laureates (2012).
5 For practical reasons, I continue to mostly ignore nonhuman victims of human-caused climate change. See Palmer (2011).
6 Engelman (2010: 97).
7 Robinson (2010: xviii).
8 Global Humanitarian Forum (2009: 22).
9 Global Humanitarian Forum (2009), DARA (2012).
10 Christian Aid (2007: 6). See Myers and Kent (2005: 51), Doyle and Chaturvedi (2011), and White (2011).
11 World Health Organization (2009).
12 Global Humanitarian Forum (2009).
13 African Development Bank et al. (2003: ix).
14 Cited in Villamizar (2011: 203–4).
15 Bulkeley and Newell (2010: 49).
16 Humphreys (2010b: 1). On loss of culture, see Figueroa (2011).
17 Bell (2012).
18 Caney (2010: 75–83). See Mearns and Norton (2010: 11–14).
19 Robinson (2010: xix). See McDonald (2010: 68–76).
20 Mearns and Norton (2010: 13). See also McInerney-Lankford, Darrow, and Rajamani (2011).
21 Humphreys (2010b: 2). See Adger et al. (2006), Harris and Symons (2010).
22 Limon (2009: 440).
23 UNDP (2007: 4), cited in Limon (2009: 443). See Nanda (2011).
24 International Council on Human Rights Policy (2008: 1).
25 Kang (2007: 2), cited in Limon (2009: 442).
26 McInerney-Lankford, Darrow, and Rajamani (2011: 56)
27 Robinson (2010: xviii).
28 Kang (2007: 4–5).
29 Kang (2007: 2).
30 Cullet (2010: 184).

31 See United Nations (2011). The council was ambivalent about whether it was the appropriate forum for discussing and responding to climate change.

32 Commission on Human Security (2003: 4), cited in O'Brien, St Clair, and Kristofferson (2010: 13). See United Nations (2010).

33 O'Brien, St Clair, and Kristofferson (2010: 5).

34 O'Brien, St Clair, and Kristofferson (2010: 4). The concept of human security is not without controversy (see Gasper 2010: 38–42).

35 Barnett (2001: 124).

36 Dalby (2009: 41–2).

37 Barnett (2001: 128). See Matthew et al. (2010).

38 For a survey of these principles and related proposals for climate justice, see, for example, Toth (1999) and Climate Action Network (2011).

39 Gardiner (2011b: 310–12).

40 Gardiner (2011b: 311).

41 See, for example, Howarth (2011).

42 Humphreys (2010a: 40–6).

43 Gardiner (2011b: 319).

44 The remainder of this section is based on ideas detailed in Harris (2010c).

45 I hesitate to use the term "cosmopolitan" because it tends to evoke quite emotional responses. For persuasive defenses of cosmopolitanism, see Brock (2009), van Hooft, (2009) and Held (2010, especially pp. 208–38).

46 See Brock (2009).

47 Held (2005: 10).

48 Heater (1996: 180).

49 Pogge (2008: 175).

50 Dower (2007: 28).

51 Elliott (2006: 350).

52 Elliott (2006: 350).

53 Elliott (2006: 351).

54 Attfield (2005: 41).

55 Vanderheiden (2008: 104).

56 Global Humanitarian Forum (2009: 62).

57 See Harris (2010c) for an analysis of global justice in climate politics.

58 For a detailed discussion of this corollary, particularly its

underlying justifications and normative merits, see Harris (2010c).
59 Maltais (2008: 594).
60 Cullet (2010: 185).
61 International Council on Human Rights Policy (2008: 6–9).
62 See, for example, United Nations Human Rights Council (2011: 2).
63 United Nations Human Rights Council (2011: 3).
64 Limon (2009: 445).
65 Limon (2009: 450–5).
66 Limon (2009: 450–1).
67 Limon (2009: 451). Here Limon is quoting a 2008 statement of the then Maldives president, Maumoon Abdul Gayoom.
68 Limon (2009: 451).
69 Limon (2009: 451).
70 Limon (2009: 451–2).
71 Limon (2009: 452).
72 Limon (2009: 455).
73 Limon (2009: 467).
74 See Harris (2010c).
75 Limon (2009: 467). Limon was more specifically proposing outcomes for the 2009 Copenhagen conference of the parties.
76 See, for example, Athanasiou and Baer (2002: 76–97), Humphreys (2010b: 12–16).
77 Meyer (2000).
78 Baer et al. (2008), Baer et al. (2009a), Baer et al. (2009b).
79 Baer et al. (2008: 5).
80 Baer, Fieldman, Athanasiou and Kartha (2009: 195).
81 Baer, Athanasiou, Kartha, and Kemp-Benedict (2009: 267).
82 Baer, Athanasiou, Kartha, and Kemp-Benedict (2009: 267).
83 Bear et al. (2008: 10). This income level is chosen because it is the point at which people start to join the global consuming class.
84 Baer et al. (2008: 13).
85 Chakravarty et al. (2009).
86 Chakravarty et al. (2009: 11884).
87 Chakravarty et al. (2009: 11885).
88 Chakravarty et al. (2009: 11888).
89 Chakravarty et al. (2009: 11888).

CHAPTER 6 DIFFERENTIATED RESPONSIBILITY:
NATIONAL AND INDIVIDUAL

1 See Ritter (2012).
2 Rafferty (2011), referring specifically to those nations outside the OECD.
3 Rafferty (2011).
4 Holland (2012a).
5 Holland (2012a).
6 Holland (2012a).
7 Holland (2012a).
8 For example, according to one study, in the United States about 40 percent of the carbon emissions arise directly from individual consumption (Szasz 2011).
9 McIntosh and Sarker (2011: 223).
10 Hertwich and Peters (2009), UNDP (2009: 195–6), Harris 2010a: 10861.
11 Boston Consulting Group (2010). The middle- and affluent-class households are defined here as those earning roughly US$9,000 per year.
12 Hurun Research Institute (2010).
13 Paterson and Stripple (2007: 159–60).
14 Paterson and Stripple (2007: 159).
15 Ananthapadmanabhan, Srinivas, and Gopal (2007).
16 One might argue that nation-states cannot be blamed for emissions because they have no physical existence; they are essentially ideas and sets of institutions.
17 Exceptions include flying to escape severe poverty (but such people cannot afford air travel), to escape persecution, and to receive life-saving medical care, as well as flying human organs for transplant.
18 Quoted in Kanter (2012).
19 Much of the illustration in this section is adapted from Harris (2010b).
20 See Elzen and Höhne (2008). A good way to picture these sources of pollution is by reference to a photograph of the world at night, revealing roughly where the most energy is used and thus where the most greenhouse pollution is emitted. See, for example, NASA's depiction at http://apod.nasa.gov/apod/ap001127.html.

21 For data and trends, see Baer et al. (2008) and Baer et al.
    (2009a).
22 See Beeson (2010).
23 Hamilton (2010: 94).
24 Gough and Meadowcroft (2011: 496).
25 Gough and Meadowcroft (2011: 496–8).
26 Gough and Meadowcroft (2011: 498).
27 Gough and Meadowcroft (2011: 500).
28 Gough and Meadowcroft (2011: 500).
29 Fawcett and Parag (2010: 329).
30 Fawcett and Parag (2010: 334). See House of Commons (2008)
    and Doran (2010).
31 Fawcett (2010: 6871–3); Fawcett and Parag (2010: 333).
32 Szasz (2011: 602–4).
33 Dobson (2009: 137).

CHAPTER 7 CONSUMPTION OF HAPPINESS:
SUSTAINABILITY AND WELLBEING

 1 Lane (1998).
 2 Princen (2005).
 3 Easterlin (2003: 11176).
 4 Gilding (2011: 203).
 5 Myers and Kent (2004: 121). See Singer (1997) and Crocker and
    Linden (1998).
 6 Jackson (2006a: 1).
 7 Gardiner (2011a: 70–1).
 8 Sheth, Sethia, and Srinivas (2011: 25).
 9 Sheth, Sethia, and Srinivas (2011: 25).
10 Compare Durning (1992: 40).
11 See Layard (2011).
12 Brennan and Lo (2011: 130).
13 Brennan and Lo (2011: 131).
14 Brennan and Lo (2011: 132).
15 Etzioni (2006: 169).
16 Speth (2008: 134).
17 Etzioni (2006: 166–7)
18 Bill McKibben's Foreword to Jackson (2009: xiii).
19 Myers and Kent (2004: 122).

20 Etzioni (2006: 166).
21 Diener and Seligman (2004: 10).
22 Jackson (2009: 40).
23 Jackson (2009: 59).
24 New Economics Foundation (2009: 3).
25 Jackson (2009: 40).
26 Cashman and Twaite (2009: 3).
27 Etzioni (2006: 167).
28 Etzioni (2006: 168).
29 Gardiner (2011a: 69), original emphasis.
30 Easterlin et al. (2012: 4).
31 Easterlin et al. (2012: 5).
32 Easterlin et al. (2012: 5).
33 Compare Jackson (2009: 41).
34 Barry (2012: 137).
35 Hamilton (2010: 71).
36 Hamilton (2010: 71), added emphasis.
37 Reuters (2012).
38 Durning (1992: 48).
39 Durning (1992: 48).
40 Barry (2012: 137).
41 See Leonard (2010).
42 Jackson (2009).
43 Jackson (2009: 16).
44 See Argyle (2002); compare Layard (2011). These account for roughly half of people's sense of happiness. The other half comes from genes, parenting, and other things beyond the direct control of individuals, such as social and economic policies to provide the best care during childhood. Simms and Smith (2008: 9–11).
45 Michaelis (2001), cited in Myers and Kent (2004: 142).
46 "Green growth" is also no solution. See U. Hoffman (2011).
47 George (2010: 276).
48 See UNDP (1990) on the original index, and UNDP (2011) on equity and sustainability.
49 UNU-IHDP and UNEP (2012).
50 See Bartelmus and Douglas (2008).
51 New Economics Foundation (2009: 3).
52 Bryner (2011: 119).
53 New Economics Foundation (2009: 9).
54 New Economics Foundation (2009: 9).

55 For analysis of this assertion, see Maniates and Meyer (2010).
56 Princen (2010a: 146).
57 Meyer (2010: 20–1).
58 Wapner (2010: 50).
59 Wapner (2010: 50).
60 Gilding (2011: 204).
61 Gilding (2011: 204–5).
62 Alexander and Ussher (2012).
63 Urry (2011).
64 Urry (2011: 166).
65 Compare Myers and Kent (2004: 144).
66 Simms and Smith (2008: 21).
67 Brown and Kasser (2005), cited in Jackson (2009: 151).
68 Elgin (2010)
69 Etzioni (2006: 167).
70 Jackson (2009: 151).
71 Elgin (2010: 4–5).
72 Sheth, Sethia, and Srinivas (2011: 27).
73 Sheth, Sethia, and Srinivas (2011: 21).
74 Sheth, Sethia, and Srinivas (2011: 27)
75 Sheth, Sethia, and Srinivas (2011: 27).
76 Sheth, Sethia, and Srinivas (2011: 28–9).
77 Sheth, Sethia, and Srinivas (2011: 28).
78 Jackson (2009: 14).
79 Jackson (2009: 15).
80 Barry (2012: 136).
81 Barry (2012: 138–9).
82 Boyle and Simms (2009: 99), quoted in Barry (2012: 140).
83 Harris (2004).
84 See Southerton, Chappells, and Van Vliet (2004), Jackson
    (2006b), and Lewis and Potter (2011).
85 Myers and Kent (2004: 24).
86 Bacon et al. (2008).
87 See Paterson (2008).
88 Hamilton (2010: 81–4).
89 Hansen (2009). There is no reason to believe yet that carbon
    capture is anything more than a dream. It will not come soon
    enough, even if it is possible to implement it on a grand scale.
    See Hamilton (2010: 159–67).
90 Brown (2011: 187).

91 Hansen (2009: 209–22).
92 Pielke (2010: 230) argues for a very small carbon tax imposed where fuels are taken from the ground, not to push down energy use but to provide funds to support energy technology innovation. On advantages of carbon taxes, see Nordhaus (2008: 148–64).
93 Pan et al. (2012).
94 Goodland and Anhang (2009), Worldwatch Institute (2011).
95 Eshel and Martin (2006), cited in Garnaut (2011: 126). This actually understates the benefits of changing to a meat-free diet because it does not account for emissions from deforestation related to livestock production.
96 Berners-Lee et al. (2012).
97 Hamerschlag (2011), Kissling and Singer (2012).
98 Sheth, Sethia, and Srinivas (2011: 27).
99 Sheth, Sethia, and Srinivas (2011: 27–8).
100 Lichtenberg (1998).
101 See, for example, Newell and Paterson (2010).

CHAPTER 8 CONCLUSION

1 See chapter 1 for some examples.
2 This assertion is not to diminish the vital importance of protecting other species and ecosystems, but it recognizes that people's interests (right or wrongly, depending on one's viewpoint) will come first in practical responses to climate change.
3 Compare Oxfam (2008).
4 For analyses of alternatives, see Letcher (2008).
5 Koch (2012: 178). By "Western way of life," Koch is referring more broadly to the practice of capitalism.
6 Simms (2005: ix–x).
7 Barnett (2001: 146).
8 Barnett (2001: 146–7).
9 See, for example, Stern (2009b: xv) and King, Richards, and Tyldesley (2011: 22). Some calculations put the maximum per capita emissions for avoiding dangerous climate change at less than 1 ton.
10 On how to live simply, see Alexander, Trainer, and Ussher (2012).

11 This rather obvious way to limit future climate pollution is of course highly controversial. See Burkeman (2010).

12 For encouragement, see Goodstein (2007).

13 Baxter (1999).

14 Cock (2007).

15 Peters (2009).

16 To alleviate doubt about the latter point, see UNEP (2012).

17 See Princen (2010b) and Cripps (2011).

18 See Reay (2005).

19 Speth (2004: 191).

20 Raskin et al. (2002: 44–5).

References

Adger, W. Neil, Paavola, Jouni, Huq, Saleemul, and Mace, M. J. (eds) (2006) *Fairness in Adaptation to Climate Change.* Cambridge, MA: MIT Press.

African Development Bank et al. (2003) *Poverty and Climate Change: Reducing the Vulnerability of the Poor through Adaptation.* Washington, DC: World Bank.

Agnew, John (1994) "The territorial trap: The geographical assumptions of international relations theory." *Review of International Political Economy* 1(1): 53–80.

Alexander, Samuel and Ussher, Simon (2012) "The Voluntary Simplicity Movement: A multi-national survey analysis in theoretical context." *Journal of Consumer Culture* 12(1): 66–86.

Alexander, Samuel, Trainer, Ted, and Ussher, Simon (2012) *The Simpler Way: A Practical Action Plan for Living More on Less.* Available at http://simplicityinstitute.org/wp-content/uploads/2011/04/The-Simpler-Way-Report-12a.pdf, last accessed 1.10.2012.

Ananthapadmanabhan, G., Srinivas, K., and Gopal, Vinuta (2007) "Hiding behind the poor." Bangalore: Greenpeace India Society.

Ananthaswamy, Anil and Le Page, Michael (2012, 28 January) "Power paradox: Clean might not be green forever." *New Scientist* 2849. Available at www.newscientist.com/article/mg21328491.700-power-paradox-clean-might-not-be-green-forever.html, last accessed 1.10.2012.

Anderson, J. W. (2001) "How the Kyoto Protocol developed: A brief history." In Michael A. Toman (ed.), *Climate Change Economics and Policy.* Washington: Resources for the Future, pp. 11–23.

Annan, Kofi (2006, 15 November) "Citing 'frightening lack of leadership' on climate change." UN Doc. SG/SM/10739. New York: UN Department of Public Information.

Argyle, Michael (2002) *The Psychology of Happiness.* London: Routledge.

Asia Society and Pew Center on Global Climate Change (2009) *Common Challenge, Collaborative Response: A Roadmap for US–China Cooperation on Energy and Climate Change.* Arlington, VA: Pew Center on Global Climate Change.

Athanasiou, Tom and Baer, Paul (2002) *Dead Heat: Global Justice and Global Warming.* New York: Seven Stories Press.

Attfield, Robin (2005) "Environmental values, nationalism, global citizenship and the common heritage of humanity." In Jouni Paavola and Ian Lowe (eds), *Environmental Values in a Globalizing World.* London: Routledge, pp. 75–104.

Austin, Andrew and Phoenix, Laurel (2005) "The neoconservative assault on the Earth: The environmental imperialism of the Bush administration." *Capitalism Nature Socialism* 16(2): 25–44.

Bacon, Christopher M., Mendez, V. Ernesto, Gliessman, Stephen R., and Fox, Jonathan A. (eds) (2008) *Confronting the Coffee Crisis: Fair Trade, Sustainable Livelihoods and Ecosystems in Mexico and Central America.* Cambridge, MA: MIT Press.

Baer, Paul and Sagar, Ambuj (2010) "Ethics, rights, and responsibilities." In Stephen H. Schneider, Armin Rosencranz, Michael D. Mastrandrea and Kristin Kuntz-Duriseti (eds), *Climate Change Science and Policy.* London: Island Press, pp. 262–9.

Baer, Paul, Athanasiou, Tom, Kartha, Sivan, and Kemp-Benedict, Eric (2008) *The Greenhouse Development Rights Framework: The Right to Development in a Climate Constrained World.* Berlin: Heinrich Boll Foundation, available at www.ecoequity.org/docs/TheGDRsFramework.pdf, last accessed 22.11.2012.

Baer, Paul, Athanasiou, Tom, Kartha, Sivan, and Kemp-Benedict, Eric (2009a) "Greenhouse development rights: A proposal for a fair global climate treaty." *Ethics, Place & Environment* 12(3): 267–81.

Baer, Paul, Fieldman, Glenn, Athanasiou, Tom, and Kartha, Sivan (2009b) "Greenhouse development rights: Towards an equitable framework for global climate policy." In Paul G. Harris (ed.), *The Politics of Climate Change.* London: Routledge, pp. 192–212.

Bang, Guri (2011) "Signed but not ratified: Limits to US participation in international environmental agreements." *Review of Policy Research* 28(1): 65–81.

Bardi, Ugo (2011) *The Limits to Growth Revisited.* New York: Springer.

Barnett, Jon (2001) *The Meaning of Environmental Security: Ecological Politics and Policy in the New Security Era.* London: Zed Books.

Barry, John (2012) "Climate change, the 'cancer stage of capitalism' and the return of limits to growth." In Mark Pelling, David Manuel-Navarrete, and Michael Redclift (eds), *Climate Change and the Crisis of Capitalism*. London: Routledge, pp. 129–42.

Barry, John and Eckersley, Robyn (eds) (2005) *The State and the Global Ecological Crisis*. Cambridge, MA: MIT Press.

Bartelmus, Peter and Douglas, Graham (2008) "Indicators of sustainable development." In Cutler J. Cleveland (ed.), *Encyclopedia of Earth*. Washington, DC: National Council for Science and the Environment.

Baumert, Kevin A., Herzog, Timothy, and Pershing, Jonathan (2005) *Navigating the Numbers: Greenhouse Gas Data and International Climate Policy*. Washington: World Resources Institute.

Baxter, Brian (1999) *Ecologism: An Introduction*. Edinburgh: Edinburgh University Press.

Beeson, Mark (2010) "The coming of environmental authoritarianism." *Environmental Politics* 19(2): 276–94.

Bell, Derek (2012) "Does anthropogenic climate change violate human rights?" In Gideon Calder and Catriona McKinnon (eds), *Climate Change and Liberal Priorities*. London: Routledge, pp. 9–34.

Benedick, Richard E. (1998) *Ozone Diplomacy: New Directions in Safeguarding the Planet*, 2nd edn. Cambridge, MA: Harvard University Press.

Berners-Lee, Mike (2011) *How Bad Are Bananas? The Carbon Footprint of Everything*. Vancouver: Greystone.

Berners-Lee, M., Hoolohan, C., Cammack, H., and Hewett, C. N. (2012) "The relative greenhouse gas impacts of realistic dietary choices." *Energy Policy*, DOI: 10.1016/j.enpol.2011.12.054.

Betsill, Michele M. (2000) "The United States and the evolution of international climate change norms." In Paul G. Harris (ed.), *Climate Change and American Foreign Policy*. New York: St Martin's Press, pp. 205–24.

Betsill, Michele M. and Bulkeley, Harriet (2006) "Cities and the multilevel governance of global climate change." *Global Governance* 12: 141–59.

Biermann, Frank (2006) "Global governance and the environment." In Michele M. Betsill, Kathryn Hochstetler, and Dimitris Stevis (eds), *Palgrave Advances in International Environmental Politics*. New York: Palgrave Macmillan, pp. 237–61.

Blue Planet Laureates (2012) "Environment and Development Challenges: The Imperative to Act." Final draft available at www.

unep.org/pdf/pressreleases/Blue_Planet_synthesis_paper.pdf, last accessed 1.10.2012.

Bodansky, Daniel (2007) "Targets and timetables: Good policy but bad politics?" In Joseph E. Aldy and Robert N. Stavins (eds), *Architectures for Agreement*. Cambridge: Cambridge University Press, pp. 57–66.

Bodansky, Daniel (2010) *The Art and Craft of International Environmental Law*. Cambridge, MA: Harvard University Press.

Boden, T. A., Marland, G., and Andres, R. J. (2009) "Global, regional and national fossil-fuel CO_2 emissions." Oak Ridge, TN: Oak Ridge National Laboratory. Available at http://cdiac.ornl.gov/trends/emis/overview_2006.html, accessed 1.10.2012.

Bolin, Burt (2008) *A History of the Science and Politics of Climate Change: The Role of the Intergovernmental Panel on Climate Change*. Cambridge: Cambridge University Press.

Bord, Richard J., O'Conner, Robert E., and Fisher, Ann (2000) "In what sense does the public need to understand global climate change?" *Public Understanding of Science* 9: 205–18.

Boston Consulting Group (2010) "The keys to the kingdom: Unlocking China's consumer power." BCG Report. Boston: Boston Consulting Group, available at www.bcg.co.jp/documents/file39807.pdf, last accessed 22.11.2012.

Botzen, W. J. W., Gowdy, J. M., and Van Den Bergh, J. C. J. M. (2008) "Cumulative CO_2 emissions: Shifting international responsibilities for climate debt." *Climate Policy* 8: 569–76.

Boykoff, Maxwell T. (2011) *Who Speaks for the Climate? Making Sense of Media Reporting on Climate Change*. Cambridge: Cambridge University Press.

Boykoff, Maxwell T. and Roberts, J. Timmons (2007) "Media coverage of climate change: Current trends, strengths, weaknesses." United Nations Development Program, Human Development Report Office, Occasional Paper.

Boyle, David and Simms, Andrew (2009) *The New Economics: A Bigger Picture*. London: Earthscan.

Bradley, Raymond S. (2011) *Global Warming and Political Intimidation: How Politicians Cracked Down on Scientists as the Earth Heated Up*. Boston: University of Massachusetts Press.

Brennan, Andrew and Lo, Y. S. (2011) "Two global crises, ethics renewal, and governance reform." In Ved P. Nanda (ed.), *Climate Change and Environmental Ethics*. London: Transaction, pp. 123–42.

Brewer, Paul R. and Pease, Andrew (2008) "Federal climate politics in the United States: Polarization and paralysis." In Hugh Compston and Ian Bailey (eds), *Turning Down the Heat*. Basingstoke: Palgrave Macmillan, pp. 85–103.

Brock, Gillian (2009) *Global Justice: A Cosmopolitan Account*. Oxford: Oxford University Press.

Broder, John M. (2011, 9 December) "At climate talks, China and US set to spar again." *International Herald Tribune*, p. 19.

Brown, Kirk and Kasser, Tim (2005) "Are psychological and ecological wellbeing compatible? The role of values, mindfulness, and lifestyle." *Social Indicators Research* 74(2): 349–68.

Brown, Lester (2009) *Plan B 4.0: Mobilizing to Save Civilization*. New York: W. W. Norton.

Brown, Lester (2011) *World on the Edge: How to Prevent Environmental and Economic Collapse*. London: Earthscan.

Bryner, Gary C. (2011) *Protecting the Global Environment*. London: Paradigm.

Bulkeley, Harriett (2011) "Cities and subnational governments." In John S. Dryzek, Richard B. Norgaard, and David Schlosberg (eds), *Oxford Handbook of Climate Change and Society*. Oxford: Oxford University Press, pp. 464–78.

Bulkeley, Harriett and Betsill, Michele (2003) *Cities and Climate Change: Urban Sustainability and Global Environmental Governance*. London: Routledge.

Bulkeley, Harriett and Newell, Peter (2010) *Governing Climate Change*. London: Routledge.

Bull, Hedley (2002) *The Anarchical Society: A Study of Order in World Politics*, 3rd edn. New York: Columbia University Press.

Burkeman, Oliver (2010, 13 February) "Climate change: Calling planet birth." *Guardian*, Weekend, p. 30.

Bush, George W. (2001a, 11 June) "President Bush discusses global climate change." Washington: White House Office of the Press Secretary, available at http://georgewbush-whitehouse.archives.gov/news/releases/2001/06/20010611-2.html, last accessed 1.10.2012.

Bush, George W. (2001b, 13 March) "Text of a letter from the President to Senators Hagel, Helms, Craig, and Roberts." Washington: White House Office of the Press Secretary, available at http://georgewbush-whitehouse.archives.gov/news/releases/2001/03/20010314.html, last accessed 1.10.2012.

Bush, George W. (2002, 14 February) "President announces clear skies & global climate change initiatives." Washington: White House

Office of the Press Secretary, available at http://georgewbush-white-house.archives.gov/news/releases/2002/02/20020214-5.html, last accessed 1.10.2012.

Calvin, William H. (2008) *Global Fever: How to Treat Climate Change.* Chicago: University of Chicago Press.

Campbell, Kurt M. (ed.) (2008) *Climate Cataclysm: The Foreign and National Security Implications of Climate Change.* Washington: Brookings Institution Press.

Caney, Simon (2010) "Climate change, human rights and moral thresholds." In Stephen Humphreys (ed.), *Human Rights and Climate Change.* Cambridge: Cambridge University Press, pp. 69–90.

Carson, Marcus (2012) "Paradigm shift in US climate policy but where is the system shift?" In Mark Pelling, David Manuel-Navarrete, and Michael Redclift (eds), *Climate Change and the Crisis of Capitalism.* London: Routledge, pp. 69–84.

Carson, Marcus and Roman, Mikael (2010) "Tipping point: Crossroads for US climate policy." In Constance Lever-Tracy (ed.), *Routledge Handbook of Climate Change and Society.* London: Routledge, pp. 379–404.

Cashman, Orla and Twaite, James A. (2009) *Toxic Wealth: How the Culture of Affluence Can Harm Us and Our Children.* Oxford: Praeger.

Chakravarty, Shoibal, Chikkatur, Ananth, Coninck, Heleen, Pacala, Stephen, Socolow, Robert, and Tavoni, Massimo (2009) "Sharing global CO_2 emissions among one billion high emitters." *PNAS* 106(29): 11884–8.

Chatrchyan, Allison M. and Doughman, Pamela M. (2008) "Climate policy in the USA: State and regional leadership." In Hugh Compston and Ian Bailey (eds), *Turning Down the Heat.* Basingstoke: Palgrave Macmillan, pp. 241–60.

China Daily (2011, 6 December) "China to accept binding climate treaty with conditions." *China Daily*, available at www.chinadaily.com.cn/china/2011-12/06/content_14220414.htm, last accessed 1.10.2012.

Christian Aid (2007) *Human Tide: The Real Migration Crisis.* London: Christian Aid, available at www.christianaid.org.uk/images/human-tide.pdf, last accessed 1.10.2012.

Christoff, Peter (2010) "Cold climate in Copenhagen: China and the United States at COP15." *Environmental Politics* 19(4): 637–56.

Chua, Beng-Huat (2000) "Consuming Asian: Ideas and issues." In Beng-Huat Chua (ed.), *Consumption in Asia.* London: Routledge, pp. 1–34.

Clapp, Jennifer and Dauvergne, Peter (2011) *Paths to a Green World*. Cambridge, MA: MIT Press.

Claussen, Eileen and Peace, Janet (2007) "Energy myth twelve: Climate policy will bankrupt the US economy." In Benjamin K. Sovacool and Marilyn A. Brown (eds), *Energy and American Society*. Dordrecht: Springer, pp. 311–40.

Climate Action Network (2011) "Fair effort sharing discussion paper." Beirut: Climate Action Network – International, available at www.climatenetwork.org/sites/default/files/CAN_effort_sharing_discussion_paper_25July2011_v2.pdf, last accessed 1.10.2012.

Cock, Jacklyn (2007) *The War Against Ourselves: Nature, Power and Justice*. Johannesburg: Witwatersrand University Press.

Cohen, Joel E. (2010) "Human population grows up." In Laurie Mazur (ed.), *A Pivotal Moment*. Washington, DC: Island Press, pp. 27–37.

Commission on Human Security (2003) *Human Security Now*. New York: Commission on Human Security.

Conner, Steve (2011, 1 July) "Extreme weather link 'can no longer be ignored.'" *The Independent*.

Cripps, Elizabeth (2011) "Climate change, collective responsibility and individual duties: What *I* must do if *we* fail to act." Paper for the general conference of the European Consortium for Political Research, University of Iceland, Reykjavik, 25–27 August.

Crocker, David A. and Linden, Toby (eds) (1998) *Ethics of Consumption: The Good Life, Justice and Global Stewardship*. New York: Rowman and Littlefield.

Cullet, Philippe (2010) "The Kyoto Protocol and vulnerability: Human rights and equity dimensions." In Stephen Humphreys (ed.), *Human Rights and Climate Change*. Cambridge: Cambridge University Press, pp. 183–206.

Curry, Patrick (2011) *Ecological Ethics: An Introduction*. Cambridge: Polity.

Dalby, Simon (2009) *Security and Environmental Change*. Cambridge: Polity.

DARA (2012) *Climate Vulnerability Monitor: A Guide to the Cold Calculus of a Hot Planet*. Geneva: DARA.

Davis, Steven J. and Caldeira, Ken (2010) "Consumption-based accounting of CO_2 emissions." *PNAS* 107(12): 5687–92.

De Graaf, John, Wann, David, and Naylor, Thomas H. (2001) *Affluenza: The All-Consuming Epidemic*. San Francisco: Berrett-Koehler.

Depledge, Joanna and Yamin, Farhana (2009) "The global

climate-change regime: A defence." In Dieter Helm and Cameron Hepburn (eds), *The Economics and Politics of Climate Change*. Oxford: Oxford University Press, pp. 433–53.

Derber, Charles (2010) *Green to Greed: Solving Climate Change and Remaking the Economy*. Boulder, CO: Paradigm.

Desombre, Elizabeth R. (2011) "The United States and global environmental politics: Domestic sources of US unilateralism." In Regina S. Axelrod, Stacy D. Vandeveer, and David L. Downie (eds), *The Global Environment*. Washington: CQ Press, pp. 192–212.

Diamond, Jared (2008, 2 January) "What's your consumption factor?" *New York Times*, available at www.nytimes.com/2008/01/02/opinion/02diamond.html?pagewanted=all&_r=0, last accessed 1.10.2012.

Diener, Ed and Seligman, Martin E. (2004) "Beyond money: Toward an economy of wellbeing." *Psychological Science in the Public Interest*, 5(1): 1–31.

Dilworth, Craig (2010) *Too Smart for Our Own Good: The Ecological Predicament of Humankind*. Cambridge: Cambridge University Press.

Dinar, Shlomi (2011) "Environmental security." In Gabriela Kutting (ed.), *Global Environmental Politics*. London: Routledge, pp. 56–71.

Dobkowski, Michael N. and Wallimann, Isidor (2002) "Introduction: On the edge of scarcity." In Michael N. Dobkowski and Isidor Wallimann (eds), *On the Edge of Scarcity*. Syracuse, NY: Syracuse University Press, pp. xxi–xxxi.

Dobson, Andy (2009) "Citizens, citizenship and governance for sustainability." In W. Neil Adger and Andrew Jordan (eds), *Governing Sustainability*. Cambridge: Cambridge University Press, pp. 125–41.

Doran, Peter (2010) "After Copenhagen: Bringing personal carbon trading home." In Duncan French (ed.), *Global Justice and Sustainable Development*. Leiden: Martinus Nijhoff Publishers, pp. 341–61.

Dower, Nigel (2007) *World Ethics: The New Agenda*. Edinburgh: Edinburgh University Press.

Dower, Nigel (2011) "Climate change and the cosmopolitan responsibility of individuals: Policy vanguards." In Paul G. Harris (ed.), *Ethics and Global Environmental Policy*. Cheltenham: Edward Elgar, pp. 42–65.

Doyle, Timothy and Chaturvedi, Sanjay (2011) "Climate refugees and security: Conceptualizations, categories, and contestations." In John S. Dryzek, Richard B. Norgaard, and David Schlosberg (eds), *Oxford*

Handbook of Climate Change and Society. Oxford: Oxford University Press, pp. 278–91.

Drexhage, John and Murphy, Deborah (2009) "Copenhagen: A memorable time for all the wrong reasons?" Winnipeg: International Institute for Sustainable Development.

Dryzek, John S., Norgaard, Richard B., and Schlosberg, David (eds) (2011) *Oxford Handbook of Climate Change and Society*. Oxford: Oxford University Press.

Dunlap, Riley E. and McCright, Aaron M. (2010) "Climate change denial: Sources, actors and strategies." In Constance Lever-Tracy (ed.), *Routledge Handbook of Climate Change and Society*. London: Routledge, pp. 240–59.

Dunlap, Riley E. and McCright, Aaron M (2011) "Organized climate change denial." In John S. Dryzek, Richard B. Norgaard, and David Schlosberg (eds), *Oxford Handbook of Climate Change and Society*. Oxford: Oxford University Press, pp. 144–60.

Durning, Alan (1992) *How Much Is Enough? The Consumer Society and the Future of the Earth*. New York: W. W. Norton.

Easterlin, Richard A. (2003) "Explaining happiness." *PNAS* 100 (19): 11176–83.

Easterlin, Richard A., Morgan, Robson, Switek, Malgorzata, and Wang, Fei (2012) "China's life satisfaction, 1990–2010." *PNAS* (14 May early online edn, doi: 10.1073/pnas. 1205672109), available at www. pnas.org/content/early/2012/05/09/1205672109.full.pdf+html, last accessed 1.10.2012.

Economy, Elizabeth C. (2010) *The River Runs Black: The Environmental Challenge to China's Future*, 2nd edn. Ithaca, NY: Cornell University Press.

Egger, Garry and Swinburn, Boyd (2010) *Planet Obesity: How We're Eating Ourselves and the Planet to Death*. Crows Nest, NSW: Allen and Unwin.

Elgin, Duane (2010) *Voluntary Simplicity*, 2nd edn. New York: Harper.

Elliott, Lorraine (2006) "Cosmopolitan environmental harm conventions." *Global Society* 20(3): 345–63.

Elmer-Dewitt, Philip (1992, 1 June) "Summit to save the Earth: Rich vs. poor." *Time*, available at www.time.com/time/magazine/article/0,9171,975656,00.html, last accessed 1.10.2012.

Elzen, Michel G. J. and de Moor, Andre P. G. (2002) "Analyzing the Kyoto Protocol under the Marrakesh Accords: Economic efficiency and environmental effectiveness." *Ecological Economics* 43: 141–58.

Elzen, Michel and Höhne, Niklas (2008) "Reductions of greenhouse gas emissions in Annex I and non-Annex I countries for meeting concentration stabilisation targets." *Climatic Change* 91: 249–74.

Energy Information Administration (2009) *International Energy Outlook 2009*. Washington: US Department of Energy.

Energy Information Administration (2010) *International Energy Outlook 2010*. Washington: US Department of Energy.

Engelman, Robert (2010) "Fair Weather, Lasting World." In Laurie Mazur (ed.), *A Pivotal Moment: Population, Justice and the Environmental Challenge*. Washington, DC: Island Press, pp. 95–107.

Erlich, Paul R. (1968) *The Population Bomb*. New York: Ballantine.

Erlich, Paul R. and Holdren, John P. (1971) "Impact of population growth." *Science* 171: 1212–17.

Eshel, Gidon and Martin, Pamela A. (2006) "Diet, energy and global warming." *Earth Interactions* 10(9): 1–17.

Etzioni, Amitai (2006) "Voluntary simplicity: Characterization, select psychological implications and societal consequences." In Tim Jackson (ed.), *The Earthscan Reader in Sustainable Consumption*. London: Earthscan, pp. 157–77.

Falkner, Robert, Stephan, Hannes, and Vogler, John (2011) "International climate policy after Copenhagen: Toward a 'building blocks' approach." In David Held, Angus Hervey, and Markia Theros (eds), *The Governance of Climate Change*. Cambridge: Polity, pp. 202–22.

Farrell, Diana, Gersch, Ulrich A., and Stephenson, Elizabeth (2006) "The value of China's emerging middle class." *The McKinsey Quarterly*, Special edn: 61–9.

Fawcett, Tina (2010) "Personal carbon trading: A policy ahead of its time?" *Energy Policy* 38: 6868–76.

Fawcett, Tina and Parag, Yael (2010) "An introduction to personal carbon trading." *Climate Policy* 10: 329–38.

Field, C. B. et al. (2011) *Managing the Risks of Extreme Events and Disasters to Advance Climate Change Adaptation*. Cambridge: Cambridge University Press.

Figueroa, Robert Melchior (2011) "Indigenous peoples and cultural losses." In John S. Dryzek, Richard B. Norgaard, and David Schlosberg (eds), *Oxford Handbook of Climate Change and Society*. Oxford: Oxford University Press, pp. 232–47.

Fingar, Thomas (2008) *National Intelligence Assessment on the National*

Security Implications of Global Climate Change to 2030. Washington: Office of the Director of National Intelligence.

Fischer, Caroline (2011) "Trade's growing footprint." *Nature Climate Change* 1: 146–7.

Fischer, Douglas (2011) "2010 in review: The year climate coverage 'fell off the map.'" *The Daily Climate*, available at wwwp.dailyclimate.org/tdc-newsroom/2011/01/climate-coverage, last accessed 1.10.2012.

Fisher, Dana R. (2006) "Bringing the material back in: Understanding the US position on climate change." *Sociological Forum* 21(3): 467–94.

Flannery, Tim (2005) *The Weather Makers: The History and Future Impact of Climate Change.* London: Allen Lane/Penguin.

Fleming, James Rodger (2010) *Fixing the Sky: The Checkered History of Weather and Climate Control.* New York: Columbia University Press.

Foley, Jonathan A. et al. (2011) "Solutions for a cultivated planet." *Nature* 478: 337–42.

Food and Agriculture Organization (2007) *Livestock's Long Shadow.* Rome: Food and Agriculture Organization, available at www.fao.org/docrep/010/a0701e/a0701e00.HTM, last accessed 1.10.2012.

Friedman, Lisa and ClimateWire (2012, 3 February) "China greenhouse gas emissions set to rise well past US." *Scientific American*, available at www.scientificamerican.com/article.cfm?id=china-greenhouse-gas-emissions-rise-past-us, last accessed 1.10.2012.

Fromkin, David (1970) "Entangling alliances." *Foreign Affairs* 48(4): 688–700.

Frost, Mervyn (2011) *International Ethics*, 4 vols. Thousand Oaks, CA: Sage.

Gallagher, Kelly Sims (2006) *China Shifts Gears.* Cambridge, MA: MIT Press.

Gallagher, Kelly Sims (2009) "Breaking the climate impasse with China: A global solution." Discussion Paper 09–32. Cambridge, MA: Harvard Project on International Climate Agreements.

Gardiner, Stephen M. (2011a) *A Perfect Moral Storm: The Ethical Tragedy of Climate Change.* New York: Oxford University Press.

Gardiner, Stephen M. (2011b) "Climate justice." In John S. Dryzek, Richard B. Norgaard, and David Schlosberg (eds), *Oxford Handbook of Climate Change and Society.* Oxford: Oxford University Press, pp. 309–22.

Garnaut, Ross (2011) *The Garnaut Review 2011: Australia in the Global Response to Climate Change.* Cambridge: Cambridge University Press.

Gasper, Des (2010) "The idea of human security." In Karen O'Brien, Asuncion Lera St Clair, and Berit Kristofferson (eds), *Climate Change, Ethics and Human Security*. Cambridge: Cambridge University Press, pp. 23–46.

George, Susan (2010) *Whose Crisis, Whose Future? Toward a Greener, Fairer, Richer World*. Cambridge: Polity.

German Advisory Council on Climate Change (2009) *Climate Change as a Security Risk*. London: Earthscan.

Gerth, Karl (2010) *As China Goes, So Goes the World: How Chinese Consumers are Transforming Everything*. New York: Hill and Wang.

Giddens, Anthony (2008) "The politics of climate change: National responses to the challenge of global warming." Policy Network Paper. London: Policy Network, available at www.policy-network.net/publications_detail.aspx?ID=2590, last accessed 1.10.2012.

Giddens, Anthony (2009) *The Politics of Climate Change*. Cambridge: Polity.

Gilding, Paul (2011) *The Great Disruption: Why the Climate Crisis Will Bring On the End of Shopping and the Birth of a New World*. London: Bloomsbury.

Global Change Research Program (2009) *Climate Change Impacts in the United States*. Washington: United States Global Change Research Program.

Global Humanitarian Forum (2009) *The Anatomy of a Silent Crisis: Human Impact Report – Climate Change*. Geneva: Global Humanitarian Forum.

Goodland, Robert and Anhang, Jeff (2009) "Livestock and climate change." *World Watch* (November/December): 10–19.

Goodstein, Eban (2007) *Fighting for Love in the Century of Extinction: How Passion and Politics Can Stop Global Warming*. Burlington, VT: University of Vermont Press.

Gough, Ian and Meadowcroft, James (2011) "Decarbonizing the welfare state." In John S. Dryzek, Richard B. Norgaard, and David Schlosberg (eds), *Oxford Handbook of Climate Change and Society*. Oxford: Oxford University Press, pp. 490–503.

Grieneison, Michael L. and Zhang, Minghua (2011) "The current status of climate change research." *Nature Climate Change* 1(1): 72–3.

Grubb, Michael, Vrolijk, Christiaan, and Brack, Duncan (1999) *The Kyoto Protocol: A Guide and Assessment*. London: Royal Institute of International Affairs.

Hallding, Karl, Han, Guoyi, and Olsson, Marie (2009) *A Balancing Act:*

China's Role in Climate Change. Stockholm: Government Offices of Sweden.

Hamerschlag, Kari (2011) *Meat Eater's Guide to Climate Change and Health*. Washington: Environmental Working Group, available at www.ewg.org/meateatersguide/a-meat-eaters-guide-to-climate-change-health-what-you-eat-matters/, last accessed 1.10.2012.

Hamilton, Clive (2010) *Requiem for a Species: Why We Resist the Truth about Climate Change*. London: Earthscan.

Hamilton, Clive and Denniss, Richard (2006) *Affluenza: When Too Much is Never Enough*. Sydney: Allen & Unwin.

Hansen, James (2009) *Storms of My Grandchildren: The Truth about the Coming Catastrophe and Our Last Chance to Save Humanity*. New York: Bloomsbury.

Hansen, James et al. (2008) "Target atmospheric CO_2: Where should humanity aim?" *Open Atmospheric Science Journal*, available at www.benthamscience.com/open/toascj/articles/V002/217TOASCJ.pdf, last accessed 1.10.2012.

Hardin, Garrett (1968) "The tragedy of the commons." *Science* 162: 1243–8.

Harris, Paul G. (ed.) (2000) *Climate Change and American Foreign Policy*. New York: St Martin's Press.

Harris, Paul G. (2001) *International Equity and Global Environmental Politics: Power and Principles in US Foreign Policy*. Aldershot: Ashgate.

Harris, Paul G. (2004) "'Getting rich is glorious': Environmental values in the People's Republic of China." *Environmental Values* 13(2): 145–65.

Harris, Paul G. (2007) "Collective action on climate change: The logic of regime failure." *Natural Resources Journal* 47(1): 195–224.

Harris, Paul G. (2008a) "Bringing the in-between back in: Foreign policy in global environmental politics." *Politics & Policy* 36(6): 914–43.

Harris, Paul G. (2008b) "Implementing climate equity: The case of Europe." *Journal of Global Ethics* 4(2): 121–40.

Harris, Paul G. (2009) "Beyond Bush: Environmental politics and prospects for US climate policy." *Energy Policy* 37(3): 966–71.

Harris, Paul G. (2010a) "China and climate change: From Copenhagen to Cancun." *Environmental Law Reporter News & Analysis* 40(9): 10858–63.

Harris, Paul G. (2010b) "Misplaced ethics of climate change: Political vs. environmental geography." *Ethics, Place and Environment* 13(2): 215–22.

Harris, Paul G. (2010c) *World Ethics and Climate Change: From International to Global Justice*. Edinburgh: Edinburgh University Press.

Harris, Paul G. (ed.) (2011a) *China's Responsibility for Climate Change: Ethics, Fairness and Environmental Policy*. Bristol: Policy Press.

Harris, Paul G. (2011b) "Climate change." In Gabriela Kutting (ed.), *Global Environmental Politics*. London: Routledge, pp. 107–18.

Harris, Paul G. (ed.) (2011c) "Reconceptualizing global governance." In John S. Dryzek, Richard B. Norgaard, and David Schlosberg (eds), *Oxford Handbook of Climate Change and Society*. Oxford: Oxford University Press, pp. 639–52.

Harris, Paul G. (2012) "The United States and BRIC countries: Climate policy in bilateral relations." In I. Bailey and H. Compston (eds), *Feeling the Heat*. Basingstoke: Palgrave Macmillan.

Harris, Paul G. and Symons, Jonathan (2010) "Justice in adaptation to climate change: Cosmopolitan implications for international institutions." *Environmental Politics* 19(4): 617–36.

Harris, Paul G. and Symons, Jonathan (2013) "Norm conflict in climate governance: Greenhouse gas accounting and the problem of consumption." *Global Environmental Politics* 13(1): 9–29 .

Harris, Paul G. and Yu, Hongyuan (2009) "Climate change in Chinese foreign policy: Internal and external responses." In Paul G. Harris (ed.), *Climate Change and Foreign Policy*. London: Routledge, pp. 53–67.

Harte, John (2010) "Numbers matter: Human population as a dynamic factor in environmental degradation." In Laurie Mazur (ed.), *A Pivotal Moment*. Washington, DC: Island Press, pp. 136–44.

Hartmann, Betsey (2011) "Population alarmism is dangerous." *Policy Innovations*, September, available at www.policyinnovations.org/ideas/briefings/data/000220, last accessed 1.10.2012.

Harvey, Fiona and Vidal, John (2011, 12 December) "Durban deal will not avert catastrophic climate change, say scientists." *Guardian* (London), p. 12.

Hawkins, David (2010) "Coal capture and storage." In Stephen H. Schneider, Armin Rosencranz, Michael D. Mastrandrea, and Kristin Kuntz-Duriseti (eds), *Climate Change Science and Policy*. London: Island Press, pp. 476–83.

Heater, Derek (1996) *World Citizenship and Government: Cosmopolitan Ideas in the History of Western Political Thought*. London: Macmillan.

Heimann, Martin and Reichstein, Markus (2008) "Terrestrial

ecosystem carbon dynamics and climate feedbacks." *Nature* 451: 289–92.

Held, David (2005) "Principles of cosmopolitan order." In Gillian Brock and Harry Brighouse (eds), *The Political Philosophy of Cosmopolitanism*. Cambridge: Cambridge University Press, pp. 10–27.

Held, David (2010) *Cosmopolitanism: Ideals and Realities*. Cambridge: Polity.

Hertsgaard, Mark (2012, 2 January) "Durban: Where the climate deniers-in-chief ran the show." *The Nation*, available at www.thenation.com/article/165155/durban-where-climate-deniers-chief-ran-show, last accessed 1.10.2012.

Hertwich, Edgar and Peters, Glen (2009) "Carbon footprint of nations: A global, trade-linked analysis." *Environmental Science and Technology* 43: 6414–20.

Ho, Mae-Wan (2008) "Carbon capture and storage: A false solution." Institute of Science in Society, available at www.i-sis.org.uk/CCSAFalseSolution.php, last accessed 1.10.2012.

Hoffman, Matthew J. (2011) *Climate Governance at the Crossroads: Experimenting with a Global Response after Kyoto*. Oxford: Oxford University Press.

Hoffman, Ulrich (2011) "Some reflections on climate change, green growth illusions and development space." United Nations Conference on Trade and Development, Discussion Paper No. 205, UNCTAD/OSG/DP/2011/5.

Hohne, Niklas et al. (2011) "China emission paradox: Cancun emissions intensity pledge to be surpassed but emissions higher." *Climate Tracker Update*. Potsdam: Climate Analytics, available at www.climateactiontracker.org/press_briefing_panama.pdf, last accessed 1.10.2012.

Holland, Tom (2010, 29 July) "Bad news for the greenies, and for Beijing's bigwigs." *South China Morning Post*: B10.

Holland, Tom (2012a, 2 April) "Beijing can't put all blame for climate change on West." *South China Morning Post*: B12.

Holland, Tom (2012b, 28 March) "The huge fracture down the middle of the BRICS." *South China Morning Post*: B14.

Honkonen, Tuula (2009) *The Common but Differentiated Responsibility Principle in Multilateral Environmental Agreements*. Alphen aan den Rijn, The Netherlands: Wolters Kluwer.

House of Commons, Environmental Audit Committee (2008) *Personal Carbon Trading*. London: The Stationery Office.

Howarth, Richard B. (2011) "Intergenerational justice." In John S. Dryzek, Richard B. Norgaard, and David Schlosberg (eds), *Oxford Handbook of Climate Change and Society*. Oxford: Oxford University Press, pp. 338–52.

Huesemann, Michael and Huesemann, Joyce (2011) *Techno-Fix: Why Technology Won't Save Us or the Environment*. Gabriola Island, BC: New Society Publishers.

Hulme, Mike (2009) *Why We Disagree about Climate Change: Understanding Controversy, Inaction and Opportunity*. Cambridge: Cambridge University Press.

Humphreys, Stephen (2010a) "Competing claims: Human rights and climate harms." In Stephen Humphreys (ed.), *Human Rights and Climate Change*. Cambridge: Cambridge University Press, pp. 37–68.

Humphreys, Stephen (2010b) "Introduction: Human rights and climate change." In Stephen Humphreys (ed.), *Human Rights and Climate Change*. Cambridge: Cambridge University Press, pp. 1–33.

Hunt, Colin (2011) "Greenhouse gas abatement in Asia: Imperatives, incentives and equity." In Moazzem Hossain and Eliyathamby Selvanathan (eds), *Climate Change and Growth in Asia*. Cheltenham: Edward Elgar, pp. 99–128.

Hurun Research Institute (2010, 1 April) "2010 Hurun Wealth Report," available at www.hurun.net/hurun/listreleaseen451.aspx, last accessed 1.10.2012.

Inglehart, Ronald (1990) *Culture Shift in Advanced Industrial Society*. Princeton: Princeton University Press.

Intergovernmental Panel on Climate Change (IPCC) (2007) *Climate Change 2007: Impacts, Adaptation and Vulnerability*. Cambridge: Cambridge University Press.

International Council on Human Rights Policy (2008) *Climate Change and Human Rights: A Rough Guide*. Geneva: International Council on Human Rights Policy.

International Energy Agency (2011a) "Executive Summary." *World Energy Outlook 2011*. Paris: International Energy Agency.

International Energy Agency (2011b, 30 May) "Prospects of limiting the global increase in temperature at 2°C is getting bleaker," available at www.iea.org/newsroomandevents/news/2011/may/name,19839,en.html, last accessed 1.10.2012.

International Energy Agency (2012, 24 May) "Global carbon-dioxide

emissions increase by 1.0 Gt in 2011 to record high," available at www.
iea.org/newsroomandevents/news/2012/may/name,27216,en.html,
last accessed 1.10.2012.

International Institute for Sustainable Development (IISD) (2009a) "A
brief analysis of the Copenhagen climate change conference." New
York: IISD Reporting Services.

International Institute for Sustainable Development (IISD) (2009b)
"Summary of the Copenhagen climate change conference." *Earth
Negotiations Bulletin* 12 (459), available at www.iisd.ca/vol12/
enb12459e.html, last accessed 1.10.2012.

International Institute for Sustainable Development (IISD) (2011)
"Summary of the Panama City climate change talks." *Earth
Negotiations Bulletin* 12(521), available at www.iisd.ca/vol12/
enb12521e.html, last accessed 1.10.2012.

Jackson, Tim (2006a) "Readings in sustainable consumption." In
Tim Jackson (ed.), *The Earthscan Reader in Sustainable Consumption*.
London: Earthscan, pp. 1–23.

Jackson, Tim (ed.) (2006b) *The Earthscan Reader in Sustainable
Consumption*. London: Earthscan.

Jackson, Tim (2009) *Prosperity without Growth: Economics for a Finite
Planet*. London: Earthscan.

James, Oliver (2007) *Affluenza*. London: Vermilion.

Jamieson, Dale (2008) *Ethics and the Environment*. Cambridge:
Cambridge University Press.

Kagawa, Fumiyo and Selby, David (eds) (2009) *Education and Climate
Change: Living and Learning in Interesting Times*. London: Routledge.

Kang, Kyung-wha (2007) "Climate change and human rights."
Address to the Conference of the Parties to the United Nations
Framework Convention on Climate Change and its Kyoto Protocol,
3–14 December 2007, Bali, Indonesia. Geneva: Office of the High
Commissioner for Human Rights.

Kanter, James (2012, 14 June) "'Lone ranger' faces critics on emissions." *International Herald Tribune*, p. 18.

Kasa, Sjur, Gullberg, Anne T., and Heggelund, Gørild (2008) "The
Group of 77 in the international climate change negotiations: Recent
developments and future directions." *International Environmental
Agreements* 8: 113–27.

Kaufman, Alison Adcock (2010) "The 'Century of Humiliation' then
and now: Chinese perceptions of the international order." *Pacific
Focus* 25(1): 1–33.

Kent, Peter (2011, 12 December) "Statement by Minister Kent," Media Release. Gatineau, Quebec: Environment Canada, available at www. ec.gc.ca/default.asp?lang=En&n=FFE36B6D-1&news=6B04014B-54 FC-4739-B22C-F9CD9A840800, last accessed 1.10.2012.

Keohane, Robert O. and Victor, David G. (2011) "The regime complex for climate change." *Perspectives on Politics* 9(1): 7–23.

Kharas, Homi (2010) "The emerging middle class in developing countries." OECD Development Centre Working Paper No. 285. Paris: Organization for Economic Cooperation and Development.

King, David, Richards, Kenneth, and Tyldesley, Sally (2011) "International climate change negotiations: Key lessons and next steps." Oxford: Smith School of Enterprise and the Environment.

Kissling, Frances and Singer, Peter (2012, 16 June) "To fix the climate, take meat off the menu." *Washington Post*, available at www.wash ingtonpost.com/opinions/why-are-they-serving-meat-at-a-climate-ch ange-conference/2012/06/15/gJQAUnoafV_story.html, last accessed 1.10.2012.

Kobayashi, Yuka (2003) "Navigating between 'luxury' and 'survival' emissions: Tensions in China's multilateral and bilateral climate change diplomacy." In Paul G. Harris (ed.), *Global Warming and East Asia*. London: Routledge, pp. 86–108.

Koch, Max (2012) *Capitalism and Climate Change: Theoretical Discussion, Historical Development and Policy Responses*. Basingstoke: Palgrave Macmillan.

Krasner, Stephen D. (ed.) (1983) *International Regimes*. Ithaca, NY: Cornell University Press.

Krugman, Paul (2011, 29 August) "Republicans against science," op-ed. *New York Times*: A23.

Ladislaw, Sarah O. (2010) "A post-Copenhagen pathway." Washington: Center for Strategic and International Studies.

Lane, Robert E. (1998) "The road not taken: Friendship, consumerism and happiness." In David A. Crocker and Toby Linden, *Ethics of Consumption*. New York: Rowman and Littlefield, pp. 218–48.

Launder, Brian and Thompson, Michael T. (2010) *Geo-Engineering Climate Change: Environmental Necessity or Pandora's Box?* Cambridge: Cambridge University Press.

Layard, Daniel (2011) *Happiness: Lessons from a New Science*. London: Penguin.

Leal-Arcas, Rafael (2011) "Kyoto and the COPs: Lessons learned and looking ahead." In Nikos Lavranos and Ruth Kok (eds),

Hague Yearbook of International Law 2010. Koninklijke: Brill, pp. 17–90.

Leiserowitz, Anthony et al. (2012) "Extreme weather and climate change in the American mind." New Haven, CT: Yale Project on Climate Change Communication.

Leonard, Annie (2010) *The Story of Stuff: How Our Obsession with Stuff Is Trashing the Planet, Our Communities, and Our Health – and a Vision for Change.* New York: Free Press.

Lester, Libby (2010) *Media and Environment.* Cambridge: Polity.

Letcher, Trevor M. (ed.) (2008) *Future Energy: Improved, Sustainable and Clean Options for Our Planet.* Oxford: Elsevier.

Lewis, Joanna I. and Gallagher, Kelly Sims (2011) "Energy and environment in China: Achievements and enduring challenges." In Regina S. Axelrod, Stacy D. Vandeveer, and David L. Downie, *The Global Environment.* Washington: CQ Press, pp. 259–84.

Lewis, Tania and Potter, Emily (eds) (2011) *Ethical Consumption: A Critical Introduction.* London: Routledge.

Lichtenberg, Judith (1998) "Consuming because others consume." In David A. Crocker and Toby Linden (eds), *Ethics of Consumption.* New York: Rowman and Littlefield, pp. 155–75.

Limon, Marc (2009) "Human rights and climate change: Constructing a case for political action." *Harvard Environmental Law Review* 33: 439–76.

Lipschutz, Ronnie D. and McKendry, Corina (2011) "Social movements and global civil society." In John S. Dryzek, Richard B. Norgaard, and David Schlosberg (eds), *Oxford Handbook of Climate Change and Society.* Oxford: Oxford University Press, pp. 369–83.

Lipschutz, Ronnie D. and Peck, Felicia Allegra (2010) "Climate change, globalization, and carbonization." In Bryan S. Turner (ed.), *The Routledge International Handbook of Globalization Studies.* London: Routledge, pp. 182–204.

Lovbrand, Eva, Rindefjall, Teresia, and Nordqvist, Joakim (2009) "Closing the gap in global environmental governance? Lessons from the emerging CDM market." *Global Environmental Politics* 9(2): 74–100.

Lovelock, James (2009) *The Vanishing Face of Gaia: A Final Warning.* New York: Basic Books.

Lumsdaine, David H. (1993) *Moral Vision in International Politics: The Foreign Aid Regime, 1949–1989.* Princeton: Princeton University Press.

Lynas, Mark (2009, 22 December) "How do I know China wrecked the

Copenhagen deal? I was in the room." *Guardian*, available at www. guardian.co.uk/environment/2009/dec/22/copenhagen-climate-ch ange-mark-lynas, last accessed 1.10.2012.

Maltais, Aaron (2008) "Global warming and the cosmopolitan political conception of justice." *Environmental Politics* 17(4): 592–609.

Malthus, Thomas R. (1959[1798]) *Malthus-Population: The First Essay.* Ann Arbor: University of Michigan Press.

Maniates, Michael and Meyer, John M. (eds) (2010) *The Environmental Politics of Sacrifice.* Cambridge, MA: MIT Press.

Marsden, William (2011) *Fools Rule: Inside the Failed Politics of Climate Change.* Toronto: Alfred A. Knopf.

Matthew, Richard A., Barnett, Jon, McDonald, Bryan, and O'Brien, Karen L. (eds) (2010) *Global Environmental Change and Human Security.* Cambridge, MA: MIT Press.

Mazur, Laurie (2010) "Introduction." In Laurie Mazur (ed.), *A Pivotal Moment.* Washington, DC: Island Press, pp. 1–23.

McCright, Aaron M. and Dunlap, Riley E. (2010) "Anti-reflexivity: The American conservative movement's success in undermining climate science and policy." *Theory, Culture & Society* 27(2–3): 100–33.

McCright, Aaron M. and Dunlap, Riley E. (2011) "Cool dudes: The denial of climate change among conservative white males in the United States." *Global Environmental Change* 21(4): 1163–72.

McDonald, Bryan L. (2010) *Food Security.* Cambridge: Polity.

McInerney-Lankford, Siobhan, Darrow, Mac, and Rajamani, Lavanya (2011) *Human Rights and Climate Change: A Review of the International Legal Dimensions.* Washington, DC: World Bank.

McIntosh, Malcolm and Sarker, Tapan (2011) "Climate change and human security issues in the Asia–Pacific region." In Moazzem Hossain and Eliyathamby Selvanathan (eds), *Climate Change and Growth in Asia.* Cheltenham: Edward Elgar, pp. 214–31.

McKibben, Bill (2010, 6 October) "Hot mess: Why are conservatives so radical about climate change?" *The New Republic*, available at www. tnr.com/article/environment-energy/magazine/78208/gop-global-warming-denial-insanity#, last accessed 1.10.2012.

McMullen, Catherine P. and Jabbour, Jason (eds) (2009) *Climate Change Science Compendium 2009.* Nairobi: United Nations Environment Programme.

Meadows, Donella H., Meadows, Dennis L., Randers, Jorgen, and Behrens III, William W. (1972) *The Limits to Growth: A Report of the Club of Rome's Project on the Predicament of Mankind.* New York: Universe Books.

Meadows, Donella H., Meadows, Dennis L., and Randers, Jorgen (1992) *Beyond the Limits: Confronting Global Collapse, Envisioning a Sustainable Future.* White River Junction, VT: Chelsea Green Publishing.

Meadows, Donella, Randers, Jorgen, and Meadows, Dennis (2004) *Limits to Growth: The 30-Year Update.* White River Junction, VT: Chelsea Green.

Mearns, Robin and Norton, Andrew (2010) "Equity and vulnerability in a warming world: Introduction and overview." In Robin Mearns and Andrew Norton (eds), *Social Dimensions of Climate Change.* Washington, DC: World Bank, pp. 1–44.

Meckling, Jonas (2011) *Carbon Coalitions: Business, Climate Politics, and the Rise of Emissions Trading.* Cambridge, MA: MIT Press.

Metz, Bert (2010) *Controlling Climate Change.* Cambridge: Cambridge University Press.

Meyer, Aubrey (2000) *Contraction and Convergence: The Global Solution to Climate Change.* Totnes: Green Books.

Meyer, John M. (2010) "A democratic politics of sacrifice?" In Michael Maniates and John M. Meyer (eds), *The Environmental Politics of Sacrifice.* Cambridge, MA: MIT Press, pp. 13–32.

Miao, Bo and Lang, Graeme (2010) "China's emissions: Dangers and responses." In Constance Lever-Tracy (ed.), *Routledge Handbook of Climate Change and Society,* pp. 405–22.

Michaelis, Laurie M. (2001) "Drivers of consumption patterns." In Brian Heap and Jennifer Kent (eds), *Towards Sustainable Consumption.* London: The Royal Society, pp. 75–84.

Miliband, David (2011) "Green peace: Energy, Europe and the global order." In David Held, Angus Hervey, and Markia Theros (eds), *The Governance of Climate Change.* Cambridge: Polity, pp. 185–93.

Miliband, Ed (2009, 20 December) "The road from Copenhagen." *Guardian,* available at www.guardian.co.uk/commentisfree/2009/dec/20/copenhagen-climate-change-accord, last accessed 1.10.2012.

Minx, Jan C. et al. (2011) "A 'Carbonizing Dragon': China's fast growing CO_2 emissions revisited." *Environmental Science and Technology* (September), DOI: 10.1021/es201497m.

Mitchell, Ronald B. (2010) *International Politics and the Environment.* London: Sage.

Mitchell, Ronald B. (2012) "Technology is not enough: Climate change, population, affluence, and consumption." *Journal of Environment and Development* 21(1): 24–7.

Monbiot, George (2006) *Heat: How to Stop the Planet Burning*. London: Allen Lane.

Moran, Daniel (ed.) (2011) *Climate Change and National Security: A Country-Level Analysis*. Washington: Georgetown University Press.

Myers, Norman and Kent, Jennifer (2004) *The New Consumers: The Influence of Affluence on the Environment*. Washington, DC: Island Press.

Myers, Norman and Kent, Jennifer (eds) (2005) *The New Atlas of Planet Management*. Berkeley: University of California Press.

Nanda, Ved P. (2011) "Climate change, developing countries, and human rights: An international law perspective." In Ved P. Nanda (ed.), *Climate Change and Environmental Ethics*. London: Transaction, pp. 145–70.

National Aeronautics and Space Administration (NASA) (2011) "Key indicators: Carbon dioxide concentration," available at http://climate.nasa.gov/keyIndicators/, last accessed 22.11.2012.

National Development and Reform Commission (2007) *China's National Climate Change Programme*. Beijing: National Development and Reform Commission.

National Oceanic and Atmospheric Administration (NOAA) (2011, 12 January) "2010 tied for warmest year on record," available at www.noaanews.noaa.gov/stories2011/20110112_globalstats.html, last accessed 1.10.2012.

Netherlands Environmental Assessment Agency (2007) "China now no. 1 in CO_2 emissions; USA in second position" (press release). The Hague: Netherlands Environmental Assessment Agency, available at www.pbl.nl/en/dossiers/Climatechange/moreinfo/Chinanowno1inCO2emissionsUSAinsecondposition, last accessed 1.10.2012.

Netherlands Environmental Assessment Agency (2008) "China contributing two thirds to CO_2 emissions" (press release). The Hague: Netherlands Environmental Assessment Agency, available at www.pbl.nl/en/news/pressreleases/2008/20080613ChinacontributingtwothirdstoincreaseinCO2emissions, last accessed 1.10.2012.

New Economics Foundation (2009) *The Happy Planet Index 2.0: Why Good Lives Don't Have to Cost the Earth*. London: New Economics Foundation.

Newell, Peter and Paterson, Matthew (2010) *Climate Capitalism: Global*

Warming and the Transformation of the Global Economy. Cambridge: Cambridge University Press.

Nikiforuk, Andrew (2010) *Tar Sands: Dirty Oil and the Future of the Continent.* Vancouver: Greystone Books.

Nisbet, Matthew C. (2009) "Communicating climate change: Why frames matter for public engagement." *Environment* 52(2): 12–23.

Noone, Kevin, Sumaila, Rashid, and Diaz, Robert J. (2012) *Valuing the Ocean.* Stockholm: Stockholm Environment Institute.

Nordhaus, William (2008) *A Question of Balance: Weighing the Options on Global Warming Policies.* New Haven, CT: Yale University Press.

Norgaard, Kari Marie (2011) "Climate denial: Emotion, psychology, culture, and political economy." In John S. Dryzek, Richard B. Norgaard, and David Schlosberg (eds), *Oxford Handbook of Climate Change and Society.* Oxford: Oxford University Press, pp. 399–413.

O'Brien, Karen, St Clair, Asuncion Lera, and Kristofferson, Berit (2010) "The framing of climate change: Why it matters." In Karen O'Brien, Asuncion Lera St Clair, and Berit Kristofferson (eds), *Climate Change, Ethics and Human Security.* Cambridge: Cambridge University Press, pp. 3–22.

O'Lear, Shannon (2010) *Environmental Politics: Scale and Power.* Cambridge: Cambridge University Press.

Olivier, Jos G. J., Janssens-Maenhout, Greet, Peters, Jeroen A. H. W., and Wilson, Julian (2011) "Long-term trend in global CO_2 emissions: 2011 report." The Hague: Netherlands Environmental Assessment Agency, available at www.pbl.nl/en/publications/2011/long-term-trend-in-global-co2-emissions-2011-report, last accessed 1.10.2012.

O'Neill, Brian (2010) "Climate change and population growth." In Laurie Mazur (ed.), *A Pivotal Moment.* Washington, DC: Island Press, pp. 81–94.

O'Neill, Brian, MacKellar, F. Landis, and Lutz, Wolfgang (2001) *Population and Climate Change.* Cambridge: Cambridge University Press.

O'Neill, Kate (2009) *The Environment and International Relations.* Cambridge: Cambridge University Press.

Oreskes, Naomi and Conway, Erik M. (2010) *Merchants of Doubt: How a Handful of Scientists Obscured the Truth on Issues from Tobacco Smoke to Global Warming.* New York: Bloomsbury.

Organization for Economic Cooperation and Development (OECD) (2012) *OECD Environmental Outlook to 2050.* Paris: OECD Publishing.

Oxfam (2008) "Climate wrongs and human rights: Putting people at the heart of climate-change policy." Oxfam Briefing Paper. Oxford: Oxfam International.

Palmer, Clare (2011) "Does nature matter? The place of the nonhuman in the ethics of climate change." In Denis G. Arnold (ed.), *The Ethics of Global Climate Change*. Cambridge: Cambridge University Press, pp. 272–91.

Pan, An et al. (2012) "Red meat consumption and mortality." *Archives of Internal Medicine* 172(7): 555–63.

Park, Jacob (2000) "Governing climate change policy: From scientific obscurity to foreign policy prominence." In Paul G. Harris (ed.), *Climate Change and American Foreign Policy*. New York: St Martin's Press, pp. 73–87.

Parks, Bradley C. and Roberts, J. Timmons (2009) "Inequality and the global climate regime: Breaking the North–South impasse." In Paul G. Harris (ed.), *The Politics of Climate Change*. London: Routledge, pp. 164–91.

Paterson, Matthew (2007) *Automobile Politics: Ecology and Cultural Political Economy*. Cambridge: Cambridge University Press.

Paterson, Matthew (2008) "Sustainable consumption: Legitimation, regulation and environmental governance." In Jacob Park, Ken Conca, and Matthias Finger (eds), *The Crisis of Global Environmental Governance*. London: Routledge, pp. 110–31.

Paterson, Matthew (2009) "Post-hegemonic climate politics?" *British Journal of Politics and International Relations* 11(1): 140–58.

Paterson, Matthew and Stripple, Johannes (2007) "Singing climate change into existence: On the territorialization of climate policymaking." In Mary E. Pettenger (ed.), *The Social Construction of Climate Change*. Aldershot: Ashgate, pp. 149–72.

Pelling, Mark, Manuel-Navarrete, David, and Redclift, Michael (eds) (2012) *Climate Change and the Crisis of Capitalism: A Chance to Reclaim Self, Society and Nature*. London: Routledge.

Peters, Anne (2009) "Humanity as the A and Ω of sovereignty." *European Journal of International Law* 20(3): 513–44.

Peters, Glen P. and Hertwich, Edgar G. (2008) "Post-Kyoto greenhouse gas inventories: Production versus consumption." *Climate Change* 86: 51–66.

Peters, Glen P. et al. (2012) "Rapid growth in CO_2 emissions after the 2008–2009 global financial crisis." *Nature Climate Change* 2(1): 2–4.

Pew Center on Global Climate Change (2007a) "Climate change mitigation measures in the People's Republic of China" (briefing paper).

Arlington, VA: Pew Center on Global Climate Change, available at www.c2es.org/docUploads/Pew_China_Factsheet_April_07.pdf, last accessed 1.10.2012.

Pew Center on Global Climate Change (2007b) *Summary of COP13*. Arlington, VA: Pew Center on Global Climate Change, available at www.c2es.org/docUploads/Pew%20Center_COP%2013%20Summ ary.pdf, last accessed 1.10.2012.

Pielke, Roger, Jr (2010) *The Climate Fix: What Scientists and Politicians Won't Tell You about Global Warming*. New York: Basic Books.

Pinkse, Jonathan and Kolk, Ans (2009) *International Business and Global Climate Change*. London: Routledge.

Pogge, Thomas W. (2008) *World Poverty and Human Rights*. Cambridge: Polity.

Pooley, Eric (2010) *The Climate War: True Believers, Power Brokers, and the Fight to Save the Planet*. New York: Hyperion.

Princen, Thomas (2005) *The Logic of Sufficiency*. Cambridge, MA: MIT Press.

Princen, Thomas (2010a) "Consumer sovereignty, heroic sacrifice: Two insidious concepts in an endlessly expansionist economy." In Michael Maniates and John M. Meyer (eds), *The Environmental Politics of Sacrifice*. Cambridge, MA: MIT Press, pp. 145–64.

Princen, Thomas (2010b) *Treading Softly: Paths to Ecological Order*. Cambridge, MA: MIT Press.

Rafferty, Kevin (2011, 16 November) "Leaders deaf to the climate alarm bell." *South China Morning Post*, p. B14.

Raskin, Paul et al. (2002) *Great Transition: The Promise and Lure of the Times Ahead*. Stockholm: Stockholm Environment Institute.

Reay, Dave (2005) *Climate Change Begins at Home: Life on the Two-Way Street of Global Warming*. London: Macmillan.

Reuters (2012, 12 February) "World is happier despite four years of upheaval." *South China Morning Post*, p. 11.

Richerzhagen, Carmen and Scholz, Imme (2008) "China's capacities for mitigating climate change." *World Development* 36(2): 308–24.

Ritter, Karl (2012, 26 May) "Is China poor? Key question at climate talks." *Salon/Associated Press*, available at www.salon.com/2012/05/25/is_ china_poor_key_question_at_climate_talks/, last accessed 1.10.2012.

Ritzer, George (2010) *The McDonaldization of Society 6*. London: Sage.

Roberts, J. Timmons (2011) "Multipolarity and the new world (dis)order: US hegemonic decline and the fragmentation of the global climate regime." *Global Environmental Change* 21: 776–84.

Roberts, J. Timmons and Parks, Bradley C. (2007a) *A Climate of Injustice: Global Inequality, North–South Politics and Climate Policy.* Cambridge, MA: MIT Press.

Roberts, J. Timmons and Parks, Bradley C. (2007b) "Fueling injustice: Globalization, ecologically unequal exchange and climate change." *Globalizations* 4(2): 193–210.

Robinson, Mary (2010) "Foreword." In Stephen Humphreys (ed.), *Human Rights and Climate Change.* Cambridge: Cambridge University Press, pp. xvii–xx.

Roozendaal, Gerda van (2009) "The inclusion of environmental concerns in US trade agreements." *Environmental Politics* 18(3): 431–8.

Ropke, Inge (2010) "Ecological economics: Consumption drivers and impacts." In Constance Lever-Tracy (ed.), *Routledge Handbook of Climate Change and Society.* London: Routledge, pp. 121–30.

Rosenau, James N. (1990) *Turbulence in World Politics: A Theory of Change and Continuity.* Princeton: Princeton University Press.

Rosenthal, Elizabeth and Lehren, Andrew W. (2012, 22 June) "Modern comforts, environmental woes." *International Herald Tribune*: 1, 4.

Royal Society (2012) *People and the Planet.* London: The Royal Society.

Russell, Muir (2010) "The independent climate change emails review," available at www.cce-review.org/pdf/FINAL%20REPORT.pdf, last accessed 1.10.2012.

Schiermeier, Quirin (2011) "Climate and weather: Extreme measures." *Nature* 477: 148–9.

Schipper, E. Lisa F. (2006) "Conceptual history of adaptation in the UNFCCC process." *Review of European Community and International Environmental Law* 15(91): 82–92.

Schneider, Stephen H., Rosencranz, Armin, Mastrandrea, Michael D., and Kuntz-Duriseti, Kristin (eds) (2010) *Climate Change Science and Policy.* London: Island Press.

Schor, Juliet (1999) "The new politics of consumption: Why Americans want so much more than they need." *Boston Review*, Summer, available at www.bostonreview.net/BR24.3/summer99.pdf, last accessed 1.10.2012.

Schreurs, Miranda A. (2008) "From the bottom up: Local and subnational climate change politics." *Journal of Environment and Development* 17(4): 343–55.

Schreurs, Miranda A. (2011) "Climate change politics in an authoritarian state: The ambivalent case of China." In John S. Dryzek, Richard B. Norgaard, and David Schlosberg (eds), *Oxford Handbook of Climate Change and Society*. Oxford: Oxford University Press, pp. 449–63.

Schreurs, Miranda A. and Tiberghien, Yves (2007) "Multi-level reinforcement: Explaining European Union leadership in climate change negotiation." *Global Environmental Politics* 7(4): 19–46.

Schroeder, Miriam (2009a) "The construction of China's climate politics: Transnational NGOs and the spiral model of international relations." In Paul G. Harris (ed.), *The Politics of Climate Change*. London: Routledge, pp. 51–71.

Schroeder, Miriam (2009b) "Varieties of carbon governance: Utilizing the Clean Development Mechanism for Chinese priorities." *Journal of Environment and Development* 18(4): 371–94.

Shaffer, Gary (2010) "Long-term effectiveness and consequences of carbon dioxide sequestration." *Nature Geoscience* 3: 464–67.

Sharman, Tom (2012) "Into unknown territory: The limits to adaptation and reality of loss and damage from climate impacts." Action Aid International, Care, Germanwatch, and WWF Briefing Paper, available at http://germanwatch.org/de/download/4108.pdf, last accessed 1.10.2012.

Sheth, Jagdish N., Sethia, Nirmal K., and Srinivas, Shanthi (2011) "Mindful consumption: A customer-centric approach to sustainability." *Journal of the Academy of Marketing Science* 39: 21–39.

Shi, Jiangtao (2010, 15 March) "Wen offers his personal account of Copenhagen climate summit snub." *South China Morning Post*, pp. A5–6.

Shi, Jiangtao (2011, 13 December) "Deal on carbon emissions hailed a victory for China." *South China Morning Post*, p. A3.

Shin, Sangbum (2010) "The domestic side of the Clean Development Mechanism: The case of China." *Environmental Politics* 19(2): 237–54.

Shirk, Susan L. (2007) *China: Fragile Superpower*. Oxford: Oxford University Press.

Shue, Henry (1996) *Basic Rights: Subsistence, Affluence and US Foreign Policy*. Princeton: Princeton University Press.

Siegenthaler, Urs et al. (2005) "Stable carbon cycle: Climate relationship during the late Pleistocene." *Science* 310(5752): 1313–17.

Simms, Andrew (2005) *Ecological Debt: The Health of the Planet and the Wealth of Nations*. London: Pluto.

Simms, Andrew and Smith, Joe (2008) "Introduction." In Andrew Simms and Joe Smith (eds), *Do Good Lives Have to Cost the Earth?* London: Constable.

Simms, Brendan and Trimm, D. J. B. (eds) (2011) *Humanitarian Intervention: A History*. Cambridge: Cambridge University Press.

Simon, Julian (1981) *The Ultimate Resource*. Princeton: Princeton University Press.

Simon, Julian and Kahn, Herman (1984) *The Resourceful Earth: A Response to 'Global 2000'*. London: Blackwell.

Singer, Peter (1997) *How Are We to Live? Ethics in an Age of Self-Interest*. Oxford: Oxford University Press.

Smith, Michael J. (1986) *Realist Thought from Weber to Kissinger*. Baton Rouge, LA: Louisiana State University Press.

Sorrell, Steve (2009) "Improving energy efficiency: Hidden costs and unintended consequences." In Dieter Helm and Cameron Hepburn (eds), *The Economics and Politics of Climate Change*. Oxford: Oxford University Press, pp. 340–61.

Southerton, Dale, Chappells, Heather, and Van Vliet, Bas (eds) (2004) *Sustainable Consumption: The Implications of Changing Infrastructures of Provision*. Cheltenham: Edward Elgar.

Spahni, Renato et al. (2005) "Atmospheric methane and nitrous oxide of the late Pleistocene from Antarctic ice cores." *Science* 310(5752): 1317–21.

Speth, James Gustave (2004) *Red Sky at Morning: America and the Crisis of the Global Environment*. New Haven, CT: Yale University Press.

Speth, James Gustave (2008) *The Bridge at the End of the World: Capitalism, the Environment, and Crossing from Crisis to Sustainability*. New Haven, CT: Yale University Press.

Stern, Eric K. (1999) "The case for comprehensive security." In Daniel H. Deudney and Richard A. Matthew (eds), *Contested Grounds*. Albany: State University of New York Press, pp. 127–54.

Stern, Nicholas (2007) *The Economics of Climate Change: The Stern Review*. Cambridge: Cambridge University Press.

Stern, Nicholas (2009a) *A Blueprint for a Safer Planet: How We Can Save the World and Create Prosperity*. London: Vintage.

Stern, Nicholas (2009b) "Foreword." In Arnaud Brohe, Nick Eyre, and Nicholas Howarth (eds), *Carbon Markets*. London: Earthscan, pp. xii–xvii.

Sunstein, Cass R. (2007) "The complex climate change incentives of China and the United States." Public Law and Legal Theory Working Paper No. 176. Chicago: University of Chicago, available at http://papers.ssrn.com/sol3/papers.cfm?abstract_id=1008598, last accessed 1.10.2012.

Sussman, Glen (2004) "The USA and global environmental policy: Domestic constraints on effective leadership." *International Political Science Review* 25(4): 349–69.

Szasz, Andrew (2011) "Is green consumption part of the solution?" In John S. Dryzek, Richard B. Norgaard, and David Schlosberg (eds), *Oxford Handbook of Climate Change and Society*. Oxford: Oxford University Press, pp. 594–608.

Tankersley, Jim (2009, 18 December) "US, China concessions give climate talks big boost." *Los Angeles Times*, available at http://articles.latimes.com/2009/dec/18/world/la-fg-climate-talks18-2009dec18, last accessed 1.10.2012.

Tobin, Richard J. (2010) "Environment, population and the developing world." In Norman J. Vig and Michael E. Kraft (eds), *Environmental Policy*. Washington: CQ Press, pp. 286–307.

Tollefson, Jeff and Gilbert, Natasha (2012) "Rio report card." *Nature* 486: 20–3.

Toth, Ferenc L. (ed.) (1999) *Fair Weather? Equity Concerns in Climate Change*. London: Earthscan.

Union of Concerned Scientists (2012) *A Climate of Corporate Control: How Corporations Have Influenced the US. Dialogue on Climate Science and Policy*. Cambridge, MA: Union of Concerned Scientists, available at www.ucsusa.org/assets/documents/scientific_integrity/a-climate-of-corporate-control-report.pdf, last accessed 1.10.2012.

United Nations (1992) "United Nations Framework Convention on Climate Change." UN Doc FCCC/INFORMAL/84. New York: United Nations, available at http://unfccc.int/resource/docs/convkp/conveng.pdf, last accessed 1.10.2012.

United Nations (2010) *Human Security: Report of the Secretary-General*. UN Doc A/64/701. New York: United Nations, available at http://docs.unocha.org/sites/dms/HSU/Publications%20and%20Products/GA%20Resolutions%20and%20Debate%20Summaries/A-64-701%20English%20%282%29.pdf, last accessed 1.10.2012.

United Nations (2011) "Security Council, in statement, says 'contextual information' on possible security implications of climate change important when climate impacts drive conflict." UN Doc SC/10332. New York: United Nations, available at www.un.org/News/Press/docs/2011/sc10332.doc.htm, last accessed 1.10.2012.

United Nations Department of Economic and Social Affairs (2004) *World Population to 2300*. New York: United Nations.

United Nations Department of Economic and Social Affairs (2010) *World Population Prospects: The 2010 Revision*. New York: United Nations.

United Nations Development Program (UNDP) (1990) *Human Development Report 1990*. New York: Oxford University Press.

United Nations Development Program (UNDP) (2007) *Human Development Report 2007/2008: Fighting Climate Change – Human Solidarity in a Divided World*. New York: Palgrave Macmillan.

United Nations Development Program (UNDP) (2009) *Human Development Report 2009*. New York: Palgrave Macmillan.

United Nations Development Program (UNDP) (2011) *Human Development Report 2011: Sustainability and Equity – A Better Future for All*. New York: Palgrave Macmillan.

United Nations Environment Program (UNEP) (2012) *Global Environment Outlook 5*. Nairobi: United Nations Environment Program.

United Nations Framework Convention on Climate Change (UNFCCC) (2009) *Copenhagen Accord*. UN Doc. FCCC/CP/2009/L.7. New York: United Nations, available at http://unfccc.int/resource/docs/2009/cop15/eng/l07.pdf, last accessed 1.10.2012.

United Nations Framework Convention on Climate Change (UNFCCC) (2011) "Establishment of an Ad Hoc Working Group on the Durban Platform for Enhanced Action." Draft decision -/CP.17. Durban: United Nations, available at http://unfccc.int/files/meetings/durban_nov_2011/decisions/application/pdf/cop17_durbanplatform.pdf, last accessed 1.10.2012.

United Nations Human Rights Council (2011) "Human rights and climate change." A/HRC/RES/18/22, available at www.ohchr.org/Documents/Issues/ClimateChange/A.HRC.RES.18.22.pdf, last accessed 22.11.2012.

United Nations University-International Human Dimensions Programme and United Nations Environment Programme (UNU-IHDP and UNEP) (2012) *Inclusive Wealth Report 2012: Measuring Progress toward Sustainability*. Cambridge: Cambridge University Press.

United States Census Bureau (2011) "US and world population clocks," available at www.census.gov/main/www/popclock.html, last accessed 1.10.2012.

Urry, John (2011) *Climate Change and Society*. Cambridge: Polity.

Vanderheiden, Steve (2008) *Atmospheric Justice: A Political Theory of Climate Change*. Oxford: Oxford University Press.

van Hooft, Stan (2009) *Cosmopolitanism: A Philosophy for Global Ethics.* Stocksfield: Acumen.

Vezirgiannidou, Sevasti-Eleni (2008) "The Kyoto agreement and the pursuit of relative gains." *Environmental Politics* 17(1): 40–57.

Victor, David G. (2011) *Global Warming Gridlock: Creating More Effective Strategies for Protecting the Planet.* Cambridge: Cambridge University Press.

Vidal, John and Harvey, Fiona (2011, 11 December) "Climate deal salvaged after marathon talks in Durban." *Observer* (London), p. 7.

Villamizar, Alicia (2011) "Climate change and poverty: Confronting our moral and ethical commitments: some reflections." In Ved P. Nanda (ed.), *Climate Change and Environmental Ethics.* London: Transaction, pp. 203–13.

Vlek, Charles and Steg, Linda (2007) "Human behavior and environmental sustainability: Problems, driving forces, and research topics." *Journal of Social Issues* 63(1): 1–19.

Wang, Haifeng and Firestone, Jeremy (2010) "The analysis of country-to-country CDM permit trading using the gravity model in international trade." *Energy for Sustainable Development* 14: 6–13.

Wapner, Paul (2010) "Sacrifice in an Age of Comfort." In Michael Maniates and John M. Meyer (eds), *The Environmental Politics of Sacrifice.* Cambridge, MA: MIT Press, pp. 33–59.

Washington, Haydn and Cook, John (2011) *Climate Change Denial: Heads in the Sand.* London: Earthscan.

Watts, Jonathan (2010) *When a Billion Chinese Jump: Voices from the Frontline of Climate Change.* London: Faber and Faber.

Watts, Jonathan, Carrington, Damien, and Goldenberg, Suzanne (2010, 11 February) "China's fears of rich nation 'climate conspiracy' at Copenhagen revealed." *Guardian*, available at www.guardian.co.uk/environment/2010/feb/11/chinese-thinktank-copenhagen-document, last accessed 1.10.2012.

Weiss, Thomas G. (2009) *What's Wrong with the United Nations and How to Fix It.* Cambridge: Polity.

Wendt, Alexander (1999) *Social Theory of International Politics.* Cambridge: Cambridge University Press.

White, Gregory (2011) *Climate Change and Migration: Security and Borders in a Warming World.* New York: Oxford University Press.

Wiener, Jonathan B. (2008) "Climate change policy and policy change in China." *UCLA Law Review* 55: 1805–26.

Willman, Dale (2010) "Media and public education." In Stephen H. Schneider, Armin Rosencranz, Michael D. Mastrandrea, and Kristin Kuntz-Duriseti (eds), *Climate Change Science and Policy*. London: Island Press, pp. 414–20.

World Health Organization (2009) "Health impact of climate change needs attention." Geneva: World Health Organization, available at www.who.int/mediacentre/news/notes/2009/climate_change_20090311/en/index.html, last accessed 1.10.2012.

World Meteorological Association (2012) "WMO statement on the status of the global climate in 2011." WMO-No. 1085. Geneva: World Meteorological Association, available at www.wmo.int/pages/pub lications/showcase/documents/WMO_1085_en.pdf, last accessed 1.10.2012.

Worldwatch Institute (2011) "Global meat production and consumption continue to rise." Washington: Worldwatch Institute, available at www.worldwatch.org/global-meat-production-and-consumption-continue-rise-1, last accessed 1.10.2012.

WWF (2010) *Living Planet Report 2010: Biodiversity, Biocapacity and Development*. Gland, Switzerland: WWF International.

Xinhua (2010, 25 February) "China has 'no intention' of capping emissions." Beijing: Xinhua News Agency, available at www.chinadaily.com.cn/china/2010-02/25/content_9499066.htm, last accessed 1.10.2012.

Yamin, Farhana and Depledge, Joanna (2004) *The International Climate Change Regime: A Guide to Rules, Institutions and Procedures*. Cambridge: Cambridge University Press.

Young, Oran R. (2011) *Institutional Dynamics: Emergent Patterns in International Environmental Governance*. Cambridge, MA: MIT Press.

Zhang, Zhihong (2003) "The forces behind China's climate change policy: Interests, sovereignty and prestige." In Paul G. Harris (ed.), *Global Warming and East Asia*. London: Routledge, pp. 66–85.

Zhang, Zhongxiang (2009a) "In what format and under what time-frame would China take on climate commitments? A roadmap to 2050." East–West Center Working Paper No. 66, available at www.eastwestcenter.org/publications/what-format-and-under-what-time-frame-would-china-take-climate-commitments-roadmap-2050, last accessed 22.11.2012.

Zhang, Zhongxiang (2009b) "The US proposed carbon tariffs and China's responses." *Energy Policy* 38: 2168–70.

Index

Lightning Source UK Ltd.
Milton Keynes UK
UKHW022236220120
357436UK00010B/954

9 780745 652511